BEATRIX POTTER'S JOURNAL

BEATRIX POTTER'S JOURNAL

Abridged with an Introduction by
Glen Cavaliero

Frederick Warne

FREDERICK WARNE
Penguin Books Ltd, Harmondsworth, Middlesex, England
Viking Penguin Inc., 40 West 23rd Street, New York, New York 10010, U.S.A.
Penguin Books Australia Ltd, Ringwood, Victoria, Australia
Penguin Books Canada Limited, 2801 John Street, Markham, Ontario, Canada L3R 1B4
Penguin Books (N.Z.) Ltd, 182–190 Wairau Road, Auckland 10, New Zealand

The Journal of Beatrix Potter, 1881–97 first published 1966
This abridged edition first published 1986

Journal Copyright © Frederick Warne & Co., 1966
Introduction and abridgement copyright © Glen Cavaliero, 1986
Copyright in all countries signatory to the Berne Convention

ISBN 07232.3334.9

Typeset, printed and bound in Great Britain by
Hazell Watson & Viney Limited,
Member of the BPCC Group,
Aylesbury, Bucks
Filmset in VIP Bembo

CONTENTS

LIST OF PLATES

Beatrix Potter with John Bright.
L to R, Rupert Potter, Beatrix, Mɪ Gaskell, Unknown,
  Helen Potter.
Beatrix Potter's first cousins, Kate and Blanche Potter, 1874.
Mrs Potter, Beatrix and Mr Potter at Wray Castle in 1882.
Sir John Millais with, probably, his daughter Effie.
Caroline Hutton.
Beatrix Potter, aged twenty-three.
Bertram and Beatrix Potter.
Number Two, Bolton Gardens, October 1889.
Hill Top Farm, Sawrey (*photo: Michael Mable, courtesy of the
  National Trust*)
In Sawrey Village (*photo: Michael Mable, courtesy of the
  National Trust*)
View from Sawrey towards the Langdale Pikes (*photo: Michael
  Mable, courtesy of the National Trust*)
Beatrix Potter in the porch at Hill Top.

Leech Family Tree

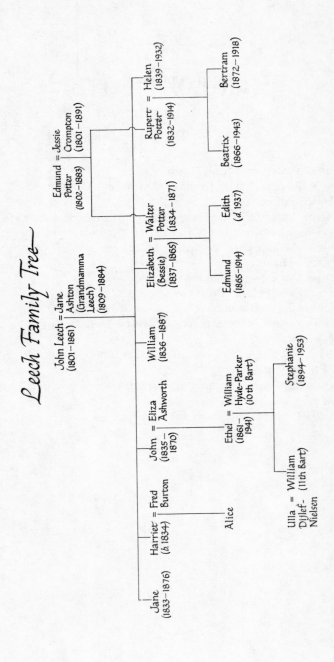

Edmund Potter (1802–1883) = Jessie Crompton (1801–1891)

John Leech (1801–1861) = Jane Ashton (Grandmamma Leech) (1809–1884)

Jane (1833–1876)

Harriet (b. 1834) = Fred Burton

John (1835–1870) = Eliza Ashworth

William (1836–1887)

Elizabeth (Bessie) (1837–1865) = Walter Potter (1834–1871)

Rupert Potter (1832–1914) = Helen (1839–1932)

Alice

Ethel (1861–1941) = William Hyde-Parker (10th Bart)

Edmund (1865–1914)

Edith (d. 1937)

Beatrix (1866–1943)

Bertram (1872–1918)

Stephanie (1894–1953)

Ulla = William Dijlef-Nielsen (11th Bart)

Potter and Hutton Family Tree

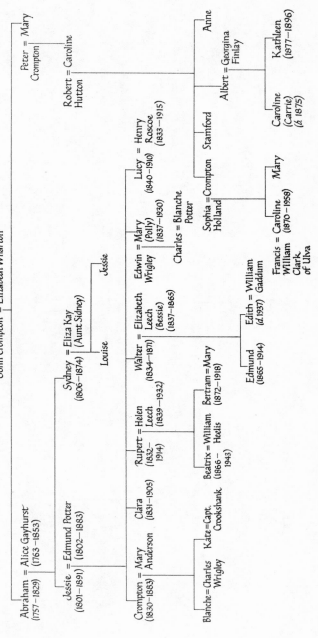

ACKNOWLEDGEMENTS

Among those who have helped me in the preparation of this book I would like especially to thank Mr Eugene Fisk, Mr David Lowe, Mr John Skidmore and Miss Judy Taylor.

NOTE ON THE TEXT

Apart from making two or three small amendments I have followed Leslie Linder's text throughout (*The Journal of Beatrix Potter, 1881–97*, Warne, 1966). No individual sentences have been abridged, but, in the interest of continuity, paragraph units have been retained without the use of spaced dots to indicate omissions. I have added a number of footnotes: the remainder are by Leslie Linder, and carry his initials. A few of these have been shortened. The family trees have been simplified, the more easily to locate people mentioned in the Journal.

INTRODUCTION

Few twentieth-century English writers have been so continuously popular as Beatrix Potter. The twenty-one small tales she wrote for children, all but two of them published before 1914, are held in undiminishing affection by successive generations of readers. Her work has been translated into a dozen different languages, including Swedish, Afrikaans and Japanese; and people of all ages and nationalities make the journey to her farmhouse in the English Lake District. Such an accolade seems out of all proportion: the books are short, designed specifically for children, and intensely local in their style and setting. And yet her appeal transcends these limitations. She herself, with the arrogance proper to a genuine artist, had no doubt as to what she had achieved, confiding to one of her relations that she knew her stories were as sure of immortality as those of Hans Andersen. Indeed, it is only a snobbery concerning scale that would find her books too small to warrant serious consideration. For they do warrant it: they are far more than merely 'children's books'. They exert a lasting influence upon their readers, a spell which is at once familiar and mysterious. Beatrix Potter's Journal not only throws light on how the books came to be written, it goes some way to accounting for their particular appeal.

Beatrix Potter was born in London in 1866 at a time of prosperity and confidence, halfway through Queen Victoria's reign. Overseas, British power and influence were strong. At home, more and more middle-class people were able to live off unearned incomes: money had become self-propagating. The average home became more comfortable and filled with furniture and other forms of portable property. In the world of art the Pre-Raphaelite school of painters, with their microscopic attention to detail, backed by the powerful advocacy of John Ruskin, were encouraging other artists to produce pictures that were celebrations of the visible world and appealed strongly to prosperous families like the Potters. In the field of literature, Tennyson was Poet Laureate: his work, too, was full of meticulous, detailed observation, and his popularity was a measure of public taste. Architects, on the other hand, favoured the grandiose and the monumental: public buildings reflected a hopefulness about the future which typified the age.

At the same time, a programme of electoral and educational reform was under way which in due course would partly undermine the hierarchical ordering of society. A year after Beatrix Potter was born the Second Reform Act all but doubled the electorate; three years after that the Education Act of 1870 inaugurated universal elementary education. By 1881, when Beatrix began to keep her Journal, British prosperity was being threatened by competition in world markets, Home Rule for Ireland was an issue that had erupted into violence, while terrorism was a growing threat to European stability. Imperial policies led to unfortunate military entanglements; scientific discovery was undermining the grounds of religious belief. It was a time of gradually increasing uncertainty and unrest, as society attempted to absorb the shock of new discoveries and the decay of long-established institutions.

Beatrix Potter's Journal reflects the thoughts and reactions of a clear-sighted young woman between the ages of sixteen and thirty, whose secure but unusually solitary life enabled her to respond with absolute integrity to what she heard and saw. Changes were in the air which would affect her attitudes; unconsciously, she was changing too. Outwardly she may have seemed undisturbed, but in her Journal she reflects an anxiety about her times as well as doubts about her own future.

Her birthplace, Number Two, Bolton Gardens, stood at the end of a terrace of gloomy five-storey houses in West Brompton, which at that period was a prosperous residential district. The road was not far from the two great South Kensington museums, the Victoria and Albert Museum, dedicated to the arts and sciences, and the Natural History Museum. Both were expanding while she was growing up, and both helped to form the tastes and interests of the girl whose work would one day be exhibited in the former, and who was to live in Bolton Gardens for nearly fifty years. Beatrix had little love for the house and was quite untroubled when she heard of its destruction in the air raids of the Second World War. It was a vertical, stratified house, with the servants inhabiting the basement and attics, the master and mistress presiding on the ground and first floors, and the children kept out of the way at the top. Inevitably such terrace houses were dark, and Victorian taste in furnishing and decoration made them darker still. Beatrix Potter, whose books are full of a sense of the country, of living, breathing things, and fresh air and hilly landscapes, grew up in a home in which a strict routine kept everything and everyone in order and whose only garden was a small square of grass. Such self-imposed predictability was essential for people of the Potters' social standing, if they were to make a life of unbounded leisure seem morally respectable.

Beatrix was their elder child and only daughter. Rupert and Helen Potter were a wealthy couple who had inherited fortunes made in the Lancashire cotton trade by their respective families. The families were closely connected, for Helen Potter's sister Elizabeth Leech had married Rupert's younger brother Walter. Rupert and Walter's father, Edmund Potter, was a man of outstanding gifts and character, who had at one time been Liberal Member of Parliament for Carlisle, and who was a friend of the radical politician and reformer John Bright. Beatrix Potter was proud of this North Country ancestry: 'I am a believer in "Breed",' she wrote. 'I am descended from generations of Lancashire yeomen and weavers; obstinate, hard-headed, *matter-of-fact* folk.' Such forthright practicality was to be her most conspicuous attribute in later life.

Rupert Potter had been called to the Bar; but although he kept chambers in Lincoln's Inn, he never practised. Instead, he lived the self-regulating life open to a gentleman of private means, interesting himself in the art of photography and taking his family away each year for lengthy holidays. The places chosen for the spring holiday tended to alternate between the smaller seaside towns, such as Sidmouth or Lyme Regis (for this was the period when, thanks to the speeding-up of rail travel, even the more distant resorts were becoming accessible to Londoners and day trippers), and seaports such as Falmouth. The Potters were true Victorians in their diligent exploration not only of sites of historic interest but also of scenes of contemporary activity such as Portsmouth dockyard. Beatrix Potter shared with her father an alert interest in topography, which she put to good use in her painting and writing. In the late summer and the autumn the family would go to Scotland or the Lake District, renting spacious houses which, in due course, would figure in Beatrix's paintings. It was here, in the North Country, that she felt she was really coming home.

In addition to pride in her ancestry, Beatrix Potter possessed a keen interest in her family connections, showing an especial affection for her grandparents and their contemporaries: the intermediate generation, as is not unusual, comes in for more critical appraisal. Her parents do not seem to have been an imaginative couple. Rupert Potter was a man of definite opinions combined with nervous irritability, an oppressive mixture. He was difficult to live with. Photographs of him in later life reveal a stern, unsmiling face with overpowering whiskers; but he appears to have been a more enlivening personality than his wife. Helen Potter, to judge from the Journal, was extremely conventional, unadventurous and something of a killjoy. Beatrix displays little warmth towards her, and at one point remarks despairingly, 'I was born to be a discredit to my parents.' Her detachment from them is evident in another entry: 'They have been married twenty years today.' That terse 'they' is very telling.

But if her parents were restrictive and discouraging, other members of the family succeeded in arousing a more cordial response in her. Her maternal grandmother's recollections of a journey from Manchester to London are the first thing she records; while Camfield Place in Hertfordshire was beloved not only for its own sake but as the home of her Potter grandparents: it was the place of childhood safety to which she turned for reassurance, 'the place I love best in the world'. To old Mrs Potter she was especially close, and it was she who fed the young Beatrix's mind with stories of the past and strengthened her imagination with her wit and humour. By the time of the Journal the formidable Edmund Potter had grown a little childish; but his granddaughter records his simplicity and comical sayings with affection. Her great-aunt Sidney is also charmingly described in two accounts of visits to her home in Manchester: 'I never saw a kinder, sweeter old lady.' One can well believe it.

Several other members of the two families make an appearance in the Journal. Her father had two brothers and three sisters. The eldest brother, Crompton (named after his mother's family, in whom Beatrix was especially interested), married Mary Anderson; references to her in the Journal are generally uncomplimentary. Their two daughters, Blanche and Kate, were applauded beauties, and occasionally played with Beatrix, being her near contemporaries in age. The announcements of their engagements were not only matters of keen interest, but also occasions for sharp comment. Two other cousins, Edmund and Edith, were the children of Walter Potter whose wife, Bessie (Helen's sister), had died the year before Beatrix's birth. She was evidently remembered warmly by the family. Of the three Potter sisters, the eldest, Clara, never married; she turned up to join Beatrix and her parents at Windermere in 1895 with a companion whom Beatrix considered to be 'odious'. The second sister, Mary (Aunt Polly), was the mother of Charles who married his cousin Blanche, to Beatrix's expressed approval; while the youngest, Lucy, married Henry Roscoe, a distinguished scientist who became a Professor at Owen's College, Manchester, and was knighted in 1895 for services to chemistry. He was to play a temporarily important role in Beatrix's life by encouraging her interest in the study and drawing of fungi: her account of her visit with him to discuss the project with the Director of Kew Gardens is a little masterpiece of understated humour. (This resulted in her writing a paper read, though not by her, to the Linnean Society in 1896.) More distantly related on the Potter side were the Hutton family. Caroline Hutton and Beatrix became close friends; their grandfathers had been first cousins. The maintenance of such distant family ties is a characteristic of Victorian family life, which was distinctly clannish.

On the Leech side, two families must be mentioned. Helen Potter's sister Harriet (whom her disrespectful niece likened to a weasel) married another cotton magnate and eventually went to live near Denbigh in an old house lovingly described in the Journal: its interior and garden were to be potent influences on Beatrix's imagination. And John Leech, the elder of Helen Potter's two surviving brothers, was the father of Beatrix's cousin Ethel: her marriage to Sir William Hyde-Parker brought about visits to Melford Hall in Suffolk, another house whose garden appears in Beatrix's books. Their daughter, Stephanie, was the dedicatee of

Mr Jeremy Fisher and in due course inherited Castle Cottage, Beatrix's home following her marriage. Ulla Ditlef-Nielsen, Stephanie's Danish sister-in-law, is the author of *Cousin Beatie*, an interesting portrayal of Beatrix in her old age.

Despite all these family friendships, Beatrix Potter endured a lonely childhood. Her mother would allow neither her nor her young brother, Bertram, to mix with children other than members of the family, supposedly for fear they might pick up germs. Instead, the pair were confined to the upper storeys of the house, where they consoled themselves with the company of the small animals and insects which their parents rather inconsistently allowed them to keep as pets and to take with them on the family holidays. In such a secluded existence Beatrix was thrown upon her own resources, occupying herself with drawing and painting, the activities which soon became her main interest. She had in any case inherited a natural gift for painting from her father who seems, at least initially, to have encouraged her. Her mother also went in for water-colour painting, in the amateur way that so many Victorian ladies did. But Beatrix was a professional at heart. In 1881, the year the Journal commences, she received an Art Student's Certificate from the Science and Art Department of the Committee of Council on Education. She drew not only her pets but also plants, furniture and fungi: the latter became an absorbing interest to her as the years went by. Bertram was sent away at the age of eleven to a preparatory school at Eastbourne, but Beatrix stayed at home and was taught by governesses. 'Thank goodness, my education was neglected,' she wrote in later years. She developed an observant, humorous and inquiring cast of mind, independent without being rebellious. Portraits of her show a steady gaze, a sensitive mouth and a determined chin: she was not a formal beauty but her face had decided charm. She created her own life so far as she could, and was clearly aware of the need to do so. Commenting on Bertram's character in 1884 she notes, 'He has an absorbing interest, which is a very great help in keeping anyone straight.'

It is difficult nowadays to understand how any young unmarried woman could have endured such a constricted way of life. In the late nineteenth century, however, English daughters of the middle and upper classes were expected to live with their parents until they married. In prosperous households it was unthinkable that a girl should go out to work, so the result was that financial dependence combined with inherited notions of filial duty to produce a situation in which any movement of revolt was construed as ingratitude. Gradually, the plight of the unmarried daughter was modified to the extent that part-time employment became permissible and even to some extent encouraged; but it was not until the outbreak of the Second World War in 1939, with the subsequent recruitment of the civilian population for various kinds of war work, that emancipation was finally achieved. Beatrix Potter's ties with her parents, however reluctantly she may have acquiesced in them, were normal: it was her seclusion from other children that was not. None the less, it was that very seclusion which bred the peculiarly adult, self-sufficient awareness which gives her books their distinctive quality.

Self-sufficiency was forced upon her, but she put it to good use. The Journal records her entry into professional life, the negotiations with Hildescheimer & Faulkner concerning her offer to supply them with designs for Christmas cards. In her middle thirties she at last began to make social contacts through her own efforts and not simply as an adjunct to her parents' lives. As a result of illustrating a small booklet of verses for children by Frederick Weatherly (later the author of the famous First World War song, 'Roses in Picardy'), Beatrix decided to illustrate a story of her own which she published privately in an edition of 250 copies as *The Tale of Peter Rabbit*. In the following year, 1902, the little book was published by Frederick Warne & Co., with the author's illustrations printed in colour; the format was to become world-famous and is substantially the same today. *Peter Rabbit* was followed over the next eleven years by eighteen other stories, including two brief and simple tales for tiny children in panoramic, pull-out form. Their success was immediate and sustained.

These years were for the most part happy and creative, despite her parents' lukewarm enthusiasm over her new interest; indeed, it is doubtful if they realized just how successful she was. They were certainly less than enthusiastic over her engagement in 1905, at the age of thirty-nine, to the youngest of her publishers, Norman Warne: disregarding the origins of their own wealth they were opposed to the idea of their daughter marrying into 'trade'. As it turned out, the engagement was to end tragically, for Norman Warne died later that year. Beatrix bore his loss with courageous resignation and she went steadily on with the work in which he had been so closely and sympathetically involved.

A more lasting resource was the purchase, in the same year, of Hill Top Farm, a small property at Sawrey (a village near Hawkshead in the Lancashire portion of the Lake District). The two villages of Near and Far Sawrey lie between Windermere and Esthwaite Water. Beatrix's village was Near Sawrey, so-called for its greater proximity to Hawkshead, at one time the market town. It lies close to the foot of Esthwaite Water, the gentlest and most pastoral scenery of the Lakes. Hill Top Farm is on a slight rise behind the Tower Bank Arms. The rest of the village snuggles between low wooded hills with outcrops of rock, its high stone walls and tranquil fields a blend of the homely and the picturesque, both workaday and rugged. Its atmosphere resembles that of Beatrix Potter's books, in several of which it appears and is still recognizable today.

The purchase of Hill Top allowed Beatrix Potter to develop her growing interest in farming and sheep breeding – when she was free to get away from home, with all its ties and duties. She employed a tenant farmer and built a wing on to the farmhouse for him and his family to occupy, retaining the original portion for herself. Over the years she filled it with the beautiful antique furniture that she used to buy in local sales. Her marriage to William Heelis, her solicitor, took place in 1913: she was by then forty-eight years old. He had acted for her in the purchase of a neighbouring property called Castle Cottage, which became their home. Her marriage resulted in final deliverance from parental bonds, and in thirty years of personal happiness; it also led, in part, to the gradual dwindling of her artistic powers. But her work had served its turn, and she settled down contentedly to the countrywoman's life she had always craved. Fiercely defensive of her privacy where English admirers were concerned, she confined her literary friendships to Americans. Her contacts with them, both by letter and as host, led to the writing (for American publication only) of her longest and most personal book, *The Fairy Caravan*. It did not appear in England until 1952.

She died in December 1943, at the age of seventy-seven. Her story has been memorably told by Margaret Lane in two biographies, but even so it remains less familiar than that of Peter Rabbit. This is understandable. There was good reason for the popularity of her books for, in addition to their perfect match of text with illustrations, they did not talk down to their young readers. The author assumes her readers are as intelligent and informed as she is herself, and writes about her animal characters as though they were personal friends – as indeed they were. Her books and her life were all of a piece; her imagination, nurtured by long years of self-discipline and study of the natural order, was akin to the abilities that made her a successful farmer. To realize this one has only to turn to the Journal. Here, in the record of some fifteen years of her early life, one sees the emergence not only of the shrewd, tough, clear-thinking woman, Mrs Heelis of Sawrey, but also of the imaginative artist, Beatrix Potter.

The Journal was not intended for publication. Written in minus-cule handwriting and in code, it was only transcribed by the late Leslie Linder after more than nine years of patient study. How he succeeded in discovering the key to the code is recorded in his introduction to the first edition of the Journal, published in 1966 (it also precedes this abridged version, see p. 39). As a glance at the original manuscript of the code-writing will confirm, it describes an achievement of a most exacting and dedicated kind.

Admirers of Beatrix Potter's writing and painting owe an immense debt to Leslie Linder. Through his research into her manuscripts and sketch books, and his patience in deciphering the Journal, he has made us aware of Beatrix Potter not only as the author of *Peter Rabbit* and its successors, but as a remarkable woman in her own right. His work is a characteristic example of that single-minded dedication which can turn a private hobby into a monument of scholarship, unaided by professional bodies, grants or scholar-ships. Leslie Linder was not an academic, nor was he a professional literary critic or a professional art critic; he was an engineer, working for the British Standard Institute, with an especial expertise in the field of tackle-lifting. There is something satisfying and appropriate about this practicality being associated with the emi-nently practical Beatrix Potter. Linder's home was at Buckhurst Hill on the borders of Epping Forest, not far from Beatrix Potter's beloved Camfield Place. He was a loyal Congregationalist, opening the large house which he shared with his sister to the children of the local church, and taking charge of the children's library there. It was the library that led to his interest in children's literature; and it was the reading of Margaret Lane's *The Tale of Beatrix Potter* that began what was to be a lifelong quest: the collecting of everything that could be found concerning the life and writings of this hitherto all but anonymous author. How successful he was may be deduced from Marcus Crouch's comment: 'It has been said, only half in jest, that he could tell you what she had for dinner on 20th August 1891.'

A shy and modest man, he was not given to publicizing his achievement, in this again resembling Beatrix Potter. But he succeeded in amassing a vast amount of valuable material, and persevered with work on her Journal despite the guarded response of her relations. His sister Enid shared his interest, and collaborated in his books by providing notes and photographs.

By 1953 he was at work among the papers at Hill Top Farm. The present writer remembers encountering him in the late summer of that year, and being amused when told that the man in the library was engaged upon 'research' – it seemed at first an inappropriate term in that particular house, so full of magical associations. But it was not long before its suitability became apparent. I had been puzzled by a discrepancy at one point between the text of my own copy of *Pigling Bland* and that belonging to a friend. Mine contained the quintessential Potterism, 'Alexander was hopelessly volatile'; his merely had 'Alexander danced about'. Leslie Linder was ready with the explanation. The passage had been altered without the author's approval, in the name, presumably, of intelligibility; and she had angrily insisted on its replacement. The difference between the two phrases used in a book for children is the measure of her quality. Her books can be appreciated by adults at an adult level, without evoking knowingness or whimsy; there is nothing childish about them, in the bad sense of that term. There was no danger of their young readers becoming soporific while attending to her particular kind of prose.

The result of these labours among the Potter papers at Hill Top and Castle Cottage is to be found in the three books that are Linder's monument. *The Art of Beatrix Potter* (1955) is a collection of her published and unpublished paintings and drawings. Although the compilation was almost entirely Linder's own work, it is character-istic that his name should have appeared not on the title page of the

24

first edition but inconspicuously on the reverse side, together with that of W. A. Herring, who had seen the *Peter Rabbit* books through the press at Warne's. However, a revised enlarged edition carries notes by Leslie and Enid Linder, with their names on the title page; and *A History of the Writings of Beatrix Potter* is unquestionably his. It is an exhaustive and continuously interesting account of how her books came into being, a classic instance of interpretative research, close to its subject both in style and outlook. It was published in 1971. In 1973 Leslie Linder died. He bequeathed his collection of manuscripts, sketches, first editions, and the miniature letters and mail-bags which Beatrix Potter used to send to her young correspondents, to the National Book League and the Victoria and Albert Museum. His inaugural lecture at the latter on the occasion of the Beatrix Potter Exhibition in 1972, an ordeal for an essentially retiring man, reflected his nervous energy and commitment to his task. Beatrix Potter was fortunate indeed in having Leslie Linder as her champion: few writers can have been so selflessly and so appropriately served.

The Journal is not a continuous work. The surviving entries run from 1881 to 1897, with a number of intermissions. Beatrix Potter was fifteen years old when she set down her grandmother's recollections. One is immediately aware of her interest in the past, an interest that manifests itself not only in such stories as *The Tailor of Gloucester* but also through her furnishing of Hill Top farmhouse. Even in these early entries nostalgia is qualified by a humorous concentration on everyday realities: she was anything but misty-eyed. The only real indication the Journal gives of what must have at times been great loneliness (Bertram, who shared her interest in painting and in animals, was only at home with her in the school holidays) is the evocation of the imaginary 'Esther', with whom Beatrix could pretend to correspond – but in whom she evidently found it unnecessary to confide. There are no self-analytical, psychological revelations here, only honest exhibitions of feeling, the evidence of a richly lived imaginative life. Considering its private nature, the Journal is remarkably free from introspection or self-pity.

Her gaze is turned outwards. The early portions, staccato in manner, are full of what she read in the newspapers and of what she must have overheard in talk between her parents and their friends and also, presumably, from the servants. She takes a keen and partisan interest in politics: some of her most pungent writing is elicited by her intense dislike of Gladstone, who was Prime Minister for some eight or nine years of the time covered by the Journal. (Prime Ministers, then as now, tend to attract fears, antipathies and prejudices not otherwise politically motivated; but in any case Gladstone had a knack of inspiring dislike, from Queen Victoria and Disraeli down. A contemporary lampoon refers to him as 'God's One Mistake'.) The times were less stable than they appeared: Beatrix gives graphic accounts of a number of riots and disturbances that show the London of the late 1880s to have been far from the calmly prosperous capital that some naïve admirers of the Victorian age suppose. The early portions of the Journal are alive with rumour, scandal and excitement. They were not written for posterity, so they are the more reliable as a reflection of their time. We read of the Phoenix Park murders, of the catastrophic expedition to relieve Gordon in Khartoum, of dynamite outrages, of the 'spring-heeled Jacks', of murders and of upsets on the Stock Market that even the placid Potter household found disturbing.

Interspersed with such dramatic events are records of visits to the art galleries and exhibitions that seem to have provided Beatrix's principal source of amusement outside her home. The somewhat pompous reports on what she saw on these occasions are qualified from time to time by the sardonic comments of her older self. But she knew what she was writing about. Rupert Potter's friendship with Sir John Millais put her in direct contact with the world of artists and sculptors, and her accounts of Millais and his wife Effie, of Holman Hunt and Ruskin, are lacking in any awe-struck sense of their importance. Indeed, her comments on Ruskin are downright disrespectful, as might be expected from a friend of John Millais.

Many readers will be interested in details such as the progress of Millais' famous 'Bubbles'; while there is an interesting glimpse of the speculation about the Laureateship following the death of Tennyson. And then, as now, the Royal Family were a source of interest, though the Queen is treated in a less friendly manner than she would be today: not until the Golden Jubilee of 1887 did Victoria recover the popularity she forfeited by her retirement following the Prince Consort's death five years before Beatrix Potter was born.

As for the Prince of Wales, his visit to the Holborn slums is summed up as that of 'a middle aged gentleman in a four-wheeler with his trousers rolled up, and probably holding his nose' – seventeen can be a sceptical as well as an impressionable age. (And 'the slums of Holborn' – it is the Tom-all-Alone's of *Bleak House* that she is talking about.)

Other well-known figures of the time are glimpsed. We see Oscar Wilde and his wife arriving at an exhibition; Henry Irving making his audience laugh without meaning to; Ellen Terry being the victim of an inauspicious stage debut; Catherine Booth, the redoubtable Salvation Army leader, dealing with a rowdy meeting. Beatrix Potter displays a lively interest in what was going on in the outside world. Understandably shy and self-conscious when in society, she seems to have enjoyed the extravagant activities and absurdities of those engaged in public life. But she remains unenvious and unimpressed. At the June Exhibition at the Royal Academy in 1882, for instance, she describes a portrait of her cousin Kate (whose engagement to Captain Crookshank was to provoke such disapproval) in terms of cool detachment. The picture was called 'Cupboard Love: Portrait of Miss Kate Potter and her poodle "Figaro".' Beatrix comments:

> After all one has heard, it is not as bad as I expected. Should not have known Kate, but it is rather a pretty picture. The chief part of it, however, is taken up by the cupboard.

From an early age she possessed that steady eye, that capacity to measure and discern, which she shared with another woman writer: Jane Austen comes to mind in more than one of Beatrix Potter's comments and observations. Indeed, the former's cool amusement at human folly and the dry playfulness of her letters are frequently echoed in the Journal. As Margaret Lane observes, Beatrix Potter possessed 'that rare kind of commonsense temperament which is more or less impervious to vanity'.

Another interesting feature of the earlier portion of the Journal is the reportage of jokes and comic anecdotes that exhibit a style of humour much in evidence at the time: Mr Pooter might have told a number of them. One also recognizes a Victorian taste, by no means peculiar to the age, for the ghoulish and macabre: like most people, the young Beatrix Potter was inclined to relish a murder or multiple disaster. It is gruesome to read of cats and dogs being boiled down for margarine; unlike some other entries at this time, the information is not prefaced by 'It is said that'. All in all, the early pages of the Journal focus on public events, oral traditions and local history: the prisoner of the nursery has her nose to the window but at other times her ear is at the door. Beatrix Potter had the makings of an interesting novelist.

As the years pass, her ambition to become a painter begins to be apparent: in her impatient endurance of lessons with the dulcet Mrs A., for example; her increasingly technical interest in materials and methods; and her assessment of the work of such diverse contemporaries among the artists of the day as Whistler, Alma-Tadema and Dante Gabriel Rossetti. She was unfriendly to the Aesthetic movement and the affectations of the later Pre-Raphaelites. On 3 April 1886, when she was nineteen, she wrote:

> The Rossettis have sold very high. To my mind they are bad, their only claim to attention is their colour, and that is hot, and of course one must not judge them by nature, but their artificiality is not beautiful as is sometimes the case with the Burne-Jones. Not that I like the latter either, but they are a shade better than the Rossettis, particularly such as contain harmonious combinations of blues and greys like the panels of creation, otherwise they are very weak in drawing, morbid in style, and forced and ridiculous in sentiment.

It could be the older Beatrix Potter speaking.

The Journal also provides evidence of the way in which photography was used as an aid to Victorian portraiture. As a result, one realizes that the seemingly idle and useless Rupert Potter did in fact have a hobby that was of benefit to others beside himself. Beatrix's emerging detachment from her father's moods and tantrums is amusing to follow. Despite her criticism of him, or possibly because of it, she appreciated and respected him more, one suspects, than she did her mother – who seems to have played a largely repressive role in her daughter's life. Only once is Helen Potter recorded as waxing enthusiastic over anything, while the very unIbsen-like episode of the wild duck suggests that much of the nursery research took place not so much with her approval as without her knowledge.

Beatrix's interest in painting was, however, not solely an interest in the art itself: she was concerned to record what was before her eyes and regarded her abilities as a means to an end. There was a streak of the social historian in her, and also of the scientist. She observed closely and with care. She searched for fossils and chronicled the hibernation of her hedgehog, while the study of fungi – which at one stage of the Journal appears to be her main interest, and which she considered as a possible full-time occupation – gave her something to paint that suited her gift for delineating the most intricate detail with exactitude and grace. Her knowledge of the working methods of Millais served her well. And yet this particular interest seems to have arisen mainly from the want of something more satisfying to do. The Journal, among other things, is a record of how time can be filled by a resourceful and imaginative mind when confronted with too much solitude and leisure.

Not unnaturally, in view of such a monotonous existence, the family holidays released her spirits and with them her capacity to write at length. The account of a visit to Falmouth in 1892, set down when she was twenty-four years old, is her first piece of sustained descriptive narrative, as compared with the more static, free-associating recollections of her childhood written two years before; and it also gave her practice and backgrounds for *Little Pig Robinson* (begun the following year but not published until 1929). It was written when the holiday was over, and reflects both her keen appraisal of the characteristics of a landscape and her sharp and often humorous eye for detail. Like *Pig Robinson* itself, it is rather conventional compared with some of her later efforts, but it is full of thumb-nail sketches and an ability to select the telling phrase. In the complete Journal it covers twenty-seven pages. She had already shown that she could master a literary portrait or character sketch. In the first half of the Journal there are noteworthy pictures of elderly people such as her great-aunt Sidney and her grandmother Potter, the latter captured impressionistically in a passage that anticipates similar entries in the Diary of Virginia Woolf.

Beatrix really begins to come into her own as a descriptive writer with her record of the family holiday in Scotland later in 1892. The country around the small town of Dunkeld, on the southern edge of the Scottish Highlands, is opulent, well wooded and well watered. She had long regarded the area as 'home', thanks to ten childhood summers spent at Dalguise House on the banks of the River Tay. Her reluctance to return to the house reflects her awareness of, and recoil from, a nostalgia she must have felt to be debilitating. But now the Journal takes on a spontaneous, liberated quality not found in the earlier pages. Her interest and delight in the region is accompanied, even excelled, by her interest in its inhabitants. Her gifts for portraiture and her love for the small, quirky, comic detail, blend with her response to the past and to the mind's capacity to dramatize and colour its experiences. The reported conversations of the old washerwoman Kitty MacDonald (in due course to be transformed into Mrs Tiggy-Winkle) are a good example of her art. But the carefree nature of most of the entries at this time does not exclude a touch of caustic resignation. She was making the most of such liberty as was available.

The Journal is not resumed until the following year. When it is, it becomes more animated and abrupt in style. The Torquay holiday is recorded with a briskness that foreshadows the crusty personality she would become in later life: 'It is possible to see too much of Ada Smallfield.' (No doubt; but the reader would like to see a little more.) And she writes with a certain irony of her visit the following year to her Hutton cousins at Stroud in Gloucestershire. Her departure had been something of an achievement, for at the age of twenty-eight she was only allowed to go away from home by herself against her mother's protests. The Stroud entries show how she responds to the rare stimulus of company of her own age, and are also of interest in indicating her attitude to religious belief. A Unitarian by upbringing, scrupulously honest in intellectual matters, she was strongly attracted to the simplicity and above all, perhaps, to the silence of Quaker worship, so seemingly consonant with

> The silence that is in the starry sky,
> The sleep that is among the lonely hills.

Wordsworth's lines evoke the quietness and sense of space that became increasingly important to her.

In *Cousin Beatie* Ulla Hyde-Parker recalls her first visit to Hill Top in Beatrix Potter's company:

> We reached the front door, and as she placed the key in its lock, she said, 'It is in here I go to be quiet and still with myself.'

Such a need to be alone is increasingly apparent in the account of the holiday spent in 1894 at Lennel House, near Coldstream, amid the open landscape of the Scottish border. It contains some haunting descriptions of solitary drives into the hills. The north country always elicited this tranquil joy and sense of being at home. The Lennel passages of the Journal at times recall Dorothy Wordsworth in their precision and quiet delight in observing what lies to hand. But the tranquillity is offset by a rueful tartness peculiar to Beatrix Potter:

> I . . . stopped at the top of a steep bank, and walked down to the Leet which turns in a half-circle round a little meadow under a hanging golden wood. There was a rickety, high wooden foot-bridge and a ford. I watched a boy ride over on a horse, the water scarcely over the fetlocks, babbling and sunny, and read a written paper pinned on a willow tree 'This Ford is unsafe when in flood'.
>
> Went back into the Duns road, marvelling at the vast stone gate-posts with pointed stone caps in the spare hedges. Stopped at the wood at the corner and got some white scented funguses and was again bitten, as usual. Undressed during afternoon, suspect spiders, but have never found anything except an average of seventy bites, but sometimes beyond counting.

In the south of England, at Weymouth and at Swanage, she becomes more critical and restive: one senses that the restricted annual round was getting hard to bear. Gwaynynog in Denbighshire, a family home, pleases her more; here, too, we see anticipations of what she would make of her own home at Hill Top Farm – a repository for the antique north-country furniture she so admired. And in Sawrey and at Windermere in 1895 there is the feeling of a genuine homecoming. (Indeed, it is notable that she does not subject the Lake District to the kind of traveller's description that she gives of places foreign to her nature.) Simultaneously, there comes a time of stress and illness, presumably caused by the strain of her unnaturally constricted life. Eight years earlier she had suffered a serious attack of rheumatic fever, and she remained liable to bouts of headaches, sickness and exhaustion. Following the record of the contented holiday spent at Lakefield, Sawrey, in 1896, the Journal entries become relatively perfunctory and the writing of them was perhaps a burden. They are principally concerned with her preparations for the talk on the germination of spores which was read to the Linnean Society under the auspices of Sir Henry

Roscoe. This project did not lead to anything further, and four years later Beatrix Potter was at work on what would become *The Tale of Peter Rabbit.*

In abridging the Journal I have concentrated on Beatrix Potter the writer, with the aim of uncovering some of the sources of her imaginative life. Accordingly, a good deal of material from the early diaries has been omitted, including many of her comments on politics and some of the accounts of the numerous art exhibitions she attended. Although these entries are interesting from a historical point of view, in both cases her reactions are too immature and second-hand to be truly representative of the woman she was to become. But as she grows up her characteristic style grows more pronounced. The supple precision of her finest books owes much to a tone of voice perfected in the Journal entries: the terse, clinching phrases, the crisp Johnsonian appositions, and the lowered inflexion at the end of sentences which characterize her prose, are anticipated in passage after passage here. Three taken quite at random from the complete Journal underline the point. In 1887 she writes:

> At one College Mr Gladstone went up to a group of females, whom he took to be the relations and friends of the students, and shook hands with them. He found afterwards that they were the house-maids attached to the Establishment.

At Birnam, on 8 October 1892:

> On a wooden foot-bridge stood six rams, great old fellows stalking by themselves. I photographed them successfully and watched a pack of grouse scudding along the side of the hill in the shadow. The sunset light was very sweet, striking the old huts and farm buildings on the east side of the Burn.

And on 3 December 1896, during a visit to Kew:

> I saw Mr Thistleton-Dyer through the window. I sat for about ¼ hour in a small room watching a large, slow clerk cut snippets from a pink newspaper and paste them carefully on a sheet of foolscap with the Royal arms. I felt all over the patterns on the legs of a cane-bottom chair, and read an advertisement of foreign steamers.

It is this kind of self-contained paragraph, often built up in units of three, which gives the distinctive flavour to those of her books that match narrative to illustration, page by page. In *The Tale of the Flopsy Bunnies*, for instance, we are told that

> Mr McGregor's rubbish heap was a mixture. There were jam pots and paper bags, and mountains of chopped grass from the mowing machine (which always tasted oily), and some rotten vegetable marrows and an old boot or two. One day – oh joy! – there were a quantity of overgrown lettuces, which had 'shot' into flower.

And inevitably one turns the page: the passage is poised for continuation. This instinct for balance and restraint in movement was the result of the controlled self-communing she had been forced to exercise. Understatement and satirical irony are necessary weapons for those obliged to hold their emotional and imaginative energies in check. (But even so, she records her temper as on one occasion 'boiling like a kettle'.)

Beatrix Potter took great trouble with her writing. In later life she complained that her books were regarded as 'toy books – not literature. Certainly my English publishers consider the pictures first; and the words a poor second.' The imbalance of such a valuation becomes obvious as one reads the Journal. Indeed, it is arguable that as a stylist Beatrix Potter has had a wider influence than many more eminent writers; and the Journal was the means through which her prose evolved from a certain over-literary quality – evident even in such a patently sincere passage as her lament over Dalguise House – to the austere beauty of the accounts of drives taken in the pony carriage around Lennel. The medium of the change was, in part at least, the transmuted conversational observations from which her peculiarly personal tone is derived.

One result of this literary method is to afford the reader fresh perspectives in time through her reporting of other people's memories, her own interest in the past making us realize how each generation becomes a source of romantic interest to the next but one. The loving curiosity evident in Beatrix's attitude to the Leech family home at Gorse Hall was to help create the peculiarly haunting atmosphere of Hill Top Farm. This was a kind of sensibility that Beatrix Potter shared with Elizabeth Gaskell, whose widower was such a well-loved friend of the younger writer: Mrs Gaskell's John Thornton, the hero of *North and South*, is of the same moral breed as Beatrix's grandfather, Edmund Potter. Both women found happiness and fulfilment in the country bordering the Lake District, for Mrs Gaskell wrote some of her finest work at Silverdale on the shores of Morecambe Bay – a landscape associated still more closely with Beatrix Potter's near contemporary, the Westmorland novelist Constance Holme, who shared her interest in folk records and traditions, and whose most famous novel, *The Lonely Plough*, describes the marshes of the Kent Estuary, within easy reach of Sawrey. In her own way Beatrix Potter, too, was a regional writer. And just as William Wordsworth spent much of his boyhood at Hawkshead and immortalized the scenery of Windermere and Esthwaite Water in *The Prelude*, so at the very time that Beatrix Potter was discovering Hill Top the young Arthur Ransome was spending his holidays in the neighbouring valley, as a result of which Coniston Water became the setting for another series of books for children which, no less than hers, succeeded in fusing the adult world with that of the child through an effortless combination of humour, psychological realism and a feeling for natural beauty. The Furness area of Lancashire, of which all three authors wrote, must surely be accounted sacred territory in the literature of childhood.

Beatrix Potter's Journal also contains some unexpected entries. While she responded to the Scottish border and the countryside round Sawrey, she did not greatly care for mountain scenery. The landscapes she describes with most obvious pleasure are of a more spacious, fertile kind (she was, after all, to be a farmer). Nor does she say much about the books she read: she used the Waverley novels to teach herself to read, and Scott and Maria Edgeworth remained lifelong favourites. Later on, her American friends introduced her to the work of Sarah Orne Jewett and Willa Cather, both of whom she much admired, but at the period of the Journal literature seems to have interested her very little; even her admiration for Shakespeare's plays did not prevent her from using them as a memory test. Her attention was reserved for animate beings, and throughout the Journal there are references to animals, birds and reptiles – the rabbits, hedgehogs, squirrels, newts, frogs, badgers, dormice, cats and toads who were to provide her with her inimitable cast of characters. The resemblance of Mrs Tiggy-Winkle to an actual washerwoman is not the only case in point: surely Mr Alderman Ptolemy Tortoise and Sir Isaac Newton originally paid a call not on

Mr Jeremy Fisher but on Mr Rupert Potter. The perpetually purring Mary Ellen of *The Fairy Caravan* has more than a passing likeness to the debilitating painting instructress, Mrs A., with her reiterated 'smoothness, softness'. And 'A little *dog* indeed! As if there were no CATS in Sawrey!' It was not only Tabitha Twitchit who could be disdainful in conversation: the 'dignity and repose' of her tea party suggest the At Homes (if any) held at Bolton Gardens by Beatrix's mother. (But it must have been the tiny, crowded Hill Top, rather than the London terrace house, which was invaded by the affable Mr Jackson, most unyielding of intrusive visitors.) In every case her characters seem to be interchangeable with human beings. In the Journal, too, we find the 'singular dried-up but pepperish old gentleman Mr Cutter', likened to 'a wood-louse diving in and out of a rotten log'. Beatrix Potter was eighteen when she wrote that.

Insects, animals and birds are also observed and appreciated in the Journal for their own sake – the Store's cat 'couchant in a pile of biscuit canisters'; the hens scuffling in a shed at Sawrey; or Nelly the pony to whom Beatrix was so grateful for her Border drives. And the human beings are similarly portrayed as interesting phenomena – the old lady, all fidgets on the train to Alnwick; John William Wandle speaking up at Falmouth; Lady John Manners adding castor oil to her potatoes – each one seems to be a potential character for a book. It is pleasant also to note Beatrix Potter's appreciative response to circuses, put to such good use in *The Fairy Caravan*, and to share in her amusement at the antics of small boys. Evidently their lawlessness appealed to her: it is easy to see why.

The Journal contains many turns of phrase and touches of description that look forward to her books:

> The air so warm and mild and spring-like, mildness one feels sometimes at the end of the year . . . The rabbits sat out at the edge of the woods in the sunlight.

This recalls a moment from *The Tale of Mr Tod*; while *Mr Tod*, in turn, contains passages that might have come from the Journal:

> He called out that it was morning – sunrise; and that the jays were making a noise down below in the woods . . .
> Every minute the sun shone warmer on the top of the hill. In the valley there was a sea of white mist, with golden tops of trees showing through.

Again from the fields down below in the mist there came the angry
cry of a jay – followed by the sharp yelping bark of a fox!

Beatrix Potter had a poor opinion of jays; in this matter she and her
mother were at one. The perfect timing of this passage, its
truthfulness and evocation of light and sound, linger in the mind
for life. In *Mr Tod* and *Pigling Bland* her gifts as a prose writer are
at their height.

In addition to her ability to evoke atmosphere with the minimum
of words – an ability fostered by the diary entries – Beatrix Potter
had a keen sense of place which adds to the memorability of her
books. Mr McGregor's garden, a distillation of those at Gwaynynog
and at Fawe Park, near Keswick, can almost be touched and smelled;
while the depictions of Derwent Water in *Squirrel Nutkin* and of
Newlands in *Mrs Tiggy-Winkle*, in addition to being beautiful and
atmospheric, are precise and accurate. (It is distressing to contrast
the serenity of the paintings of the delicate squirrels sailing across
the lake with the real-life tragedy on Derwent Water that Beatrix
recorded while staying at Lingholm.) Other places mentioned in
the Journal reappear in the books. Esthwaite Water is visible in
Jemima Puddle-Duck, Sawrey in *Ginger and Pickles* and in *The Pie and
the Patty-Pan*, that miniature satire on polite and not so polite
manners. (Both of these last two most gossipy stories may in part
derive from memories of local people at Birnam.) The most moving
presentation of Sawrey and its gardens appears in the account
Timmy Willie gives of his country home, during his uncomfortable
visit to Johnny Town-Mouse in Hawkshead. Johnny, an urban
personage, is sceptical, commenting that the garden sounds rather
a dull place, and inquiring, 'What do you do when it rains?' The
reply of the little field mouse rises with the quiet force of absolute
contentment:

When it rains, I sit in my little sandy burrow and shell corn and
seeds from my Autumn store. I peep out at the throstles and
blackbirds on the lawn, and my friend Cock Robin. And when the
sun comes out again, you should see my garden and the flowers –
roses and pinks and pansies – no noise except the birds and bees and
the lambs in the meadows.

The words surely voice their author's own thankfulness for the life
she had achieved: *The Tale of Johnny Town-Mouse* was published in

1918, after she had been married for five years. Though based on one of Aesop's fables, it is as locally rooted as are its predecessors.

This north-country flavour became stronger with each story Beatrix Potter wrote, and nowhere is it more evident than in *The Fairy Caravan*, a book which she considered to be undervalued. Certainly it lacks the economy of style and sureness of pace which one finds in her narrative masterpieces, *The Tailor of Gloucester*, *The Roly-Poly Pudding*, *Mr Tod* and *Pigling Bland*. At times it has a weary, ramshackle quality, and only occasionally matches its predecessors in wit. But it is full of local names and references, it has a sense of space and movement, and it makes one conscious of the existence of a country community that is not only made up of animals. It is therefore all the more appropriate that in the chapter called 'Springtime in Birds' Place' Beatrix Potter should evoke her beloved Hertfordshire 'home' at Camfield Place, and put it into the mouth of Xarifa the dormouse, 'the sweetest little animal I ever knew'.

She wrote lovingly of Camfield Place in a descriptive piece composed in 1890 which was printed at the end of the complete version of the Journal. It retains that position here, where it is now followed by 'The Lonely Hills', first published in 1942 in *The Horn Book*, the well-known American magazine concerned with books for children: the editor, Bertha Mahoney Miller, was a valued friend. Beatrix Potter had planned a continuation of *The Fairy Caravan*, but only succeeded in producing a few fragments. One of these was a story called 'The Solitary Mouse', which was printed by Leslie Linder in his History of her writings. She incorporated some of it in 'The Lonely Hills', the last of her works to appear before her death. Stylistically it contrasts with the piece on Camfield Place. The former is assured and flowing; 'The Lonely Hills' is allusive and condensed. But, for all that, one senses half a lifetime of experience behind it. It constitutes Beatrix Potter's last message to the world.

From each period of her life she was to leave a benefaction. With the proceeds from her books she provided the various properties she bequeathed to the National Trust – among them not only Hill Top Farm itself, but also the extensive Monk Coniston Estate (part of which had belonged to her great-grandfather) and the upper Troutbeck valley, whose haunted loneliness she so greatly loved. And from her younger days she bequeathed the Journal. It consorts perfectly with her other writings. Not only is it a valuable record of what it was like to live as a young unmarried woman in the last two decades of the nineteenth century, it also amounts to a literary workshop for an artist. The appeal of her humorous, unsentimental but imaginative response to life shows no sign of having dwindled in the hundred years since she set down the comments and observations printed here. Nor is it likely to do so for, as she wrote to one of her American correspondents, her aim had always been to create

> that pleasant, unchanging world of realism and romance, which in our northern clime, is stiffened by hard weather, a tough ancestry and the strength that comes from the hills.

It is an imaginative landscape that was hard won and peculiarly her own. Her books domesticate its magic. The Journal tells us something of how that magic came to be.

Glen Cavaliero

THE CODE-WRITING

From about the age of fourteen until she was thirty, Beatrix Potter kept a Journal in her own privately-invented code-writing. It appears that even her closest friends knew nothing of this code-writing. She never spoke of it, and only one instance has come to light where it was mentioned. This was in a letter to her much-loved cousin, Caroline Clark (the Caroline Hutton of her younger days), written five weeks before Beatrix Potter died, in which she described it as 'apparently inspired by a united admiration of Boswell and Pepys', continuing, 'when I was young I already had the itch to write, without having any material to write about (the modern young author is not damped by such considerations). I used to write long-winded descriptions, hymns(!) and records of conversations in a kind of cipher shorthand which I am now unable to read even with a magnifying glass.' In her opinion they were 'exasperating and absurd compositions'.

In the spring of 1952 when working on *The Art of Beatrix Potter* I had the pleasure of a visit from Captain and Mrs Duke. She was the *Stephanie* to whom *The Tale of Mr Jeremy Fisher* was dedicated, and her mother was a first cousin to Beatrix Potter. When Stephanie was a little girl she lived at Melford Hall, Suffolk, and Beatrix Potter often stayed there and tried out many of her stories on the child. As I was taking leave of them at the railway station she turned to me saying, 'Do you know that we have just come across the most extraordinary collection of Papers at Castle Cottage, a large bundle of loose sheets and exercise books written in cipher-writing which we can make nothing of – I wonder if *you* could decipher them? – I wish you could see them!' At that moment the train came in and there was no time for further conversation.

It was not until several months later when I was at Hill Top that I first saw this mysterious bundle of Papers which had recently been

given to the National Trust to keep with their other Beatrix Potter
Papers. I was able to examine them in detail, but could find no clue
to the cipher-symbols, apart from the fact that some of them looked
like ordinary letters of the alphabet, also the figure *3* appeared very
frequently. There was, however, an indication of the period covered,
since the figures *'83*, *'84*, etc. had been marked in the top right-
hand corner of some of the sheets – large red-ink figures written
boldly over the cipher-writing. Also, at the beginning of some of
the exercise books, Beatrix Potter had put the year, *1892*, *1893*, etc.

In two instances some of the loose sheets had been neatly sewn
together at the top left-hand corner forming *sets*, other sheets were
of irregular shape and size, in most cases unruled. The remaining
code-writing was contained in ordinary paper-covered exercise
books of varying sizes, with ruled pages. In another exercise book,
an old school-book labelled *French Dictation*, the pages had been cut
up into long narrow strips forming hinges on which loose sheets of
code-writing were pasted. This book eventually turned out to be a
collection of reviews of the Picture Galleries which Beatrix Potter
had visited between the years 1882 and 1895.

The following year when again visiting Hill Top, I was allowed
to take away some of the code-written sheets in order to study them
at my leisure. I hoped that I could find a clue which would eventually
lead to their translation, but the next few years passed without any
definite results, and all attempts to break down the code failed. By
Easter 1958 I was beginning to think somewhat sadly that these
code-written sheets would remain a mystery for ever.

On the evening of Easter Monday, 1958, I remember thinking to
myself, I will have one *last* attempt at solving this code-writing,
more to pass the time than with any anticipation of success. I
selected a sheet at random, and then, quite by chance, noticed a line
near the bottom of the page which contained the Roman numerals
XVI and the year *1793*. Was this a clue – could something of
consequence have happened to a Pope bearing the numerals XVI,
or to King Louis XVI in the year 1793? I consulted a Dictionary of
Dates without success, and then, almost by chance, looked up Louis
XVI in the Index to the Children's Encyclopedia, where I read
'Louis XVI, French King; Born Versailles 1754; guillotined Paris
1793.' Here at last was a possible clue!

It so happened that this particular line of code-writing contained a word in which the second cipher-symbol was the letter *x*, and, while there was no justification for assuming this to represent an *x*, it immediately suggested the work *executed* as the equivalent of *guillotined*. Fortunately Beatrix Potter had left the letter *x* unchanged, and the clue was therefore valid. In actual fact the word turned out to be *execution*, and the likelihood of this word was confirmed by noticing that it appeared to contain nine cipher-symbols, of which the first and third were the same.

With the help of these assumed symbols, other words were deciphered, and by midnight on that memorable Easter Monday practically the whole of Beatrix Potter's code-alphabet had been solved, and one of the early sheets of code-writing partly translated. If this particular sheet had not been an early example, written in bold copperplate style, it is doubtful whether I would ever have discovered the basic symbols of her code-alphabet.

The Code Alphabet

a	a	ħ	k	ʊ	ü
l	b	t	l	η	v
2	c	n	m	m	w
σ	d	m	n	x	x
k	e	e	o	η	y
c	f	ᴁ	p	3	z
σ	g	q	q	2	to, too, two
ι	h	w	r	3	the, three
ι	i	ʏ	s	4	for, four
ι	j	1	t	4	and

On the other hand, had one but known it, this collection of code-written sheets contained the perfect clue – a page of note-paper headed *XC*. I recollect on more than one occasion looking at these Roman numerals and wondering what they could represent? A little more thought might have told me, for in a letter to Miss Mahoney, her American friend, Beatrix Potter had once described her method of writing, and how she 'read the Bible, un-revised version and Old Testament' if she felt her 'style needed chastening'. The Roman numerals were, in fact, the heading to verses 1–12 of the 90th Psalm, which she had written down from memory. Apart from two wrong words and three which had been omitted, it was word-perfect – a tribute to her powers of memory, and a simple and straightforward key to the code!

Since Beatrix Potter did not leave a key to the code, she probably thought that these writings would never be read by anyone else – in fact in one paragraph she wrote 'no one will read this'.

Although the key to Beatrix Potter's code-writing had now been found, it required a great deal of practice before this knowledge could be applied with any degree of certainty. One problem was learning to recognize the cipher-symbols as they gradually lost their copperplate form when she began to write fluently and at high speed. This made it desirable to learn to read *words* rather than to decipher individual symbols.

Working through the Journal word by word and sheet by sheet, it was strange how one forgot about Beatrix Potter the author of the *Peter Rabbit* books, and became conscious of a charming person called *Miss Potter*, who lived at Number Two, Bolton Gardens, London.

The early sheets of copperplate handwriting were translated first, and then as experience was gradually built up, the later and more difficult ones were attempted. In order that any desired part of the Journal could be easily checked, each page of code-writing was translated on to a single sheet of appropriate size, ruled with the same number of lines as the original, and having the same number of words in each line. When individual words could not be deciphered, spaces were left and the words re-considered at a later date after further experience had been gained.

In checking the accuracy of translation, early editions of *Whitaker's Almanack* provided much of the information needed in connection with the accounts of political activities, while large-scale Ordnance maps were used to identify place-names. People having specialized knowledge were consulted on such subjects as Botany, Natural History, Geology, etc., while the names of artists and the titles of pictures were verified from exhibition catalogues of the period and from auction sale catalogues.

With a view to obtaining first-hand knowledge of the places mentioned in the Journal, some of these were visited, including Birnam and Dunkeld in Perthshire, Sawrey in the Lake District,

Falmouth in Cornwall, also Camfield Place, Hertfordshire, where Beatrix Potter so frequently stayed with her grandmother Potter.

Beatrix Potter's code-alphabet included some of the letters in *our* alphabet, but these did not necessarily stand for the same letters in *her* alphabet. She also used characters resembling the Greek alphabet and German script. The rest were imaginary symbols, also the figures 2, 3 and 4.

The figure 3 was used to represent *three* and also the word *the*, the latter accounting for its frequent appearance on every page. Similarly, the figure 2 was used for *two*, *to* and *too*, and the figure 4 for *four* and *for*. At times, this choice of alternative words could alter the meaning of a sentence, and introduced an element of uncertainty into the translation. Occasionally the figures were used as parts of words, such as *4get* or *2gether*, which again added to the difficulty of translation as the words did not *look* right.

One of the main problems, however, arose from the fact that often when two symbols were joined together they resembled a *different* symbol, making it difficult at times to be certain of the word, particularly in the case of people's names, place names and scientific terms. Again, some of the abbreviations for example *gr.* for either grandmother or grandfather, added further to the problems of translation.

At first Beatrix Potter distinguished between capitals and small letters by placing a line underneath each capital, but this only occurred on a few of the early sheets, and from 1882 onwards she made no distinction between the two. Furthermore, she seldom indicated where one paragraph ended and the next began, as her writing was practically continuous.

Throughout the translation, in order to show more clearly the chronological sequence of events, the day and date have been added. If Beatrix Potter's day and date did not correspond, the *day* was assumed to be correct and the date amended accordingly.

It is of interest to note that throughout the whole of the Journal there are comparatively few parts which have been extensively revised, and from the general neatness of the majority of the sheets it would appear that Beatrix Potter knew exactly what she wished to say before writing it down; also, in view of an occasional word which has been altered, it is evident that she attached importance to her choice of words. (One of the few sheets with extensive corrections is illustrated in the 1892 example of her code-writing.)

Beatrix Potter's vocabulary was a large one, and searches often had to be made for confirmation of some of the more unusual words. In regard to her spelling, there were frequent instances of mis-spelt words, some of which occurred several times, for example *beautifull* for *beautiful*; also, at times her spelling was phonetic, such as *minits* for *minutes*, *Glasco* for *Glasgow*, etc. In the translation, however, the correct spelling has been used.

The earliest specimens of code-writing which have been found, belong to the year 1881 when Beatrix Potter was fifteen. It is thought, however, that earlier examples than these once existed, but were destroyed at the age of twenty when she read through and sorted out her code-written sheets. On one of these early sheets which had been retained she wrote 'looked over – all right', and on another (the Review of her uncle Crompton's pictures), we find the remark 'looked over – tall writing'. Again, on what had once been a folded sheet of note-paper, a fragment of the writing on the torn-off page still remained as proof that a part had been destroyed – either too personal, or not up to her standard of writing and the subject-matter of insufficient interest to keep.

This period of reading through and sorting out has been verified by the following comments added to a review of her visit to the 1883 Winter Exhibition at the Royal Academy of Arts – 'The preceding remarks are so amusing to me as representing childlike and simple, not to say, silly sentiments that have since passed away, that I preserve the greater part of them, though it is rather appalling to find one was such a goose only three years since.'

That Beatrix Potter was using her code-writing at the age of fourteen is suggested by a remark written at the head of a code-written sheet of verses of hymns – 'Copied off scraps of paper, probably written about 1880.' Alongside one set of verses are the words 'Bearing no date, doubtful authorship, probably a close imitation,' while alongside another set, 'Early, no date, have not the slightest recollection of writing the hymn, but believe it is original.'

In 1881 her code-writing was in a comparatively large and carefully formed copperplate hand. The fragments which exist are written in ink on single and folded sheets of note-paper.

During 1882 and 1883 the handwriting became smaller, but her symbols were still well formed. As the handwriting developed it became more flowing and individual symbols were joined together. Some of the writing of this period is in ink and some in pencil. Difficulty was encountered with sheets which were originally written in pencil and later inked over, since *both* sets of writing were visible at once and the effect was somewhat confusing. On the other hand there was the advantage that if a word could not be read from one set of writing, it could sometimes be identified from the other.

In a letter which Beatrix Potter wrote to her father from Ilfracombe in April 1883, which many years later she referred to as 'Worth keeping, an early impression leading to *Pig Robinson*,' she described events which were also recorded in the Journal, almost word-for-word. It was therefore possible in this particular instance to check the accuracy of translation.

Between 1884 and 1887 Beatrix Potter's handwriting became even smaller, and by 1886 it reached its smallest proportions. In an extreme case, a single sheet measuring 8 in. × 6½ in. contained over fifteen hundred words on the one side only.

There was apparently very little code-writing from 1888 until the beginning of 1892. This is believed to be due to ill-health, for in 1895 Beatrix Potter wrote 'We came to Holehird, Windermere, where we tarried in the summer of 89 when I could hardly walk at all . . . I think I must have been in very weak health when I was here before, though not conscious of it to complaining at the time.'

From the summer of 1892 until January 1897, the Journal was contained in ten exercise books totalling three-hundred-and-sixty pages, and throughout the whole of this period her handwriting was of normal proportions.

Beatrix Potter's Journal ended on the 31st January, 1897, when at the age of thirty she was about to submit a Paper to the Linnean Society of London 'On the Germination of the Spores of *Agaricineae*'. During the last few months of the Journal, she described in detail her preparation of this Paper and the help and encouragement she received from her uncle Sir Henry Roscoe, the distinguished chemist.

The Paper was eventually read at a Meeting of the Linnean Society on April 1st. 1897, but it was unfortunately never published.

The Minutes of a Council Meeting of the Society held on April 8th. 1897 state – 'A proposal on behalf of Miss Helen Potter to withdraw her Paper No. 2978, "On the Germination of the Spores of *Agaricineae*" was sanctioned.'

This request for withdrawal is thought to have been due to the fact that Beatrix Potter wished to bring her researches to a more advanced stage before permitting publication, and is supported by the fact that during the latter part of 1897 she prepared many highly-magnified studies of spore development.[1]

From now onwards the keeping of a Journal appears to have been put on one side as Beatrix Potter became more and more absorbed in the planning of her books. It is of interest to note, however, that in later years she sometimes wrote odd notes and even fragments of stories in code-writing, but it was never used again for the purpose of a Journal.

Leslie Linder

BEATRIX POTTER'S JOURNAL

1881

Grandmamma Leech's Recollections

LONDON

Grandmamma Leech was telling us today about when she came to London. She did not say the date. They came up by the stage coach because great grandfather was going to buy a new one and did not wish to come in his own.[1]

They were too many to go all at once, so great grandmamma and most of them went on in front, and grandmamma and great grandpapa followed, I suppose next day. He had been ill and grandma was to take great care of him and not to let him hang his head when he went to sleep, consequently she got no rest herself and when they stopped at an inn to eat, she begged for a bedroom where she might wash herself.

They went to Radcliffe Hotel in Blackfriar's! The fashionable place where all the Manchester people went. Great granddad was afraid to take them to the city on a weekday because of the great crowd, so he took them through Lombard Street etc. on Sunday.

He bought an immense family coach (bought of Silk's who supplied four succeeding generations), a great length with a dickey behind, two imperials on the top, large seat in front. The postilions rode the horses, of which four were necessary, a thing which greatly disturbed great grandpa, who thought it dreadful to keep so many.

They got on without mishap as far as Stockport. Great grandpa (nervous about four horses) wished to reach home after dark. The man did not know the way very well, and drove up a street which came to an end. There was the immense coach almost jambed between the houses.

A man in a nightcap put his head out of a window and exclaimed, 'What in the world have we here?' 'We may well ask what 'av we theer, but coom down an' 'elp us,' replied great grandpa. They had to pull the coach backwards, having taken out the horses, to the great amusement of the people of Stockport.

The final end of the family coach was to be sold to a man in Hyde who kept hearses. Great grandma was very sorry it should go but it took so much room.

The stage coaches changed horses every ten miles and reached London in twenty-four (?) hours. It was an excellent road. Reynolds[2] in later day rode Major up and back three times taking two days, and once when detained by a snowstorm, three. There was one hill where outside passengers were obliged to walk up. There was a lady on the top on grandma's first journey who grumbled much at having to do it in the middle of the night.

When the railway was opened it took eight hours to come from Manchester to London. There was a certain pompous old gentleman when grandma was young who used continually to say 'I tell you some of you will see the time when one can eat one's breakfast in Manchester and one's dinner in London.' He both saw and did it himself.

When grandma was at Miss Lawrence's school, she and some other girls used occasionally to go backward and forward between Manchester and Liverpool. There was generally some gentleman going who looked after them. One day there was an old lady who was discoursing on the danger of the times, she said she was even told they were to use steam engines, she said people would be forced to travel whether they liked or not. Mr Stuart, the gentleman, teased her finely about it.

The road from Hyde to Manchester was so bad that great grandmamma used to ride to the Assemblies on a pillion behind great-grandpa, and put on her grand dress when she got there. Some horses objected to 'double', and they always rode 'Old Jarvie'. At the bottom of the hill near the flowery field mills was a brook crossed by stepping stones which horses had to ford. One day 'Old Jarvie' was crossing carrying 'double', when the pillion came loose and great grandma slipped over his tail into the water.

At one time there was great discontent among the mill people who were disturbed by the doctrines of a sect called Luddites, who thought everyone should be equal. They had made arrangements for a riot, decided who should be killed and how the spoil should be divided. Great grandmamma was aware that when the clothes were hung up on the lines, the mill folk decided who should have this and that. She was very anxious about great grandpapa and wished him to go away for a bit but he wouldn't.

At last a letter was put through the hall door, informing great grandfather he was one of those to be killed, and that it was written by someone who knew what was going on. He resolved to go to Liverpool. Grandmamma who was two years old can just remember being left at her aunt's and seeing her father and mother ride off with the baby.

He was no sooner gone than there was a great clamour after him. He must come back, no one should hurt him. So in a few days he returned and things quieted down.

Grandmamma has still got her own and grandfather's wedding clothes. His were very tight-fitting. Uncle Willie tried to get them on but couldn't, which surprised grandmamma, though I should think it only natural.

Her wedding dress had very large loose sleeves with tight swansdown ones under them. People who could not afford swansdown had feathers. The sleeves were always made to take off, young ladies generally changing them in the evening, in the same way as was afterwards done with the long drawers.

Mamma was once walking in the garden when a little girl, when one of the gardeners called after her that she had lost something, and presented her with an elegant embroidered drawer-leg.

Grandmamma has also a bonnet and pelisse. The bonnets had great pokes which were filled up by the frills of a cap worn under them. These caps were made with great care, the great point being that they should not look prim or quakerish. The pelisse which belonged to great grandmamma is of green silk shot with blue, very pretty. It came down to the feet and had sleeves tight at the wrist and loose at the shoulder.

Grandmamma seems still to prefer post travelling for some things. She says grandfather and she drove all over England for their wedding tour in a chariot, and it was the nicest journey she ever went. Crinolines seem to have been a great trouble, particularly on tours abroad, Hannah[3] particularly disliked them. It was almost impossible to ride a mule with one on, till at last grandma found a way of tying one side of the crinoline top to her waist, when she managed very nicely.

They were also worn in the mills, in spite of all that the masters could do to keep them out, for they were both in the way and dangerous.

1882

'Papa says he never made a good bargain'

LONDON

Sunday, January 15th. Poor little Jack of the South Eastern Railway has had an accident. He is a fox terrier who has been spoken of a good deal in the papers. About a year ago he was first seen, a stray but by no means lost dog. He travelled about in the guards' vans, at first to stations near Lewes (where he was first seen) and then between Lewes, Brighton and London, invariably taking a train which would enable him to reach Lewes by bedtime. Then the Company gave him a collar with their name on it. One day he went to a wedding and turned up at Lewes next day covered with ribbons.

One day he was rather late for his return train. He was hurrying over the line when his feet slipped and the express crushed one of his front legs. He was taken to a veterinary surgeon near Lewes, who took off his leg. The dog tore off the bandages once, but was found out in time and is expected to appear shortly on three legs.

The barometer is said to be higher than it's been for forty years, delightful weather, thick white fog.

Rufus=Prince, the chestnut horse is disposed of at last. Papa sent Reynolds to the Zoological Gardens to enquire the price of cat's meat: £2 for a very fat horse, 30/- for a middling one, thin ones not taken as the lions are particular. However, he is sold to a cab owner along the road for £15. He was bought a year ago for ninety. Papa says he never made a good bargain.

They are much bothered by the scholars of a Sunday afternoon down at Miss Hammond's.[1] The bells are continually ringing. Last Sunday there was a tremendous pull. Miss Hammond and Lizzie rushed to the door to see what could be the matter. There was an old workhouse woman who enquired was Dr Goodrich (the parish doctor)'s name Alfred or Arthur. Another time, Miss Hammond's brother saw from his studio window five very small boys seated in the laburnum tree smoking. He sent down the boy he was drawing who caught the biggest by the legs and gave him a sound whipping.

Convenient way of disposing of horses once practised by someone papa knew in the North of England. They turned one loose on the road, and sold the other for 7/6. I have heard Uncle Crompton bought a donkey for seven pence.

Mr Stocker says when he was young they could tell an Oxford clergyman from a Cambridge because the Cambridge said 'amen' with a short 'a'. Miss Hammond saw a print checked brown and white dress all over flounces labelled 'aesthetic' 15/6.

Sunday, January 29th. Papa saw Mr Bright[2] yesterday. He told him he'd been to dinner at a Club he had never been to before, Brooks' I think. They showed him a very old Betting Book of 1781 in which were a great many large bets of C. J. Fox.[3] Also an old Gambling Table with seats for nine and the man who kept the money, and holes in the table before each person to keep the money in.

An old woman was buried at Paris last Saturday aged 107, who was present at the execution of Louis XVI in 1793.[4] The same week died a certain Captain Green, the last surviving naval officer present at the funeral of Nelson. The paper mentioned as an odd thing, that he died in the same room and bed he was born in.

I remember a few years ago the death of an old French soldier who had been in the Battle of Waterloo. He was found dead of starvation in his attic in Paris. It is strange what a wrong impression of the length of time one gets from history, so many things happen in a century. Within the last twenty years (?), there was a blacksmith living at Killiecrankie whose father was in the battle.

Exeter is returned to Reading, Rufus is radiant in a hansom cab, papa is disgusted.[5] As he was going down Piccadilly he saw a curious conveyance, a gentleman driving his wife in a smart little dog-cart, getting along at a fine rate with a spotted donkey! Why shouldn't we start one?

Sunday, February 5th. Walked to Notting Hill Chapel, having no means of getting to Portland Street. Such music!

Mr Millais[6] is going to paint the portrait of one of the Duchess of Edinburgh's children. The duchess is staying with Princess Mary, Kensington Palace.[7] Mr Millais went to see her yesterday, doubtless very shy. She offended him greatly. She enquired where his 'rooms' were, evidently doubtful whether a Princess might condescend to come to them. 'My *rooms* ma'am are in Palace Gate,'[8] and he told papa afterwards, with great indignation, he daresay they were much better than hers. He is right proud of his house.

He says she speaks English without the slightest accent, the Russians are wonderful at languages. They say the late Czar prided himself on his good English, till he found when he came to England that, having learnt from a Scotchman, he spoke Scotch. Lady Mallet says the Princess of Wales has a very foreign accent.[9]

Saw the Duchess's little girl come out of Mr Millais' about quarter past twelve – brown bonnet, sealskin jacket, long yellow hair to the waist. Mr Millais got a matting and an extra butler for the occasion, he's telling them, see what his rooms are like!

A pedestrian who had dropped half-a-crown before a blind person said, 'Why, you're not blind'! 'I, oh no sir, if the board says so, they've given me the wrong one, I'm deaf and dumb'! Queer thing how fast some blind folks can walk when no one is about!

Mr Stocker says that the people who tame and exhibit lions and tigers have a red-hot rod inside their whip, and that is why they have so much power over them.

In the *Christian Life* last week was the following from tombstones:

> In memory of . . . who died in Philadelphia. Had he lived he would have been buried here

and

> Here lies . . . who was accidentally shot by his brother as a mark of respect.

Saturday, June 3rd. A Sunday School little girl being asked the order of the books of the Old Testament, replied with great rapidity, 'Devonshire, Exeter, Deuteronomy, Jumbo, Ruth.' Two ladies at the Academy are said to have done this, 1st. (reading catalogue), 'Ruth and Boaz, who were they?' 2nd., giving plot of one of Mrs Gaskell's novels added, 'It ended with a confession, but I don't remember who Boaz was.'[10]

Once when Bertram was sailing his boat at the Horticultural

Gardens, an elegant young gentleman playing lawn tennis remarked to an elegant young lady, when the boat stuck in the reeds, that it reminded him of 'Moses in the Ark!'

Oil lamps were first used in London in 1694, when they were placed along Kensington High Street in order to enable William of Orange and his train to find their way back to the Palace. They did not, however, make the road safe for pedestrians after dark.

A writer of the time speaks of it as a place 'where I should advise no honest man to go after dark'. Knightsbridge had also a very bad character. It was unsafe to go along one part of the road alone. A bell used to be rung whenever a party was going to start.

The last place in London where gas was adopted was Grosvenor Square (?) in 1842, when Link-boys finally disappeared. In a Mews, somewhere in that neighbourhood, there is still an old sign and under it 'I am the only running-footman', the picture being a man with a torch.

Mr Bright a little while ago on opening a library in Birmingham, said something to the effect that he would rather enter a library than a room highly decorated by art. It gave him a solemn feeling. Now papa says he never goes into the library at the Reform Club, but into the billiard room, and his own drawing room is in such dreadful taste that it is quite unpleasant.

Mr Moody[11] (the missionary) went to the House of Commons with Mr Graham who had not been there since he was a member seven years since. He said it was much changed for the worse, it is a mere bear-garden. Mr Moody said he had often been in the House of Representatives which had a bad name, but it was nothing to the House of Commons.

Sunday, July 2nd. Mr Millais has been suspected for a dog-stealer – there is an ancient solemn Scotch stag hound who walks about this parish in a silver collar. Mr Millais, going down to town to give Mr Boehm a sitting for a bust he's making, saw this dog walking along in Onslow Gardens, and decided it was just what he wanted for his picture.

He followed and watched it for half an hour without being able to see where it would go; then he asked the gardener in the Square, who said it belonged to one of the houses, he didn't know which. Finally the dog lay down on a door step. At last the door was opened and the dog went in. Mr Millais left his card and wrote to ask if he might paint it, which he has done.

The authorities collect from the streets of Manchester and the dustbins in one year (it is said), seven tons of dead dogs and thirteen of cats. These are boiled down. The oil is worth a good deal, being in great request for making *Olio Margarine* and other artificial butters!

Mr Edwin Lawrence had the Hungarian Band last week. Father said the music was very sweet – they are mostly string instruments. The Hungarians are wild looking men with thick hair standing straight up. A gentleman who had them last year told papa they were rather bad to manage. The first thing they did was to ask leave to smoke in the house. Being sent to the dining room, they ate nearly all the peaches and nectarines.

WRAY CASTLE[12]

Monday, July 10th. Papa took Wray Castle.

Friday, July 21st. Wray Castle. We came here on 21st July. This house was built by Mr Dawson, doctor, in 1845, with his wife's money. Her name was Margaret Preston. She was a Liverpool lady. Her father Robert Preston made gin; that was where the money came from.

They say it took £60,000 to build it (probably including furniture). It took seven years to finish. The stone was brought across the lake. One old horse dragged it all up to the house on a kind of tram way. The architect, one Mr Lightfoot, killed himself with drinking before the house was finished.

Mr Dawson was married 1810 (?), died in 1875, aged 96. Mrs Dawson died in 1862, aged 72. He used to live in the cottage, but one day a storm blew off a slate and he vowed he would build a house that could stand the weather.

He lived there alone till his death, living in the little room papa photographs in. He kept three servants. The rest of the house was shut up. His sister lived in a house in the middle of Randy Pike Wood.

★

Saturday, August 19th. Went to Hawkshead on 19th. Had a series of adventures. Inquired the way three times, lost continually, alarmed by collies at every farm, stuck in stiles, chased once by cows.

Hawkshead Hall. One of the granges of Furness Abbey, nothing old remains but the gateway. Under a counting-room, now a barn, the old windows, an empty niche, old beams. Popular tradition states that an old passage exists between this grange and the Abbey – it is frequented by a white lady!

The people about here are mostly Dissenters, chiefly Methodists. The Warden of Wray Castle is a Methodist. Old Mrs Dawson was a Unitarian. When she died Mr Dawson wished to bury her in the churchyard, but the Bishop strongly objected because it was not yet consecrated. Then Mr Dawson said he would give it to the Dissenters if there was any more bother. He could get a minister to bury her fast enough. Whereupon the Bishop became very civil.

People about say Mr Dawson might have built a village with the money he spent on his house. He objected evidently to any increase of the population. He would not allow a shop or lodgers.

They are working the horses at the Ambleside Inns very hard at present. The omnibuses go eight or nine times a day to the station, some eighty or ninety miles. It is only for the season of two months, but I don't think horses could stand it, it must be exaggerated.

Grandmamma once went from the Lake of Geneva to Rome with the same horses, but slowly. They were four little black horses with long manes. The driver had a little dog which sat behind on the luggage, but it was run over by another carriage and killed, to his great sorrow. After that Hannah had to look after the luggage. People were always jumping up behind to try to cut the straps. Hannah caught and beat one.

Grandpapa is rather fond of fine phrases. Once when he went to London for the day, he told all his friends he was a 'bird of prey', meaning to say 'passage'.

The proper way to clean unpolished slate chimney-pieces is to wash them with milk.

Old Dr Hopgood of Stalybridge tells the following story. In the reign of George III there was a very wise old Lancashire doctor living at Oldham. One of the Princesses had some kind of impediment in her head which no one could cure. At last this old doctor was sent for, and gave her such a tremendous dose of snuff that she sneezed for two or three days and was cured. Then the old doctor was a privileged person and walked about the palace as he liked. One day he entered a room where the Queen and Princesses were sitting with poker backs, according to the fashion of the day. Going up to the Queen he gave her a clap on the back saying in broad Lancashire, 'Well lass I'se never seen such a straight-backed wench in my life.'

1883

'What will be blown up next?'

LONDON

Saturday, January 13th. Been to the Winter Exhibition of Old Masters at the Academy. I had been looking forward to it very much, but I never thought it would be like this. I never thought there *could* be such pictures. It is almost too much to see them all at once – just fancy seeing five magnificent Van Dyck's side by side, before *me* who never thought to see one. It is rather a painful pleasure, but I have seldom felt such a great one.

I was most impressed by the Reynolds', twenty-two in number. I liked best the five figures at the end of the room, particularly *Justice* and *Faith*. Justice is the more beautiful figure and face, but the colouring of Faith's face in strong light was extraordinary. These five figures seem to me far the highest art in the Exhibition, more beautiful than Sir Joshua's portraits. Those are beautiful from nature, but there is more than nature in *Justice* and *Faith*. His portraits are difficult to remember separately. Some are much better than others. There was one of *Mrs Abington*, I think, which was much less faded than the others, almost as bright as Gainsborough's. For his pictures of children I liked the Little Archer and Una (Miss Beauclerk) best.

Gainsborough and Van Dyck I liked next. Of the English painters I don't know which next. The former is the more beautiful, the latter the more real and powerful. Gainsborough's colour is very fine, but almost unnatural. He sees it so well that it makes him sacrifice the softness and shadows which are the chief charm in Reynolds' pictures, and his drawing is decidedly inferior. His most striking work there was the *Lady Margaret Lindsay*, standing with her arms crossed before her. The arms are not very well drawn, but Gainsborough's chief defect in my opinion. The narrowness of the chest, which takes away from the dignity of his heads and positions, is not so noticeable. The painting of the face is very fine – the landscape is a good example of Gainsborough's trees. He has used a great deal of crude green and yellow which throws out the pinks but is otherwise unpleasant. He has only one landscape there which I unfortunately missed.

There are in all nine pictures of Van Dyck. The first I came to, *Portrait of King Charles II, when a boy*, disappointed me, and I was not much pleased with the next *Ecce Homo*. I had never seen a Van Dyck and thought they were much richer in colour – but those at the other end of the room were very different – they seem to stand out of the canvas, and *The Marchese Spinola* stared in a manner quite unpleasant. They are very different from Reynolds, Gainsborough, Romney, etc. They are bold, hard (in comparison), and their beauty is the beauty of nature as we commonly see her, in plain daylight. The horse's head in Spinola's portrait was very powerful. The *Earl of Pembroke* was noticeable for the wonderful painting of the yellow satin.

Angelica Kauffmann is represented by only one picture, *Design*, a round picture rather cruelly hung near Reynolds' five figures. Rather hot and ruby, but the expression and drawing is very good. The drawing is bold and firm, the arms and hands being particularly striking. I seemed to see the hands move.

There were three Turners, nothing particular.

The finest portrait of the Exhibition, if not the most beautiful picture, was *Caterina Cornaro, Queen of Cyprus*, by Titian. Here the crude, unpleasant colour disappears, while simplicity remains. The prevailing colour is dull green, relieved by the crimson pomegranate. I shall never forget that picture, I never saw anything so lifelike. *A female portrait* by Paris Bordone would probably be striking if not hung on the same wall with the last mentioned. There are also some examples of the Venetian School which are very uninteresting.

These are the pictures I liked best at the first exhibition of the Old Masters that I ever went to –

I was most impressed by the *Queen of Cyprus*, Reynolds' five figures and Van Dyck.

It has raised my idea of art, and I have learnt some things by it. I was rather disheartened at first, but I have got over it. That picture by Angelica Kauffmann is something, it shows what a woman has done. If you ever feel uncertain remember the face of *Faith*.

The preceding remarks are so amusing to me as representing childlike and simple, not to say, silly sentiments that have since passed away, that I preserve the greater part of them, though it is rather appalling to find one was such a goose only three years since.

Thursday, February 22nd. One of the first symptoms of George III's insanity occurred when he was opening Parliament. He insisted that he ought to read the beginning of his address to *My Lords and Peacocks*. The lords and gentlemen of the court were much puzzled what to do, and decided on dropping books and making different noises when His Majesty began.

After a recent collision in the Bay of Biscay a part of the crew and passengers of one of the ships, including six ladies in their night-gowns, drifted in an open boat for two days. The only discreditable circumstance in the disaster was the behaviour of three Chinamen, who when applied to for some of their super-abundant clothing to keep the ladies warm or to stop a leak, only gave the expressive reply, 'No, me catchee cold.'

Have had a cold most of the time since Christmas, have had almost enough of it. Think it's going to stop till Easter.

Wednesday, February 28th. What funny things grandpapa does say to be sure. Papa remarked on rooks to him, and he remarked, yes, they fly by night and on Sundays. Another time papa said how muddy the ponds were, and poor old grandpapa said they were as thick as his two fingers.

Mr Whistler[1] is holding an Exhibition somewhere, termed an *Arrangement in white and yellow*. The furniture is painted yellow and the footman is dressed in white and yellow, someone said he looked like a poached egg. Mr Whistler sent the Princess of Wales and the fine ladies yellow butterflies which they wore at the private view. What a set of yellow butterflies! It's quite disgusting how people go on about these Pre-Raphaelite aesthetic painters.

Monday, March 5th. Papa asked Mr Millais yesterday what he thought of the Rossetti pictures. He said they were all rubbish, that the people had goitres – that Rossetti never learnt drawing and could not draw. A funny accusation for one P.R.B.[2] to make at another.

★

Tuesday, March 6th (and following week). Bought a wild duck Sat 10th. Mr Phillips said it would keep for three weeks. Could not help wondering if he knew from experience.

Papa asked Mr Millais about mixing the paints, and he very kindly said what I must get. He said linseed oil took two years to dry. I think that was a stretch, but it certainly takes a dreadful time and I think would crack.

Mr Millais is very careful what he uses and says he believes his pictures will last to the end of time, and not crack like Reynolds', for Reynolds used bitumen to make his pictures mellow, which time alone will safely do. Mr Millais has his linseed oil specially prepared from the best seeds. His friend, a Mr Bell of the firm of Bell in Regent Street, I believe, gets his things specially made.

He has difficulties occasionally, great painter as he is. He is painting a child now, and says he never had such a job in his life, and were it not for the trouble he has had he would give it up. She won't stand still a moment, and he has got to use strong language about her. She is the daughter of a barrister, he met her in the street.

He is painting a subject-picture of a girl walking in her sleep on a turret stair, which he says he thinks will be the finest painting he ever did. He is doing it carefully anyway. He says now, the ball of the thumb is a little too thick.

Papa went into the studio the other day and was rather put-out when he found him painting it, he thought the girl who was standing between two screens was a model and didn't look at her, but he was amused afterwards to find it was Carrie Millais. Mr Millais is using Papa's velveteen for a background and has torn it. It has done its work that same velveteen, it used to be mamma's dress more than sixteen years since.

Here's a nice state of things in the first city of the world. Builders are in the habit of digging out the gravel on which they ought to found their houses, and selling it. The holes must be filled. The refuse of London is bad to get rid of though the greater part is put to various uses. The builders buy, not the cinders and ashes, but decaying animal and vegetable matters etc. to fill the gravel parts. It is not safe to build on at first, so is spread on the ground to rot – covered with a layer of earth.

A builder in Chelsea neglected to cover it up, and the householders round proved the smell to be a legal nuisance, and he was fined, but as the judge said, it is impossible at present to prevent its use. After a while the bad smells soak through the earth and floors and cause fevers. This delightful substance is called 'dry core'.

Friday, March 16th. What will be blown up next?[3] Last night an attempt was made to blow up the Government Offices in Parliament Street. Not so much damage was done to the building, owing to its great strength, but the streets for some distance round were strewn with glass.

One thing struck me as showing the extraordinary power of dynamite, a brick was hurled 100 feet and then through a brick wall into some stables. Some one said the noise was like the 80 ton gun. I believe it was heard here.

An attempt was also made, but failed, on *The Times* office, which seems to prove it was the work of Irishmen, that paper having had a leading article in its last number in which it was stated the Irish had got enough and more than enough, and need ask for no more.

Papa says it is Mr Gladstone's fault.[4] He takes the side of these rogues and then, if they think he is slackening, they frighten him on a bit – really we shall be as bad as France soon.

There was a big riot in Paris last Friday the 9th., and a meeting on Sunday, or rather crowds, which had to be dispersed by soldiers. On Friday they say the mob only stopped from penetrating into the Elysée by the block of the omnibuses in a narrow street. People are anxious about next Sunday 18th. Foreigners are leaving Paris. As *The Times* correspondent remarks, the best thing that could happen would be a drenching wet day.

Sunday, March 18th. Sunday 18th. passed quietly. The government kept such an overwhelming force drawn up in the barracks that no out-door meetings were attempted. Here in England we have had another excitement – two a week is really getting too much.

This time it was an attack on Lady Florence Dixie.[5] She was attacked almost within sight of her house, in the shrubbery, by two men disguised as women. They struck at her with daggers, cutting her clothes. They either simply wanted to frighten her, or thought they *had* killed her, or were startled by a cart passing, and the brave conduct of a big St Bernard whom the papers call 'Beau' or 'Buiert', who dragged off one of the men.

Some of the papers, this being a sceptical age, and the lady a Tory, have tried to make out that the affair never happened, but I think there are the strongest reasons and evidence that it did. Lady Florence pays little attention to them.

She must be a lively and extraordinary person, much more like a man, strongheaded but brave and sound hearted. They must be a strange family, her mother strongly on the Irish side was a Jesuit. One of her brothers is a Jesuit priest, another was killed on the Matterhorn.

Wednesday, March 21st. Manner of catching ducks in Egypt. Man swims in the water with his head inside a hollow pumpkin and surrounded by decoy ducks, and pulls wild ones under.

My Duc d' Orleans began to smell suspicious yesterday and has been eaten. Couldn't make out what had come to him a day or two ago, but found, he having been sent to the larder on account of mamma's nose, Sara had taken the opportunity of arranging him as if for dinner.

Tuesday, April 17th. The Queen has ordered that no lambs be eaten in the Royal Establishment this season.

I wonder what the truth is about this queer affair of Lady Florence Dixie. One gentleman says he saw Lady Florence Dixie all the time she was out, and nothing occurred. Some people give her a character I should never have suspected from her writings. It is said she is subject to strange fits owing to hard drinking.

When the Prince Imperial died[6] she published a poem relating the manner and place of his death, which she said she heard in a dream seven years before. She used to go out shooting with the gentlemen and wear a kilt, the *spectable man*.

Miss Ellen Terry's[7] complexion is made of such an expensive enamel that she can only afford to wash her face once a fortnight, and removes smuts in the meantime with a wet sponge. The Crompton Potters know someone who knows her well.

I really wish I had more time, and I would keep an historical account, but I keep thinking every time something happens it is the last startling event. Latest news, attempt to blow up Salisbury cathedral.

Wednesday, April 18th. Mamma decided on Miss A. Carter[8] – today 18th. Bertram going to school tomorrow!

Today is the first day it has been warm enough to sit painting in the dressing room. It is nice and airy and the light is tolerable. I am well pleased. Never mind what they say after what he said. *Faith.*[9]

Monday, April 23rd. 18th. to 19th. heavy rain, the first for perhaps three weeks. What funny weather we have had this year! Everything goes queerly, terrible storms in January, floods all winter and early spring, snowstorms March – drought – those grumblers the farmers get in their corn and groan about the turnips.

Now, when the rain has made everything begin to get green, we have storms of hail and snow, frost, and an east wind 23rd.

19th. the second anniversary of Lord Beaconsfield's death[10] and unveiling of his monument – primroses were worn by an extraordinary number of people when you consider that some fifty per cent are indifferent. I should say the Conservatives aren't in a large minority.

Don't quite know what to think of Lady Dixie's affair. Believe it was quite true. Lord Queensberry has proved that the papers are acting unfairly, having kept back part of that gentleman's statement. He only said he saw her at 3 and 4, whereas she said she was attacked at 3.45. If, as he was reported to have said, he kept her in sight the whole time, he must have followed her in the plantation, in itself a rather singular circumstance.

It was highly probable that she should be attacked as matters are now in this country. She had incurred the deadly hatred of the Fenians,[11] and perhaps, or rather almost certainly, the Land League,[12] by her letters. The one in *The Times* a few days before the attack, in which she hinted where the Land League money had gone, has never been answered.

Papa came back from Brighton in the Pullman cars the other day, 23rd. He met a friend, an MP, who remarked that Parnell[13] was in the train. 'He's being followed,' said the MP. Presently papa remarked, 'Why, there's Sir E. Henderson!' 'Why, that's the very fellow who is following Parnell!'

He came with him from Brighton, and got out with him at Waterloo.[14] Parnell did not seem at all ill at ease. Went to a bookstall and bought a paper, probably to see how his fellow-rascals are getting on in Dublin. He is quite a young looking man.

The police are very careful. French lady saw them stop two men with a hamper and look in it. She teaches in the family of Mr— of the Custom House. He was anxious about a rumour that dynamite was being imported in the form of apples.

The affair at Salisbury was a hoax. There has been another since. It is very wicked, but it helps the newspapers almost as much as if it were true. The men were Labifying[15] at 10.30 last night, 'great explosion at a powder magazine', and others about a narrow escape of the Princess Louise,[16] but it seems all an invention.

The Duke of Wellington looks very big and ugly,[17] usually with a sparrow seated impertinently on some part of him. There is an immense space where the arch was, it looks right queerly.

Bother spring cleaning! I could have put my finger in the dark on most books in the cupboard in the drawing room. I have stared at them for hours, though hardly opened any, and when I went there the other day I couldn't believe my eyes, I took out several books and they all came wrong.

Wednesday, April 25th. I am up one day and down another. Have been a long way down today, and now my head feels empty and I am nothing particular. Will things never settle? Is this being grown-up? If I could have seen my mind as it is now, when I left Dalguise[18] I should not have known it.

I thought surely we had got into all the difficulties now, but here is another. A nice way, a lively, to begin with a new governess. If they said I must, I'd do it willingly enough only my temper'd be very nasty – but father wouldn't force me.

I thought to have set in view German, English Reading, and General Knowledge, cutting off more and more time for painting. I thought to have settled down quietly – but it seems it *can not* be.

Only a year, but if it is like the last it will be a lifetime – I can't settle to anything but my painting, I lost my patience over everything else. There is nothing to be done, I must watch things pass – Oh *Faith – Faith.*

★

Sunday, April 29th. I believe Mr Millais has nothing on hand just now but a bad cold – what a funny person he is to be sure. Papa went to see him yesterday evening (Sat). He was in bed with his head tied up in a handkersneeze, playing a game all by himself on a little board. He invited papa to sit on the bed, but after treading on his slippers he preferred a chair.

It is strange how unfortunate the Government has been at each of the two trials of Tim Kelly at Dublin[19] – no sensible person doubts his guilt, but each time he has had a personal friend among the jurors who nodded and smiled to him during the trial, and afterwards refused to agree in the verdict. The interest in the trials still continues, and a new set of trials have begun in Dublin about the attempts to murder Fenian approvers. The evidence discloses the extraordinary secret organizations of the Fenians, and the terrible moral state of a part of the population of Dublin. Lawlessness and violence seem almost incredible. In future ages people will refer to these times as we do to the crimes and violence of the Middle Ages.

The dynamite conspiracy is every bit as dreadful as the gunpowder-plot. Fancy these words spoken by one Fenian to another on crossing Westminster Bridge, 'that (the Houses of Parliament) will make a fine noise when it comes down, in the month of Guy Fawkes!' We have ceased to have explosions now, and hoaxes are in fashion.

Monday, April 30th. Went to the Museum 28th. and again 30th. 30th., also I went to the dentist (Mr Cartwright, 12, Old Burlington Street), for the first time in my life. He stopped a little hole in one of my top left double teeth.

It was a simpler business than I expected. He had a little instrument with a head about as big as a pin's head, which he whirled round and round to get out the bad, wiped it with cotton-wool and rammed in gold as if he meant to push the tooth out through the top of my head. He did not hurt me in the least, only he had only just come in when *we* did, and his fingers tasted muchly of kid glove.

Wednesday, May 2nd. The French lady gave me a most amusing account of how her brother went to a Meeting of the Salvation Army in Regent Street. He is a clerk in the City, and went in from curiosity during his dinner-hour. The hall was crammed, numerous policemen tried to keep order, and the redoubtable Mrs Booth[20] who had just returned from a journey addressed the audience in a by no means religious discourse, but in good spirits.

All through her remarks people on the floor kept shouting 'Amen! amen!' in every key, with an occasional 'Hallelujah!', though the remarks were quite secular. Then people began ascending and descending the pillars of the gallery. Mrs Booth stopped and shouted to the police 'Turn them out, turn them out!' Mr Lambert soon had enough of it and got up to go out, but behold they wouldn't let him; he remonstrated in vain and was told he must stay till the meeting was over, which, as they sometimes last all night, was not an agreeable prospect. Presently he saw a fellow victim, a clerk from the same office.

The clerk, however, was in good spirits. 'We've only got to make a row and they'll turn us out.' Accordingly, they edged up to Mrs Booth in the midst of her discourse, and the clerk said out loud, 'I think it is a shame of you to turn religion to ridicule like this!' Mrs Booth, like the Queen in Alice in Wonderland, replied 'What do you say sir? we're not turning religion into ridicule.' 'Turn him out!' 'That is just what I want,' muttered the clerk as he was taken in charge.

Monday, May 28th. A golden eagle was shot a few weeks since, which measured, if I remember rightly, 4 feet 11 inches, from tip-to-tip of the wings.

The starlings are fledged. The swallows have disappeared, I am afraid they have not built near here. There is a fine thrush for singing, in Mr Beale's garden, he has some blackbird's notes in the middle of his song.

I had my first drawing lesson with Miss Cameron in November 78, and my last May 10, 83. I have great reason to be grateful to her, though we were not on particularly good terms for the last good while. I have learnt from her freehand, model, geometry, perspective and a little water-colour flower painting.

Painting is an awkward thing to teach except the details of the medium. If you and your master are determined to look at nature and art in two different directions you are sure to stick.

Friday, June 8th. They cut down the old walnut up the new road. Poor old tree, I remember it almost as long as I remember anything hereabouts. They are cutting a road across the field, preparatory to building. It is the last bit of the orchards left.

On 15th. they cut down the big mulberry bush on the left at the bottom of Gloucester Road, and most of the other trees except the big plane. I wonder how the rooks know, they left these trees a very short time before they were felled, and they left the rookery in Kensington Gardens the autumn before the trees went.

WOODFIELD

Thursday, July 26th. We came to Woodfield[21] on Thursday, 26 July. It is such a nice place and, though very different from anywhere we have stayed the summer, one is not inclined to be particular after staying in London so long. Quiet and fresh air is everything.

There is a perfect plague of flies here. There are two old cats and an amusing kitten. The horses, an old mare and a foal, a young mare who is prettier than Phyllis excepting the head and neck, she has such nice little feet, Magistrate, an old carriage horse, gaunt, thin, and who seems not to know which foot is most uncomfortable to stand on – A cow, a heifer and two calves, and two delightful pigs who lie on their backs, smiling sweetly to be scratched.

Taylor & Co. brought the luggage in a large three-horse van. It started at 7.30 and arrived about 4. They charged nearly £17.

Friday, July 27th. Went to Camfield in the morning, and along to Tyler's Causeway in the afternoon. Two ladies called to look at the house.

Saturday, July 28th. I, seventeen. I have heard it called 'sweet seventeen', no indeed, what a time we are, have been having, and shall have –

Went to fish in the ponds, caught a perch as long as my finger. The gardens are most beautiful – I never was here in the summer before – had no idea it was so pretty.

Birds: water-hen, water-ousel (no), sparrow-hawk, dove, thrush, blackbird, bullfinch, sparrow, linnet, yellow-hammer, chaffinch, hedge-sparrow, black-cap, robin, swift, house-martin, fly-catcher, heron, kingfisher, water wag-tail, ring-dove, wood-pigeon, rook, jackdaw, wren, long-tailed and big titmouse. There are some people in the neighbourhood called Titmouse, the misses Titmice, like the waiter at the party who announced 'Mrs Foot and the Misses Feet,' 'Mr Tootle and Mrs Tootle too,' he hadn't noticed Mrs Tootle at first.

Thursday, August 2nd. Went in the carriage to St Albans. Had great difficulty in finding the way. The country is very pretty and thickly wooded. Passed within sight of the old Elizabethan house near North Mymms, Inigo Jones, architect.

St Albans is a queer old town, The High Street, St Peters, is very wide with handsome old houses. The old north road runs through it. The Alms House is rather a fine building with the Marlborough crest over the door, having been built by one of the duchesses. There is the old church, in which Lord Bacon is buried, with an immense churchyard. The old Clock Tower at one end of the high street; opposite is some Roman building dug out.

We had not time to go and see the Roman city of Verulamium,[22] they say it is very large. The streets are at right-angles and easily traced by the difference of vegetation.

The Abbey is very fine, particularly the tower, but they are spoiling it as fast as they can. I was most struck with the little chapel containing the shrine, the watching gallery and Duke Humphrey's tomb. There is a gallery all round the Abbey at a great height up the walls.

We went fishing in the ponds. Caught nearly fifty fish between us. Also caught some newts in the afternoon. Didn't know they grew so big, or that they squeaked, it is as queer as to hear a fish make a noise.

They cannot breathe under water, having no gills except in the tadpole state, but they, like frogs, can remain under the surface for a long time. They sometimes let out the air at the bottom of the water, but generally rise to the top so as to get a fresh supply. The moment they have parted with the old they breathe rapidly through the nostrils like other reptiles, as may be seen by the rapid palpitation of the throat; but there is one thing about the breathing which I never noticed in any other, the newt having put out the used-up air, draws in fresh by quick respirations through its nostril. Then, if in the water, it sinks to the bottom till the new supply is exhausted;

but the air when used, instead of returning through the nose, collects in the throat, extending it greatly. Then the newt rising to the surface, lets out the air by opening its mouth wide with a snap.

Now the thing which puzzles me is that land-newts, frogs and toads and salamanders, though they breathe the air in at their noses in the same way (taking in a good deal and then stopping to use it), do not get fresh air through the mouth, or collect it in the throat, but through the nose. Indeed, I think sometimes they breathe and discharge the air alternatively like an ordinary animal, otherwise they would burst from breathing in too much. Another thing is, how can frogs stop under water so long as they sometimes do, over half an hour? The big newts seem to have to rise oftener than the small ones.

Tuesday, August 7th. Papa and mamma went to London.

Fished in the horse pond, had great fun with the frogs. I caught one old frog four times during the afternoon. It was a very bad shot and kept going snap, snap with its great mouth, and always missing. You can't lift frogs out of the water on the string, they're too heavy. Newts you can swing about.

Wednesday, August 8th. They have been married twenty years today. Dreadfully wet and windy, first bad day we've had yet, not spoilt the corn much. A little of grandpapa's oats in. Wheat getting ripe. When we came I was very disappointed with the stiff green heads, like a forest of asparagus, but now when the golden corn is beginning to bend it is much prettier, though nothing like the bonny barley and oats up north. The oats they grow here have the grain stuck close to the stalk right queerly.

Friday, August 10th. Had a fright last night, or rather this morning. Slept soundly in spite of friends from the dog show.

Was woken up at 3.30 by a report which sounded like an explosion or a small gun under the door opposite the bed. Was sure I wasn't dreaming, but not half awake, not least use calling, two doors between everyone, a certain shivery sensation, a strong inclination to get out of bed.

Just light enough to see that the blind-cord against the eastern window is not swinging. Where are the bells? Are there any? They ring in the back passage, where their only effect would be to send the cats into hysterics. Is it the electric bells which have done it? What is to be done?

Another tremendous bang about half a minute after the first. The air full of white dust, and bits dancing in the grey dusk. I am nearly choked and the smell of plaster is dreadful. Make sure something has exploded in the drawing-room and blown up my floor. At that moment I noticed a great dark mark on the ceiling. I thought then that a water pipe had burst in the roof. I didn't care much when I knew it wasn't on the floor. I tumbled out of bed and found the floor covered, not with water, but with plaster. A big piece of the ceiling had fallen in.

Thursday, September 20th. Yesterday, 19th. we bought a little ring-snake fourteen inches long, it was so pretty. It hissed like fun and tied itself into knots in the road when it found it could not escape, but did not attempt to bite as the blind worms do. It smelled strongly when in the open road, but not unpleasantly. Blind worms smell like very salt shrimps gone bad. We have seen only one living here, but several grass-snakes, one as long as my arm. They live in holes, sun themselves same as lizards. No vipers, don't believe they are as common as people say. Grimes, who seems intelligent on the subject, can only say of two lately.

LONDON

Wednesday, November 21st. Am going to Mrs A's for the first time tomorrow, two hours, Monday and Thursday, for twelve lessons. Can have no more because Mrs A's charge is high. Lady Eastlake[23] told papa about her.

Of course, I shall paint just as I like when not with her. It will be my *first* lessons in oil or figure drawing. Of the latter I am supposed to be perfectly ignorant, never having shown my attempts to any one.

I may probably owe a good deal to Mrs A as my first teacher. I did to Miss Cameron, but I am convinced it lies chiefly with oneself. Technical difficulties can be taught, and a model will be an immense advantage. We shall see.

Thursday, November 22nd. Refrain to give any opinion till I have been again.

Rosa Bonheur[24] is said to be very ill. There is an extraordinary number of pictures forged in France every year, as many as 1,800 Rosa Bonheur's, and other modern French painters. Meissonier[25] being probably the only one they cannot manage.

Mr Du Maurier[26] was said to be rapidly going blind last spring, and his big dog was dying, but I have heard no more of it.

Soon after we came back to town papa bought a curious book at the secondhand booksellers, Ruskin's *Modern Painters*. It had Mr Ruskin's autograph[27] on the title page stating he gave the book to D. G. Rossetti.[28] Interesting copy, not that I think much of either chappy.

Lady Eastlake is very tall. Once she was in the front of a crowd in France watching some sight when a Frenchman in the background, who thought she was on a chair, shouted, 'Descendez, madame, descendez!' She used to be able to lift up her husband under her arm. I am reading her book *Five Great Painters*,[29] most interesting book I have seen for this long time. One reason for her bitterness against the Germans was that her sister married a German baron who left her and married someone else.

Papa took me to Dover Street for my paints and box. Came home with Miss Carter. Went through St Giles, queer place, very interesting all these old little streets and houses. Passed the houses of Burke and Dryden.[30]

Saturday, November 24th. Have been to Mrs A's. Am uncertain what to say about it. Believe, though I would not tell any one on any account, that I don't much like it, which is rather disappointing. Wish it did not cost so much, is the money being thrown away, will it even do me harm? Don't much like the colours, why should I not use English ones. Linseed oil horrid sticky stuff, she actually used bitumen in her big picture.

She seems to have had three stages in her painting. 1st. German, her best, strong though somewhat hard. 2nd. French, sentimental and rather contemptible (I don't like French art as a rule). 3rd. A development of the French by which it has become woolly! with pinkiness of the English school super-added. I don't mean to say but that she draws and paints pretty well, but I don't like it, it's as smooth as a plate, colour, light and shade, drawing, sentiment.

It is a risky thing to copy, shall I catch it? I think and hope my self-will which brings me into so many scrapes will guard me here – but it is tiresome, when you do get some lessons, to be taught in a way you dislike and to have to swallow your feelings out of considerations at home and there. Mrs A is very kind and attentive, hardly letting me do anything.

There has been a violent domestic explosion with Elizabeth in the lower regions, several small eruptions up here. I have a cold, my temper has been boiling like a kettle, so that things are as usual. I do wish these drawing lessons were over so that I could have some peace and sleep of nights.

Thursday, November 29th. Things are going on worse. Do not like my drawing lessons. She speaks of nothing but smoothness, softness, breaking the colours, and the lightness of the shadows, till there is nothing left.

Wednesday, December 5th. Have begun a head of myself which promises surprisingly well, I think. Am using my old paints and medium, and Rowney's rough canvas (I have the double primed). I shall not let it be in the least influenced by Mrs A, being a nice confession after all this money. I can't make out that underpainting, don't like it some way, though I know a great many painters do, and have used it. Mr Millais does not use it, I'm sure, don't think Reynolds did in his more rapidly painted heads any way. It quite destroys all orginality of execution because you never see things to be the same.

5th. More splendid sunset than ever, a blue moon! bright silvering blue. I believe it was noticed the night before, people in the streets by are looking at it. Perhaps it was something to do with the old man plucking geese, for we had our first snow next day. As sensible a theory as that the red sky is caused by volcanic dust from Java.

Had a model for the first time at Mrs A, nice little old lady, Mrs Kippel, who will come out a ghastly object with Mrs A's tones and lights.

★

Thursday, December 6th. Night fires at Harrods & Ransome's – Harrod wonderful man, sent round printed advertisement before the day was out to say he hoped to re-commence business by Tuesday.

A Scotch minister was exhorting an old woman to remember the blessing granted to her in her old age. 'Ya, but it's been taken out of me in corns.'

Saturday, December 8th. An awful tragedy was discovered Sat. 8th., the whole Bill family, old Bill and Mrs Little Bill, and ditto Grimes and Sextus Grimes his wife, Lord and Lady Salisbury, Mr and Mrs Camfield, Mars and Venus, and three or four others were every one dead and dried up. We have had old Bill more than a year. I am very much put out about the poor things, they have such a surprising difference of character, and besides it was partly our fault, but they were all asleep in bed and it seemed so cruel to water them.[31]

Deceased, Richard Doyle the designer, died aged sixty.[32] I have always from a little child had a great admiration for his drawings in the old *Punches*. He left the Paper in 1850 when the stir against Papal aggression began. He designed the *Punch* cover. I consider his designs as good and sometimes better than Leech's.[33] He must have been little over twenty when he made those drawings. How time does go, and once past it can never be regained.

Tonight a most terrible storm of wind, never recollect it striking our side of the house so heavily, didn't half like it.

Saturday, December 15th. Went to four Exhibitions. Hablot Browne's drawings at Fine Arts;[34] Doré Gallery, water colour; Pall Mall; and McLean's. I think the first was by far the most interesting.

I was much surprised at the extent of the Phiz collection, which included oils and water-colours as well as drawings in black and white. The most interesting pencil drawings were the originals of *Dombey & Son*, *Bleak House* and *David Copperfield*. These drawings and some others of the same kind were simply marvellous. They were drawn for the most part on scraps of paper, blue very often, scribbled in the pencil. I do not think the engravings, good as they are, do them justice. There is a wonderful difference of expression in the faces, however small.

Of the landscapes I was most struck by one of the City, called I believe, *Tom's all alone*. Some for *Bleak House* were very good, but that one was most striking, equal to Doré's finest illustrations. It was probably done in a few minutes, only soft pencil scribblings on a bit of paper, but what a sense of lone, dismal solitude the artist has given it, what a sermon that little drawing preaches.

The originals of the *Old Curiosity Shop* were not there. I was sorry, I should like to have seen the real little Nell. I wonder why Phiz made such a mess of some of his ladies, most in *Dombey & Son*. His young girls were natural and simple, but he could not draw a well-bred lady.

There were few drawings, if any, which could be called caricatures, and if there was a keen sense of the ridiculous, there was an equally strong one of beauty.

Next, across the road, we went to the Doré Gallery, which I had never seen before. What a contrast! I consider Doré[35] one of the greatest of artists in black-and-white, but I never had any idea of his pictures before, except that they were big, which some of them certainly are.

Perhaps coming straight from the unpretending little Phiz exhibition made me notice it more, but all along I kept being irritated by something vulgar in his exhibition. No doubt the great crimson dome and hangings, the peculiar light, and the sudden introduction to numerous pictures round dark corners may add to the impressiveness thereof, but it suggests an appeal to vulgar fancy, which a noble work of art does not at all require to be appreciated.

Most extraordinary coincidence, some three years ago Mrs A had a happy idea for a picture, of a subject which no artist had before painted, namely *Little Miss Muffet*. She could not find a model suitable till last spring, but the child was ill. This spring she sent for her, but finding she was sitting for Mr Millais she said she would wait, but imagine her surprise on finding he was painting the same child in the same subject.

Mr Brett[36] does not paint his large pictures from nature, but from small sketches and memory. He seems to have an extraordinary memory and to paint very fast, finishing a large picture in a few days. He is an enthusiastic photographer and has a big yacht. Papa has bought a small sketch by him.

Jeff Millais is trying to learn to photograph. Rather a hopeless business seeing his want of brains and pocket money. He has to borrow his mother's umbrella when he goes out.

Instance of the bad bricks they use now. A fire has been lit in an end house near here, and the smoke comes out at several places up the wall.

The Dutch houses are mostly finished. Mr Gilbert's is said to contain twenty-six bedrooms with a bath-room to each (fancy twenty-six burst water-pipes). It is a very handsome house with its marble court, but I should doubt the comfort of the little latticed-windows.[37]

Finished drawing-lessons last day of old year. Have bad colds since seven days before Christmas.

Grandmama Leech ill at Christmas, better on 28th. and 29th. Suddenly worse on the 30th., gout having attacked her lungs.

1884

'How times and I have changed!'

LONDON

Thursday, January 3rd. Grandmamma Leech *Died on 2nd. January 1884, aged seventy-four – At Gorse Hall, Stalybridge.* There will be no one soon.

Mamma went north on 1st., comes home today 3rd.

Sunday, January 6th. Grandfather died in 1861. There is an inscription on the wall at Dukinfield near grandpapa Potter's pew beginning 'Cur fles?' why dost thou weep? Papa used always to be thinking of 'Dog fleas' during service.

An old woman is lately dead in the East End and buried at Finchley who was known as the Queen of the Costermongers. She was in the habit of lending to the costermongers on Fridays at 5/- in the pound, and left £69,000. She left orders that she should be buried in white satin, and £10 should be given in drink and 10/- in tobacco, which caused an immense procession of pony-carts and donkey-barrows full of costermongers to follow her to her grave.

Mr Millais has begun a new picture of a little gypsy girl with mistletoe. He is going to take it to the country to paint a snow landscape, but in the mean time the weather is very mild. He has also been painting *News from the Sea*, a child with a letter, her head has been in and out four or five times, and her body more than once.

Mr Millais says he never painted more than 29 pictures in a year; Reynolds once painted 149. He has begun to paint a young lady – has about finished *Lord Lorne* and *Miss Muffet*, whose name is Ethel May, younger sister of the child they *got for me* to paint.

Two, perhaps three of the girls, are to go to Miss Ward's. Oh dear, it is tiresome, I really shouldn't half like to go, after the other business having been paid for, and of course wouldn't ask to. I don't

79

feel as if I've learnt much, I can't bear those horrid paints, and they've put me out for using my own.

There is no doing anything just now because mamma says the dressing-room is too cold. Its almost a year since I began. After all I don't think its so bad if I learnt as much every year.

Friday, January 18th. It is a year today since I wrote I had got the dumps. How are my prospects compared with last year. I am not, not in high spirits tonight, something unpleasant having happened, so my opinion should be bended as regards height. This time last year I hadn't tried oils, don't think I've done badly considering all things. Am going to do a group of fruit etc. to compare with last year's. If I get on as much every year I may be well satisfied.

Sunday, January 27th. A little snow. A remarkable instance of a cat's affection for her young offered at the burning of a Music Hall lately. A tabby cat had four kittens in a basket behind the stage. When the fire began she was seen rushing wildly about, and at last forced her way down a smoky corridor and returned with a kitten in her mouth. This she did three times and then eluding those who attempted to stop her, she went for the fourth and was not seen again, but her burnt body was found beside her kitten.

There was another story in the paper a week or so since. A gentleman had a favourite cat whom he taught to sit at the dinner-table where it behaved very well. He was in the habit of putting any scraps he left on to the cat's plate. One day puss did not take his place punctually, but presently appeared with two mice, one of which it placed on its master's plate, the other on its own.

Mr Millais has begun a large picture of a drummer-boy playing on a flute, and three little girls listening. He began it and did such a quantity on Saturday 26th.

I think there is a chance of Mamma's taking me north when she goes. I should so like to see Gorse Hall for the last time.

Mr Millais had the drummer-boy there on Sunday morning in uniform. He is a real drummer and not particularly good looking. He is to be dressed in the Queen Anne's time uniform, which they will get from a print of Hogarth's. A tailor was there receiving very minute instructions. The boy sits on a bed. Papa photographed him but it did not come out well.

The forked tree in the Gardens came down in the gale.

Papa went hunting about after Mr Saunders the other day on this horrid building business. In one of his offices, all alone in a big room, he found a minute red-headed clerk who turned out to be the smallest Master Reynolds![1]

Wednesday, January 30th. Papa was not very well, perhaps partly by photographing in the cupboard, and, having said so on Sunday to the all powerful Mr Castles,[2] down came Mr Millais on Wednesday evening in a state of alarm and trepidation to see, as he expressed it, 'whether he'd killed that man'. He said the wretched business of the drummer-boy had been of the greatest service to him. He likes light prints as the pen-and-ink shows clearer on it. He said he had done a lot more at the portrait of Miss Lehmann (= Lewiman, Jew dodge of name changing), and got her arms right. I wonder what a drawing master would have said of her arms in the first sketch, not that they were by the great Mr Millais!

He wanted a photograph of a running stream to assist him with the landscape in the Drummer, and of course, as it was wanted, papa had the greatest difficulty in finding any. I should have thought we had them in every variety, however we found a few. When he painted *Pomona* he wanted a photo of an apple tree, of which, strange to say papa had not one. Since, he has taken ever so many, but they haven't been wanted. Mr Millais says the professionals aren't fit to hold a candle to papa. He has an old fellow called *Old Praetorius* when he can't get him, who takes an outrageous time to expose his plates, won't come on Sunday, charges high (important item), and when his prints are at last obtained they fade within a week, not having been washed.

Mr Millais always asked very carefully whether he might take a print before doing so, which is more than can be said for some other members of his family. He is amusingly grateful for them, and, as papa says, it is a pleasure to see someone who is obliged to you for your trouble.

He almost upset the drawing room chair last time he was here. He stood through the leather of the dining chair while looking at Lord Brougham, but that was a good thing because we had them re-covered. Mamma says they must have bulky chairs in the servants' hall. Elizabeth has lately collapsed one, the legs coming off as she sat down (by no means the first catastrophe of the kind). The chairs have a history. They were the dining-room chairs bought for *Greenheys* when grandpapa Potter was married, and afterwards were used at Princes Gate.

Saturday, February 2nd. Went to Eastbourne 2nd. February, partly for papa's health, partly for sending Bertram to school. First time I'd seen the town, nice of its kind. Fine sea on Saturday.

Sunday, February 3rd. Went to Beachy Head on Sunday morning to see the wreckage from the *Simla*. Extraordinary mixture of articles, but fortunately no spirits, the heavy articles having landed nearer Brighton where they have had frightful drunkenness. Two pianos (which I did not see), sacks of yeast, timber, coconuts, paper (blue, scattered along the coast), cigar and pickle boxes and provisions, live monkey (I did not see) and many other things. Stopped at Burlington Hotel, not very comfortable.

Saturday, February 9th. Bought a tail-less cock-robin for the exorbitant price of eighteen-pence. Let go in the flower walk, where it hopped into aucuba laurel with great satisfaction.

Friday, February 22nd. The Prince of Wales lately visited the slums in Holborn in disguise. Who says the present century is not romantic? Compare the exploits of his Royal Highness with those of his ancestor James V. To be sure, instead of a gallant knight on horseback you have a middle-aged gentleman in a four-wheeler with his trousers rolled up, and probably holding his nose, but time mellows everything in a few hundred years.

The town of Banbury in Northampton used to have an unenviable notoriety for body-stealing, the London coach frequently taking away a corpse. Once when the Innkeeper's daughter died some suspicious looking men arrived, and from their questions, and what was heard of their remarks, a search was made, and the necessary instruments for their horrid trade discovered in their bags.

Near there, I believe at Daventry, a lady was buried alive. The sexton, knowing she had been buried with her rings on, went at night and opened the grave. In taking off the rings he hurt her, and she started up. The old man dropped his lantern and rushed off. The lady went home and lived several years.

A man at the same place had a favourite apple tree in his orchard. He left £5 to have his grave dug under it. He wished to be buried in an upright position so that on the day of judgement he might jump out and claim his tree!

A most amusing thing happened at Hammersmith many years ago. Some men, having stolen a body, were bringing it into town in a cart. They went into an Inn on the way, where a soldier and another young man, having found out what was in the cart, determined on a joke at their expense. They took out the body and the soldier got in, in its place. The men drove off smoking their pipes. Presently they began to talk about the cold. One of them turning to the supposed dead man said joking, 'It's a cold night friend.' 'It's warm enough where I am,' muttered the soldier in a stifled voice. The three men thinking it was a ghost rushed away, and the soldier took back the cart and horse, which were never claimed, to the Inn.

A schoolboy being asked the meaning of the term Habeas Corpus said, 'Habeas Corpus=you may have his body,' the watchword of a gang of body-snatchers of whom Burke and Hare were the chief.

Wednesday, March 5th. Went for the second time to the Academy and Grosvenor. Saw the pictures better this time. Also saw at the Academy the Duke of Westminster and Mr Ruskin, and at the Grosvenor the Princess of Wales.

Mr Ruskin was one of the most ridiculous figures I have seen. A very old hat, much necktie and aged coat buttoned up on his neck, humpbacked, not particularly clean looking. He had on high boots, and one of his trousers was tucked up on the top of one. He became aware of this half way round the room, and stood on one leg to put it right, but in so doing hitched up the other trouser worse than the first one had been.

He was making remarks on the pictures which were listened to with great attention by his party, an old lady and gentleman and a young girl, but other people evidently did not know him. He armed the old lady in the first rooms, and the girl in the others.

Didn't see the Princess well, though she must have almost touched us. Papa was so surprised at meeting her pushing about in a crowd, same as other people, that he could not believe his eyes in time to tell me till she was almost gone.

A new waitress with some Manchester people cut up a cake or some kind of sweetmeat before handing it round. She thought the old lady looked rather aghast, and next morning received a reprimand. That cake had been offered at supper for three years and now she had cut it up!

I have heard that the chicken incubators don't always act as they should. The person who told the story certainly believed it. He said his master had applied too much heat, and a great part of his batch of eggs came out with extra allowance of wings, heads, tails (!) and legs.

Monday, March 17th. Miss Ellen Terry's first appearance on the stage was peculiar. She was quite a little child, and managed to hold or get caught in the curtain, so when it went up the first the audience saw of this actress was a pair of black legs dangling and kicking in the air.

Friday, March 28th. A shocking rumour is about that Prince Leopold has died today at Nice. He and the Duke of Connaught were the most popular of the Queen's sons.[3] He was looked up to as a very respectable, good man, whatever may be said of two of his brothers. It seems doubtful how the Queen will stand the death of her favourite son. No one says much of it, but for some months it has been suspected that all is not right with her. Some say she is mad, not that that is anything uncommon, half the world is mad when you come to enquire.

Have been very unsettled this week, first mamma said I should go to Manchester, then that I could not, then I was to stop at home with the girls, then it was decided I should go to Camfield, but now I am to go to Manchester tomorrow. I am afraid grandmamma Potter will be disappointed, and I very much wished to go, but it is the last chance of seeing the old house.[4] Not that I look forward to that as an unmixed pleasure.

I have a very pleasant recollection of it, which I fear may be changed. I have now seen longer passages and higher halls. The rooms will look cold and empty, the passage I used to patter along so kindly on the way to bed will no longer seem dark and mysterious, and, above all, the kind voice which cheered the house is silent for ever.

It is six or seven years since I have been there, but I remember it like yesterday. The pattern of the door-mat, the pictures on the old music-box, the sound of the rocking-horse as it swung, the engravings on the stair, the smell of the Indian corn, and the feeling on plunging ones hands into the bin, the hooting of the turkeys and the quick flutter of the fantails' wings. I would not have it changed.

Saturday, March 29th. Came to London Road [Manchester], 29 March, being Saturday afternoon a great many people were in the streets. A small Wake was going on in one place. The people look so homely to me. I was struck by the large proportion of good-looking girls among the Lancashire voices.

Saw a grand sight in the evening, one wing of the Infirmary was burnt down. It is about four miles from here. The others went, but would not let me! Saw it well from the house.

First there were the separate masses of flame, then, as the fire burnt out that part, it spread on both sides. It was caused by a woman putting too much coal on a fire where they were going to have a dance. There were buckets and hose on the place, but never a man to use them, and, even when the firemen came, they could do nothing until the steam engines arrived because there was hardly any pressure. Only the upper part of one block is burnt. I had no idea it would make such a blaze.

Sunday, March 30th. Had a hard afternoon in six trams, never was in them before, it is delightful travelling. Am very much struck with Manchester, though I want to see it when the streets are crowded, on a week-day.

The Infirmary and Exchange are particularly fine buildings, so are some of the Warehouses and the Town Hall. We saw the Cathedral tower and heard the bell. There was grandpapa's Ware-house on Mosley Street 14, Uncle Crompton's down another street, Uncle Willy's in Pall Mall. All along the streets were familiar names on the door-plates.

When we got to Greenheys, there was the house in Exmouth

Terrace where papa was born, a small brick house, once red, second in the row from town. The house where Uncle Crompton was born has been pulled down to make room for Owen's College, and Rusholme is marked out for streets. We saw where papa went to school, and the shop I have so often heard of where he bought goodies.

We called on Aunt Sidney[5] whom I saw for the first time, a dear old lady sitting in a rocking chair before the parlour fire. She was dressed in a black-brocade silk dress, a little gauze-cap and a red knitted shawl. She wore a good many rings, and a large cameo brooch. She was rather like cousin Louisa to look at. I thought she was very nice.

We went on to Fallowfield to The Hollies and saw Aunt Harriet, perhaps for the last time. We hadn't time to go to Mr Gaskell's[6] or Alice's. I hope to go again.

Monday, March 31st. I had a quiet day. Went to Eccles, fine old cross, market cross, celebrated cookie shop – Mamma and Aunt Harriet brought back the jewellery from Gorse Hall and divided the things of little value in the evening, when the scene was at once so ridiculous and melancholy that I shall never forget it.

The jewellery was some of it very old-fashioned, which here in some instances means quaint, but in most, ugly. The things which I most admired, irrespective of value, were two cameo brooches and a bracelet composed of three small cameos. Among the rings was a wedding-ring which Aunt Harriet kept, and which has rather an interesting story, previously unknown to me, attached to it. Once when grandmamma was looking for something in grand-papa's desk she came upon this ring, and asked him rather sharply what it was. He said it was one he had bought for her because hers was worn out, but she had refused to wear it. However, the new ring in question was found also, and my grandfather was totally unable to explain the presence of the other in his desk. Aunt Harriet said it was the only time she had seen poor grandfather really angry. I came off with a farthing which I kept as a remembrance.

Wednesday, April 2nd. Went to Gorse Hall, a painful and dreary visit. My first feeling on entering the door was regret that I had come. How small the hall had grown and – there was a new doormat, but in a minute or two it had come back. It was the same old place, the same quiet light and the same smell – I wonder why houses smell so different. On thinking of a place the first recollection is the smell and amount of light.

I went into the cellars with the others who were in search of boxes. Such an extraordinary collection of lumber I never saw. Among other things, the old grey rocking-horse on whom I sat down instead of climbing, and a kind of hooped stool for holding a baby. The last strange old piece of furniture belonged to great-grandmother Ashton.

One thing was given me which I value exceedingly, an old green silk dress of my grandmother's which she wore as a girl. It was wrapped up in the same paper with her wedding dress, a white silk brocade, high-waisted, short, scolloped at the bottom, lownecked, tight long sleeves with puffs to put on over them. I thought at first they would have given it me, but Aunt Harriet thought after she *ought* to keep it. I should not have ventured to ask for either, but that they spoke of giving it to the servants! It is extraordinary how little people value old things if they are of little intrinsic value. We could not get down grandpapa's wedding clothes and the poke-bonnet as they were top of the cupboard.

Thursday, April 3rd. Went to Alice's, lunched at Aunt Sidney's. Went to see Mr Gaskell. He will not last long I am afraid. I have got the cameo bracelet if Uncle Willy does not interfere. He has no right to, but wants it.

Friday, April 4th. Came home 4th.

Saturday, April 5th. Duke of Albany buried. London has been in deep mourning. Almost everyone in black, and, the few that were not, looking ashamed of themselves. Great many blinds down, all the Clubs, most of the shops shut, many cab drivers etc. with crêpe on their whips. It is probably a long time since any death not of the reigning sovereign, caused so deep a gloom and impression. All over the country are flags half-mast high, and not an ill-word is heard of him. The only exception I have seen was the Eccles Liberal Club, which actually was insulting enough not to fly its flag.

Aunt Sidney speaking of the deaths of the sons of George III said there was no feeling of this kind shown at all, they were all rascals – the mourning for the Duke of Sussex, perhaps the most respectable, was ten days.

Thursday, May 8th. Mamma back 8th. Quite uncertain for this summer, I am afraid there is a chance of going back to Dalguise. I feel an extraordinary dislike to this idea, a childish dislike, but the memory of that home is the only bit of childhood I have left. It was not perfectly happy, childhood's sorrows are sharp while they last, but they are like April showers serving to freshen the fields and make the sunshine brighter than before.

We watch the gentle rain on the mown grass in April, and feel a quiet peace and beauty. We feel and hear the roaring storm of November, and find the peace gone, the beauty become wild and strange. Then as we struggle on, the thought of that peaceful past time of childhood comes to us like soft music and a blissful vision through the snow. We do not wish we were back in it, unless we are daily broken down, for the very good reason that it is impossible for us to be so, but it keeps one up, and there is a vague feeling that one day there will again be rest.

The place is changed now, and many familiar faces are gone, but the greatest change is in myself. I was a child then, I had no idea what the world would be like. I wished to trust myself on the waters and sea. Everything was romantic in my imagination. The woods were peopled by the mysterious good folk. The Lords and Ladies of the last century walked with me along the overgrown paths, and picked the old fashioned flowers among the box and rose hedges of the garden.

Half believing the picturesque superstitions of the district, seeing my own fancies so clearly that they became true to me, I lived in a separate world. Then just as childhood was beginning to shake, we had to go, my first great sorrow. I do not wish to have to repeat it, it has been a terrible time since, and the future is dark and uncertain, let me keep the past. The old plum tree is fallen, the trees are felled, the black river is an open hollow, the elfin castle is no longer hidden in the dark glades of Craig Donald Wood.

I remember every stone, every tree, the scent of the heather, the music sweetest mortal ears can hear, the murmuring of the wind through the fir trees. Even when the thunder growled in the distance, and the wind swept up the valley in fitful gusts, oh, it was always beautiful, home sweet home, I knew nothing of trouble then.

I could not see it in the same way now, I would rather remember it with the sun sinking, showing, behind the mountains, the purple shadows creeping down the ravines into the valley to meet the white mist rising from the river. Then, an hour or two later, the great harvest-moon rose over the hills, the fairies came out to dance on the smooth turf, the night-jar's eerie cry was heard, the hooting of the owls, the bat flitted round the house, roe-deer's bark sounded from the dark woods, and faint in the distance, then nearer and nearer came the strange wild music of the summer breeze.

Tuesday, May 13th. The *Monarch of the Glen*[7] has just been sold at Christie's among the collection of the late Dowager Lady Londesborough. It fetched £6,200 and was bought by Mr Eaton, MP, who seems to be making a collection just now. Some said before the sale that it would fetch ten or fifteen thousand, but times are bad. There were some handsome gold ornaments from the Irish bogs, and a sort of engagement ring given by William of Orange to Queen Mary. It was of gold, ornamented by *small* diamonds. Strange how poor people used to be.

Saturday, May 17th. Have begun Cicero, easier than Virgil. Mr Ruskin has got a study of laurel leaves at one of the water-colour exhibitions. Papa says it is simply dreadful.

Monday, May 19th. Such news this morning! am going to Edinburgh tomorrow with papa and mamma – the places I have always wished to see most were Manchester, Edinburgh, Rome, Venice and Antwerp, or another of the old Hansa towns.

I have seen Manchester, and now I am going to Edinburgh, O fine, I can hardly believe. Was not the scene of the story I have been telling myself in bed for the last month, and of the most ambitious of my picture theses, laid in Edinburgh? and I have the *history* nearly by heart, so I have the streets too. I wonder if they will be what I expect? There is hardly a place in the world with more romantic associations than Dunedin.

I will endeavour to write voluminously, and poetical impressions on another sheet of paper. There is only one drawback, there is the chance of going on to Dunkeld, O Home, I cannot bear to see it again. How times and I have changed!

EDINBURGH

Thursday, May 22nd. Started from King's Cross by the Flying Scotsman at ten, to go to Edinburgh. We went at a great rate at times, but always delightfully smoothly.

I only knew the line as far as Hatfield. After passing the broad corn-lands of Hitchin, and the beautiful valley of the Lea, I was much struck by the quantity of mustard grown. Field after field spread out like dazzling gold in the sun, at each side of the valley.

We passed Knebworth, Lord Lytton's place, at a little distance, and another fine old house where Oliver Cromwell had lived just south of Huntingdon. Having followed the course of the Ouse, and seen Lincoln cathedral on its hill just above the horizon, we crossed the Trent at Newark not far from the Castle.

Peterborough we saw very well, but I was not so much struck by it as by Durham and York, not because the latter were finer, though Durham has a magnificent situation, as on account of the faded light. Lumley Castle is vast and deserted looking, but the situation is poor. Not so Warkworth, standing on the sand cliffs above the sea. I was surprised by the great size and good preservation of the buildings.

Holy Island was a little disappointing, it was so flat, but the sands were pretty with a red cart coming towards the Island. The coast was very fine after this, but still more so after crossing the border. The little village of Burnmouth was particularly picturesque.

I was much struck by Newcastle, the high bridge, the smoke and the *coaly* Tyne. I did not know that the Castle still existed. But Berwick was one of the most interesting places we passed. The old town with its walls perched above the harbour, and broad river where the salmon-netting was going on in a disgusting manner, and also bathing, but, above all, the fact that we were again crossing to Scotland (at twenty-five to six), was very impressive. I saw the Bass Rock well, steeper than I expected, so was Dunslaw.

Between the sea and Edinburgh there is beautiful rich country, the Midlothian. – I was dreadfully puzzled when we got up to Edinburgh. It is always so if one has a clear idea of a place one has not seen. I knew exactly what the different places were like, the Calton Hill, Arthur's Seat, the Castle, but I had fitted them together all wrong. But I am anything but disappointed with the real form. It is impossible that there can be a finer situation for a town. I had no idea the new town was so fine, such wide streets, large shops, fine public buildings, solid and in good taste for the most part, and built of good grey ashlar which should last for ever. Charlotte Square and George Street are particularly handsome, so is Princes Street in the separate buildings, but it is not such a balanced whole, and the great attraction is in front. Another thing that is striking is the number of statues in the streets. Some are not commendable, but the effect is always good.

As to the old town, it is a most wonderful and interesting place. It is like being taken back at will into whatever century you please to walk along those streets, and look down the dark silent wynds and courts peopled by strange legends, historical or ghostly, and by very dirty but contented and lively human beings.

We are stopping at Mr Greggar's Royal Hotel, comfortable enough except as regards waiting and noise from the Station. The view is wonderful, except for the nasty railway smoking at the bottom of the Gardens.

It is extraordinary to see so many fine buildings close together. Those on the Mound, the National Gallery and the Institute, look very bold and well-proportioned from below, but slightly heavy from above.

DUNKELD

Monday, May 26th. Are leaving for Dunkeld at 1.30 today 26th. Don't know why papa is so anxious to go. I don't want to at all, particularly after what Mr Armitage has told us. However, there is no help. I must make the best of it.

Arrived at Pople's Hotel 5.30. O how homely it seems here, how different to anything I have seen since I left – I went down by the river after tea. The grass is greener, the flowers thicker and finer. It is fancy, but everything seems so much more pleasant here. The sun is warmer and air sharper. Man may spoil a great deal, but he cannot change the everlasting hills, or the mighty river, whose golden waters still flow on at the same measured pace, mysterious, irresistible. There are few more beautiful and wonderful things than a great river. I have seen nothing like it since I left; down to the smell of the pebbles on the shore, it may be drainage, but it brings back pleasant memories.

I remember *Home* clearer and clearer, I seem to have left it but yesterday. Will it be much changed? How fast the swifts fly here, how clearly the birds sing, how long the twilight lasts!

Tuesday, May 27th. Down over to Dalguise, a forlorn journey, very different to the usual one, and we had a grey horse too, poor Berry and Snowdrops. The place is the same in most ways. It is home. The bridge re-built at Inver, and some new railings on the Duke's land. Some saplings grown, others dead. Here and there a familiar branch fallen, and, on the Dalguise land, things more dilapidated then ever, and some new cows in the fields.

A horrid telegraph wire up to the house through the avenue, a Saw-Mill opposite the house and a pony-van at the back. There are deaths and changes, and the curse of drink is heavy on the land. I see nothing but ruin for the estate. How well I remember it all, yet what has not happened since we left? What may not happen before I see it again if I ever do – I am not in a hurry to do so. It was a most painful time, and I see it most as well with my eyes closed.

LONDON

When we went to the station before going to Edinburgh the Duke of Wellington was headless. It really is too bad to expose him to ridicule in that way. One thing I cannot understand, after the House of Commons had agreed it should go, the Lords moved an amendment that it should not, but the Commons have had their way. When his head was removed a starling's nest was found in the cockade hat. When the horse was first erected a dinner of twelve was held in the belly. A second horse of Troy.

These explosions are becoming commonplace, after a certain

amount of a thing it gets tiresome. Mamma heard something like a gun a bit after nine, having marked the time on the clock as we always do now when we hear a noise. It has often struck me what a risk there is of some of those rascals setting off in a picture gallery. Trafalgar Square is rather near the mark, but it must be hoped that these poeple are not art-critics, and think pictures beneath their notice. I don't see how these explosions are to be stopped, it is such a simple thing to leave a parcel. It is announced that nothing will be done till Harcourt comes back.[8] He and Chamberlain are yachting,[9] and things going from bad to worse.

I don't know what will come to this country soon, it is going at a tremendous speed. I think and hope that this extension of the Franchise may not be as bad as the Conservatives fear. No doubt if the labourers get power they will be greedy at first, but I think the sentiments of the lower-classes in the country are rather conservative on the whole, very loyal and tenacious of England's honour. Still, landed property is not a particularly secure possession at present. It is the middle-men who have pushed up, that are such mischievous radicals, like Chamberlain.

Had the misfortune to lose a favourite lizard in the garden on Sunday.

OXFORD

Tuesday, June 3rd. Came to Oxford to stay with the Wilsons yesterday, June 2nd. First time I have been here. Had no idea the Valley of the Thames was so pretty, and the River so small.

Oxford itself is a very picturesque old town, almost deserted now, before the vacation has begun. I had seen plenty of engravings and photographs of the colleges, and could never make out what the blotches on the surface were. What a state some of the stone is in!

We went out in the evening into the gardens of St Johns. Certainly the boys have every inducement to be idle. Then across the College and along St Giles, St Aldate's Street, over the bridge and back in a punt to Christ Church meadows, and under the tall old elms. I was particularly struck by the cloisters at Christ Church, so cold and dark in spite of the heat outside. They were empty and perfectly silent, except for the swallows and occasionally the sound of lively singing coming through the closed doors of the Cathedral. Cardinal Wolsey's ceiling and stairs are also very fine. Found a kind of slug in the garden which I never saw before, brown-streaked and spotted, six or seven inches long.

Sunday, June 8th. Sunday we went down by the river, morning! Evening, went to Service at the Cathedral. Most delightful singing. Service not the least unpleasant to me because I did not understand half a dozen words of it. Cathedral a magnificent building, several old windows and some frightful modern ones, also three by Burne-Jones[10] which surprised me agreeably, better drawing than he generally favours us with, and one of Faith, Hope and Charity, wonderfully rich and harmonious in colour for modern glass. I believe Morris is the maker.[11]

Monday, June 9th. Monday, went to Museum, very interesting, but too much to take in comfortably at a time. Afterwards to Keble College and Chapel. Struck me as decidedly ugly. Why with such beautiful old buildings to copy, cannot they get anything better than glaring red and white brick edifices, which remind one of a London suburb.

I was supposed to see Hunt's *Light of the World*,[12] I had never seen the original before. I have always thought little of the design, the figure much wants dignity and firmness, the management of the light is the best part of the picture. The details I was much disappointed with, there is no particularly careful and minute work as in Millais' Pre-Raphaelite pictures. No doubt when this picture was painted it was more striking, because at that time art was so conventional.

Tuesday, June 10th. Tuesday, went to a most interesting shop of furniture, china and every kind of old curiosity. The house itself was worth seeing, such stairs and passages, and crammed from basement to roof.

Mamma ended in buying a Chippendale clock, fourteen guineas. Cheap I think. Indeed, I thought the prices were extraordinary. I had an erroneous impression that Chippendale was very scarce and valuable, also old oak. We must have seen some twenty or thirty pieces of the former, and a great deal of fine old oak. Papa rather misdoubted some of the latter owing to prices. I think a great deal of it was good though, and, if it wasn't, it was very handsome. I particularly admired (with a wish to possess), a cupboard like the one at Wray, £6.

If ever I had a house I would have old furniture, oak in the dining room, and Chippendale in the drawing room. It is not as expensive as modern furniture, and incomparably handsomer and better made.

In the afternoon I went to the Museum again, and then with the Wilsons to a garden-party in the beautiful gardens of Merton College. Before that, Mrs Wilson showed us over the Chapel, and the kitchen, and a most interesting library. One of the oldest buildings in Oxford with a most beautiful oak roof, and the original tiles on the floor.

There was no one there, and we looked at the old books, and did not hurry, which I have come to the conclusion is a necessary part of the enjoyment of sight seeing. The library is said to be haunted by old Lord Chancellor Merton, the founder, who was killed by his students with their pens.

It certainly was very silent, and there was the ancient, dusty smell so suggestive of ghosts. Then at last, heavy steps, and the sound of a stick on the stairs at the further end, pat, pat, nothing visible, but it proved a little fat old lady, a very sociable ghost.

Then to Magdalen to Service. Liked the music and singing better than at Christ Church, it was lovely. The service is certainly very impressive, but somehow it awakens no feeling of devotion in me, like our own bare service does.

Thursday, June 12th. Papa heard from Mr Steinthal that Mr Gaskell died at five yesterday morning. Dear old man, he has had a very peaceful end. If ever any one led a blameless peaceful life, it was he. Another old friend gone to rest. How few are left.

There has always been a deep child-like affection between him and me. The memory of it is one of the past lights bound up with the old home. [13]

Saturday, June 14th. Four o'clock Saturday afternoon. Mr Gaskell is just being buried at Knutsford beside his wife. We have sent some flowers.

Oh how plainly I see it again. He is sitting comfortably in the warm sunshine on the doorstep at Dalguise, in his grey coat and old felt hat. The newspaper lies on his knees, suddenly he looks up with his gentle smile. There are sounds of pounding footsteps. The blue-bottles whizz off the path. A little girl in a print frock and striped stockings bounds to his side and offers him a bunch of meadow-sweet. He just says 'Thank you, dear,' and puts his arm round her.

The bees hum round the flowers, the air is laden with the smell of roses, Sandy lies in his accustomed place against the doorstep. Now and then a party of swallows cross the lawn and over the house, screaming shrilly, and the deep low of the cattle comes answering one another across the valley, borne on the summer breeze which sweeps down through the woods from the heathery moors.

Shall I really never see him again? but he is gone with almost every other, home is gone for me, the little girl does not bound about now, and live in fairyland, and occasionally wonder in a curious, carefree manner, as of something not concerning her nature, what life means, and whether she shall ever feel sorrow. It is all gone, and he is resting quietly with our fathers. I have begun the dark journey of life. Will it go on as darkly as it has begun? Oh that I might go through life as blamelessly as he!

LONDON

Wednesday, July 2nd. Went to dinner at Queens Gate. Warm. Never saw grandmamma looking better, or livelier, talking about every-thing, enjoying the jokes, playing whist with her accustomed skill.

How pretty she does look with her grey curls, under her muslin cap, trimmed with black lace. Her plain crêpe dress with broad grey linen collar and cuffs turned over. So erect and always on the move, with her gentle face and waken, twinkling eyes. There is no one like grandmamma. She always seems to me as near perfect as is possible here – she looks as if she had as long before her as many of us, but she is eighty-four.

There was a queer sight in the Brompton Road on the 2nd. Several storks escaped from Pring's the bird shop. Papa saw one circling round, and finally settled on the gable of the schools opposite Tattersall's. One was caught. Hope if the others get away that they will not be shot. Fear it. Storks in Holland, from being constantly protected, are quite dangerous if meddled with. Our common heron is a horrid customer to touch if wounded, always striking straight at the eye.

A boy went in to a graveyard and shot a white owl. Then, seized with alarm, he rushed home in the greatest excitement screaming 'I've shot a cherubim.'

Lord Selborne has taken the haunted house in Berkeley Square. It is now in the hands of the builders. It has been empty a long time. About the last who braved its horrors were a party of gentlemen who went there with their collie dogs. It is said that they gave the ghost a sound thrashing, but the difficulty is that no one seems to know what the said ghost is. Anyway, the house has a notoriously bad name.

19, Queens Gate is another house which is no canny. Nearly twenty years syne a gentleman about to marry took it, but the bride died a few hours before the wedding-time, suddenly. The gentleman would not live there, and they say that to this day the untouched breakfast is on the table.

Then the low red house second from the bottom of Palace Gardens has always been unlucky. Thackeray died there, then it was the home of the notorious Bravos.[14] The next owner's son, running down stairs at a club, could not stop himself, and went over the banisters. I believe yet another owner died suddenly.

Mrs Bravo was a Campbell of Boscat or Buscot, they are the great landowners in New Zealand, and are advertising for as many pairs of lively weasels as can be procured. Some one suggested starting consumption among rabbits, but this would be most dangerous owing to the tinned-rabbit.

Lord Randolph Churchill[15] is looked upon with mingled hope and fear. He is the only promising and spirited young politician who has spirit to go on his own path, but he wants steadiness. He shows keenness and common sense one day, but the next, his followers may find themselves the laughing stock of the country. Let us hope he'll mend. Politics seem to have come naturally to him. Mr Wilson's brother, the Master of Radley, was one of his masters when he was a boy. Lord Randolf read Demosthenes with him, and Lord Churchill kept muttering between his reading a sort of rambling comment, 'Just like old Gladstone – there he goes again!' He has a wonderful memory which is most inconvenient to the government.

It strikes me that that august body, and indeed the House of Commons itself, is regarded with very little respect by the country at large. Gladstone has got hold of power, and I suppose will stick to it till he dies, unless the opposition unite better. A certain class who owe everything to Mr Gladstone, or who hope to get something from him, stick to him.

The commoners take that side because they hope from his promises to obtain more power. If you offer a thing, commonly considered pleasant and desirable, to any person, he will be likely to take it, though he might not have asked for it. Changes are to be treated with the greatest caution, and only granted when really desired and needed.

It is nonsense to say the country longs unconsciously for the Radical reforms that are turning up now. They are simply baits. I say nothing about their merits or de-merits, but simply that there is no feeling in the country like that which animated sober, quiet men at the time of the Reform Bill or repeal of the Corn Laws. Doubtless times have changed, but Englishmen are still Englishmen, and if they want a thing they will ask for it.

As for the House of Commons, it is not likely to be much looked-up-to while scenes, sometimes disgraceful, sometimes silly and childish, take place within its walls, and as for a man being an MP, there are all kinds of people that. Some of the greatest rascals in the country are in Parliament.

Saturday, July 12th. Papa and mamma went to a Ball at the Millais' a week or two since. There was an extraordinary mixture of actors, rich Jews, nobility, literary, etc. Du Maurier had been to the Ball the week before, and Carrie Millais said they thought they had seen him taking sketches on the sly. Oscar Wilde was there.[16] I thought he was a long lanky melancholy man, but he is fat and merry. His only peculiarity was a black choker instead of a shirt-collar, and his hair in a mop. He was not wearing a lily in his button hole, but, to make up for it, his wife had her front covered with great water-lilies.

★

Monday, July 28th. Papa has been photographing old Gladstone this morning at Mr Millais'. The old person is evidently a great talker if once started. Papa said he talked in a set manner as if he were making a speech, but without affectation. They kept off politics of course, and talked about photography. Mr Gladstone talked of it on a large scale, but not technically. What would it come to, how far would the art be carried, did papa think people would ever be able to photograph in colours?

He told several long stories of which the point was exceedingly difficult to find, including one about a photographer at Aberystwyth thirty years ago, how the working classes enjoyed looking at the photos in his window, and it occurred to them to get ones of their friends, but at this point, Mr Millais broke in with the request that Mr Gladstone would sit still for a moment.

Then they talked about the judges and people they knew, and about Mr Bright going to Ouless'. The principal subject of his conversation with Mr Millais was about the election of a new master of Eton which is coming off today.

He was very inclined to talk, but it interrupted the painting. He did not seem conceited, nor yet difficult to manage like Mr Bright is when being taken. He was sitting in a gorgeous arm chair which was taken by Captain James[17] from Arabi's tent at the battle of Tel-el-Kebir.[18] How that surprising person Captain James managed in the confusion of conflict to carry off a heavy, Belgian, highly-ornamented arm-chair, is as extraordinary as the manner in which he won the Victoria Cross at the same battle.

Before he left for the war old Bill the homeopathic chemist made him a seasonable present in the shape of a case of plaster. General Wills happened to be the only commander wounded in the battle, and young James who was near him stuck a piece of plaster on his shoulder. In reward for this incident both plasterer and plastered received a Cross.

Papa thinks the portrait promises very well. There have been three sittings.

I am eighteen today. How time does go. I feel as if I had been going on such a time. How must grandmamma feel – What funny notions of life I used to have as a child! I often thought of the time when I should be eighteen – its a queer business –

BUSH HALL

Friday, August 1st. Came to Bush Hall August 1, taken till the end of October for twenty-five guineas a week.[19] Also we have a little carriage and pony, the latter aged sixteen is the neatest daisy-cropper I ever saw, and cost £6. It is the first opportunity I have had of learning to drive, like it very much, had no misfortune yet.

Have a piece of private trout fishing in the Lea, which goes past the back-door at four or five yards distance from the house. It is very picturesque, but sometimes smells shocking when the Miller at Brocket clears his dam, which appears to be once or twice a week.

The house is an extraordinary scrambling old place, red brick, two and three stories, tiled, ivied, with little attic windows, low rooms and long passages. I like old houses, and for the summer this will be all very well, but it must be uncommonly damp in winter. It has been much added to, but parts are probably as old as Hatfield House.

There is nothing of interest in the way of panelling or chimney pieces as there is in so many old houses about here. How much better the brick work used to be than now, there is scarcely a house in the neighbourhood which is not very old. The old part at Camfield, which was mostly pulled down when my grandfather built the new, was an immense age, and the manor existed in the middle-ages.

All this part and the house belongs to Lord Salisbury,[20] and is leased by our worshipful landlord Mr Kendall. There are numerous little things in which the Kendalls have not behaved nicely to us, the main one being that they carefully cleared the garden before leaving, and that the gardener does not give us a fair share of what is left. Papa bought everything, but told Mr Kendall that he might sell (that is his custom) what we do not want, but Mr Kendall has got hold of the wrong end and sells almost everything, and grumblingly gives us the leavings.

Lord Salisbury does not find that horsepower answers very well, so he employs three or four traction engines and a troupe of very fine donkeys. The former are most dangerous on the roads, and the latter are rather surprising, they are so large. Imagine suddenly meeting round a corner a tall, long-legged and eared donkey, wearing a muzzle and looking very ferocious, dragging at a hand gallop a light cart, in which are wedged the fat gardeners taking precedence on the road from the proud notice on the cart. *Robert, Marquis of Salisbury, No. 16.*

It is extraordinary how liberal his Lordship is with his Park. The public walk and drive in most parts, even close to the house. Earl Cowper does the same, it must be one disadvantage of living at a great place. We had a touch of it at Wray.

The Kendalls have left castor-oil in a locked cupboard on the stairs. If there is a smell I dislike it is castor-oil. Lady John Manners used to eat it as a regular thing in her potatoes at dinner, I believe from liking it, but old Sir William Gull gives it that way to his patients.

Tuesday, September 30th. It seems they will not give a child Christian burial at Hatfield unless it has been baptized. I believe it is still a common superstition that a child goes to the wrong place unless baptized. How can anyone believe that the power above us – call it Jehovah, Allah, Trinity, what they will – is a just and merciful father, seeing the end from the beginning, and will yet create a child, a little rosebud, the short-lived pain and joy of its mother's heart, only to consign it after a few days of innocence to eternal torment?

All outward forms of religion are almost useless, and are the cause of endless strife. What do Creeds matter, what possible difference does it make to anyone today whether the doctrine of the resurrection is correct or incorrect, or the miracles, they don't happen nowadays, but very queer things do that concern us much more. Believe there is a great power silently working all things for good, behave yourself and never mind the rest.

Saturday, October 4th. Saw the eclipse of the moon splendidly on Sat. 4th. First I ever saw.

Phyllis remembered the turning down to Woodfield perfectly well the first time she passed it after ten months' absence. It is extraordinary how some horses notice. Poor Snowdrop, who was rather lazy, could scarcely be induced to pass my grandmother's in Palace Gardens.

If one thing in nature can be said to be more perfect than another, I should say a fine horse is among the most striking. It is such a pleasure to watch the mare going, her tail whisking with satisfaction, her neck curved, her ears cocked knowingly forward, her feet lifted like a circus-horse to music. No fear of her shying or falling going down hill, she swings along with long steady strides, and when she sees a hill she takes the bit in her teeth, tucks in her chin and just tears at it. She goes faster up hill than on the flat, she has so much spirit. She would never take a whipping, I should almost as much expect one myself.

Extraordinary and wonderful intelligence, the *greenery yallery Grosvenor fellow* has come to an end. The premises have become a carriage-shop. What will become of the wretched greeneries I cannot imagine![21]

They may well be more sickly than ever, for they have the prospect of extinction before them. I am sorry for them, but it is quite time they died. When one comes to consider the other summer exhibitors, I don't think after all there will be much loss to the public. The only important artist who seems to drop out is Mr Watts.[22] Millais, Herkomer, Bell, Ouless, Alma-Tadema, all exhibit at the Academy, and it is a strong proof against the objections continually raised against that Institution's choice of pictures, that its rival can disappear without any loss to the public.

The new Institution will receive the small artists, and as to Mr Watts, I believe he is all humbug, he draws shockingly, has hardly any colour, and is given to thieving; they say he will not sell his picture – 'sour grapes'.

The unfortunate part of the Gallery's end is the stop put to the Winter Exhibitions there. They were to have had Gainsborough this winter on the same plan as the Reynolds one. Of course the Reynolds illustrated catalogue must have disappeared too. I should think the etchings must have been commenced though.

I have got something here which I have often wished for but never before attained, any amount of beautiful white clay under a bit of the river bank. I wish I had found it earlier in the summer.

It is all the same, drawing, painting, modelling, the irresistible desire to copy any beautiful object which strikes the eye. Why cannot one be content to look at it? I cannot rest, I must draw, however poor the result, and when I have a bad time come over me it is a stronger desire than ever, and settles on the queerest things, worse than queer sometimes. Last time, in the middle of September,

I caught myself in the back yard making a careful and admiring copy of the swill bucket, and the laugh it gave me brought me round.

Sunday, October 12th. This day last year, how time moves and what it brings! So cold and stormy, and yet such gleams of peace and light making the darkness stranger and more dreary. How will it end for me?

LONDON

Sunday, October 26th. If the next year takes away as many dear faces it will bring death very near home. How strange time is looking back! A great moving creeping something closing over one object after another like rising water.

The Northern suburbs seem to be quite frequently afflicted by raging elephants. The last escaped, jammed itself in a lane where the frightened inhabitants gave it an unlimited supply of buns to keep it from knocking down the houses.

When we came home from the station on Thursday through Marylebone, we were surprised to find policemen moving on and turning off the traffic, amongst great excitement. Supposed there was a riot, that being the ordinary cause of excitement now, but it seems a horrid human head and then some limbs had been found in a back street.

PORTSMOUTH

Monday, November 10th. Left Eastbourne 10.5 Monday morning 10th. November 84, and arrived at Portsmouth at half past one. I had never been here, or along the coast before.

Thought the country very pretty and exceedingly rich, reminding me of Devonshire. Among the Downs, before reaching Brighton, several ploughs were being drawn by big black oxen with brass-tipped horns. There appear to be great quantities of black cattle on the marshes, but I see comparatively few of the celebrated South-down sheep, and those few are penned on turnips. Never saw richer crops of turnips than about Arundel.

Goring and Arundel; unfortunately the mist almost hid the Castle at the latter place, but we passed several picturesque churches, notably Shoreham with a Norman tower, Chichester Cathedral, and Porchester Castle. The Forts round Portsmouth struck me as being very low, which is said to be conductive to strength. It is a singular thing that Portsmouth is the only English town which is strongly fortified.

On leaving the Station I was first struck by the poorness of the streets, the quantity of timber yards, and tricycles and the scarcity of soldiers and sailors, however, the last have become plentiful.

After wanderings in a Fly[23] we finally settled the Queens Hotel which seems comfortable, a queer old house with mountainous floors. An ironclad is anchored opposite, and this evening the electric light[24] has been dodging off it round the coast, the sea, and the sky, in a most erratic manner.

Went in the afternoon to a landing place whence we saw the old warships *St Vincent, Victory*, and *Duke of Wellington* at anchor in the middle of the channel. They look immense and very picturesque, which I should think they are not, to judge by the one opposite, though it is a great size; but there is a most odious mist hiding everything. How easy they must have been to hit!

A buoy opposite marks the sinking of the *Royal George*, at which one of the few survivors was a little child who clung to the wool of a sheep which swam ashore.

In the High Street was a charming bird-shop where they had a most incredible number of dormice in two cages. I don't believe they were dormice, too large by three or four sizes. Am considering how it would be possible to convey some home. Only saw one curiosity-shop with only old china, which is very interesting and to my taste, but not my purse.

Wonder why that bust of Charles I put up on his return from his Spanish courting has never been broken. Blake[25] must have stared at it many a time.

Signs of a little wooden midshipman and Red Indian (tobacco), dirty old back-streets, suggestive of the press-gang. Extraordinary boxes for carrying admirals' cocked-hats, also several shops with curious musical instruments. Quite a flourishing Unitarian Chapel abounding in tombstones opposite the house where Buckingham was murdered.[26]

Quantity of convicts working, several warders on wooden platforms with guns. Scotch soldiers and men-of-war men, very strong and serviceable looking, much sturdier looking and more sensibly dressed than the soldiers, except perhaps the Highlanders.

Tuesday, November 11th. Still misty unfortunately, but no rain. Morning, went by tram and, after several changes and considerable amusement from the company, we reached the Docks.

While still a considerable distance from the stopping place the tram-steps were lowered by a most determined-looking short, broad, close-shaven seafaring party with an oily black curl twisted over each ear, who planted himself on the steps, whence he looked down on his numerous fellows in the street with the contemptuous air of a man who has made a conquest.

I saw we were in for it, and, before we descended, papa had capitulated to the seafaring gentleman who marched us along the pier across the railway, facing round every few steps to see that his prey had not escaped.

At the pier-end was a broad, yellow-whiskered man, who, in obedience to the mute and mysterious signs of his superior delivered at about ¼ mile distance, had brought round a large old boat resembling a tub, into which we were put as prisoners, not without difficulty owing to the swell from two or three of the small steamers and tugs which seem positively to swarm here.

I didn't care tuppence for the water, but I was oppressed by the doubt of how the men-of-war were to be mounted, having completely forgotten the stairs, of which I must have seen drawings.

When once we were fairly captured the naval gentleman suddenly relented and became very communicative, and took us a very pleasant row to the *Victory*. I think this ship was one of the most picturesque sights imaginable, particularly from close under the stairs – looking up at the queer little portholes, and the end like a quaint carved old house. It struck me as being a great height and width, both from within and without, but not very long.

We went on the fighting deck, an extraordinary long deck which would be under water when the ship was freighted, and looked down into the hold, which extends twenty-three feet under the water. Its decks were very clean and roomy, with very few coils of rope or furniture of any kind to cumber them. The cracks between the floor boards were filled with pitch. The low beams, supports and sides were whitewashed, and very steep oak steps in the middle of the ship led from one deck to another.

On the top deck was the spot where Nelson fell, the barge which brought his body to London and several of the original twenty-four pounders, and some old flint guns and a curious case for carrying bullets. Only four of the original cannon are on board, as all the rest were thrown overboard to lighten the ship after the battle, as she was partially full of water.

Down below we saw the original fore topsail torn, with big holes. I thought the most interesting place was a very low deck above the hold, which would be below the water if the ship was in action. At each side of the deck were railed enclosures which I took for loose boxes, but which were cabins. To one of these Lord Nelson was carried, and died with his head against a beam.

There was a poor portrait of him on deck, and a very good picture in the officer's cabin, painted by one Mr Davis, one of the ship's officers. I was surprised to find that the only personal relics preserved there were two letters, one written before he lost his right hand, the other afterwards. We were shown over by a Marine.

Again looked upon those dormice. Would they carry in a biscuit canister? They are grievously afflicted with tickles. Bought some coins at a jewellers, it was mamma's doing. I would never buy them at a jewellers, even with my relation's money. It greatly detracts from the enjoyment of a purchase if you have paid an exorbitant price.

Went along the beach in the afternoon. Southsea Castle is very strong, but why so unprotected on the land?

Wednesday, November 12th. Wednesday morning we again set off in the tram, and were duly captured by the nautical gentleman who was more condescending, but took it out in a still larger exaction.

Port smoother than ever, though sometimes too rough for small boats, but unfortunately the same fog. Rowed up towards the *Excellent*, passing on the way a ship which we had seen coming in during the morning, the *Poonah*, a troop ship hired by the Government, having white officers and a black crew.

I never saw such an immense ship, we seemed as if we should never get to the other end. There was a fat brown-man in a white nightgown and turban. The ship was of a most elegant shape, but as the seaman remarked, she looked as if she would roll a great deal. The sailors were doing something to the ropes of the *Seahorse*, swarming up and down with their bare feet, and hanging on like monkeys. We could see the top of the *Euphrates* lying in the docks. We got up on board the *Excellent* which was beautifully clean as usual, and a striking contrast to the two other ships, full of sailors. What funny people they are, like children, tumbling over one another singing, and one playing gravely with the ship's cat. Fine handsome men, and very civil. They were just beginning ten minutes for lunch, and as we went up some steps we were nearly run over by some twenty or thirty tearing along. I would think sailors never have sorrows, I did not see a single grave one.

The first thing to look at was the big tub for grog, we also saw the cooking and mess-rooms and store-place, all of which seem very well regulated, also the ship's tailor with his sewing machine, and the ropes in the course of twisting by an ingenious machine.

We crossed by a gangway to the second ship, the *Calcutta*, which is included in the title *Excellent*, and considered as the same ship. We had a very civil and intelligent guide who explained everything, and showed how the guns worked. There were the rifles in stands, with swords which fitted to them as a bayonet, and the Gatling gun, whose five barrels fire at once by turning a wheel, and load themselves from a box above, throwing away the empty cartridges, also the Nordenfelt (?) guns of the same kind.

The sailors were being taught to work the big guns on two decks. On the upper the guns worked most ingeniously on runners, but the older ones had to be pulled round with ropes amid great confusion and tumbling. The teachers were very sharp, and kept the men always on the move.

One gunner made a mistake and was reproved at full length. The class became suddenly serious, and the head delinquent looked as if he was going to cry. They fired some caps, which made quite sufficient noise to be agreeable.

Came home Wednesday 12th.

LONDON

Wednesday, November 19th. Went with papa and mamma to Cutter's shop near British Museum to look for a cabinet. Most singular dried-up but pepperish old gentleman Mr Cutter, like one of the specimens in his dusty shop-window. Brisk, thin, long white hair, thin red face, necktie awry to an extraordinary extent. Old and musty from head to foot, with spectacles, he moved about among the piled-up lumber and curiosities and old bones of his shop like a wood-louse diving in and out of a rotten log.

New cabinets cost more than Mr Cutter could express, 'Good Lord! Gracious! Pound a drawer!' and old ones are rather surprising as to price.

I was amused beyond expression to see mamma rapidly opening drawer after drawer of one to see if it was clean, suddenly come to one full of human bones, 'who's feared of boggarts'. A bone leg set out on wire, skulls everywhere, and the little dust-dried old man who told us how much he paid in rates, fussing about.

A few weeks ago the officials at King's Cross Station were amazed to hear the big clock strike 'one' at twenty past four. On someone's going to the tower stair the door was found locked on the inside. At last a painter managed to crawl along the roofs and gutters so as to approach the clock on the other side.

To his surprise he heard voices within, and peering through discovered three little boys, the eldest being twelve, who were calmly breaking the works for mischief. They had gone up after pigeons.

Friday, November 28th. Went out with papa. First to the French Gallery in the Tate, where there is a very fair collection of pictures with very little rubbish, chief being landscapes and sketch by Heffner,[27] a young man whom Wallace has picked up. The large pictures are striking, the distant sky in particular, but they are a trifle sketchy.

Large Holl, of woman pawning her wedding-ring. Wonder why Holl's subjects are so much better than his portraits? Not much colour in this, but not smudgy or ill-drawn. Several Leaders, hard as sticks, and one small Corot. There is an extraordinary rage at present for Millets and sundry realistic pictures.

The daubs of melancholy, wooden peasants which one sees in the smaller exhibitions are dreadful. I have never seen a Millet, or a Corot before this one, and after what papa has said I was agreeably surprised with it. I think the smudgy slovenliness is affectation, but it was the best drawn landscape there.

Went on to the National Gallery and enjoyed myself exceedingly. How large it is! I was rather surprised at the selection of pictures which I had remembered. I wonder what governs a child's perception? I remembered more of the Turners than any others. Clearest of all the *Building of Carthage*, of which I am sure I have seen no engraving.

Swarms of young ladies painting, frightfully for the most part, O dear, if I was a boy and had courage! We did not see a single really good copy. They are as flat and smooth as ditch-water. The drawing as a rule seems pretty good, but they cannot have the slightest eye for colour. I always think I do not manage my paint in that respect, but what I have seen today gives me courage, in spite of depression caused by the sight of the wonderful pictures.

What I am troubled by is the inability to control my medium, but these copyists, content to work greasily with camel hair brushes, paint with the greatest facility, and yet can't colour in the least. If I could govern my paint I'd go better. Age imparts to pictures a peculiar glow and mellowness, varying in different pictures from green or yellow to orange, the first being the commonest, but, the stronger the green tint of age, the more persistedly do these young ladies apply a kind of sickly chocolate which they seem to have caught from one another. Their works certainly would be the better for going up the chimney a bit. I cannot understand it, and they have such perfect self reliance, uncertainty always makes the colours muddy.

What marvellous pictures the Turners are! I think *Ulysses and Polyphemus* is the most wonderful in the gallery. Well might Turner despise fame and wealth with such a world in his brain, and yet his end was hastened by drink. What a mixture of height and depth!

Mr Gladstone's health and vigour is said to be owing to his chewing every mouthful thirty-two times, but Mr Millais who has been staying there says they eat faster than he, which is saying a good deal. Disraeli, looking at Mr Gladstone's portrait by Millais in the Academy, remarked there was just one thing in the face which Millais had not caught, that was the vindictiveness.

1885

'I always thought I was born to be a discredit to my parents . . .'

LONDON

Saturday, January 24th. Intense anxiety about General Stewart's army from which there is no news whatever.[1] They say, if none comes within twenty-four hours, there will be great risk that he has been cut to pieces.

And a serious dynamite explosion on the top of this. My father says the country is going to the deuce, and his spirits get worse and worse. One explosion indeed! three! How is it they always come on a Saturday! The *Observer* must make a fortune by them. This is the first time they have happened by daylight. Before, there has always been gas extinguished.

It seems to me that the most serious damage is the shaking to the roof of Westminster Hall. The damage in the House of Commons is between twelve and fifteen thousand pounds, but of course that is modern work and can be restored. Even Westminster Bridge was shaken, and passengers, before the sound reached them, thought it was an earthquake.

It has always been asserted for some reason that there was no dust on the ancient oak boards of Westminster Hall, but on the contrary, the floor was two or three inches deep with it. People will be afraid to go sight-seeing soon. Visitors at the Tower do not bargain for a taste of the horrors of war.

Some odd things happened in the House, which Radicals who are still touched by the ancient Tory failing, superstition, will treasure up. A shield bearing a crown and Irish harp was blown from the Peers' Gallery on to the seats occupied by the Home Rulers. Mr Bradlaugh's seat[2] was hurled along the House till it touched Mr Gladstone's.

The Tories on the other hand do not fail to remark that the

opposition side of the House was scarcely damaged. Mr Gladstone and Bright's seats were destroyed, the Speaker's chair broken.

It is rumoured that the damage is greater than outsiders are informed of. The police maintain a prudent silence, the dynamiters, as is always their way, threaten larger damage. A second gunpowder plot, but I don't suppose the 24th. of January will be kept as a second Guy Fawkes. Such things were less common in the 17th. century!

Thursday, February 5th. Awful news just sent from Egypt, Khartoum fallen, Gordon a prisoner, Sir Charles Wilson and part of the army blocked up under heavy fire and probably without provisions.[3] O, if some lunatic had shot old Gladstone twelve months since. It is too dreadful to believe, what will foreigners say? Surely our cowardly Cabinet who are responsible for it will go down? Great excitement in town, great sale of newspapers.

Saturday, February 21st. General Buller being surrounded in the desert.[4] Greatest excitement in town over the probability of war with Russia. Times are awful. Father says we shall have the taxes ½ crown in a pound and conscription. I don't think we shall have the latter, I have not a high opinion of my fellow men, but I believe, if old England were in straits, her children would rise of their own accord.

The Colonies are showing the greatest enthusiasm, the troops most eager, and several people have subscribed over a thousand pounds each towards the expenses. It is incredible that the government should have hesitated a moment in accepting their help. It seems to me England's only hope lies in her Colonies, and what with Russian and German, and French and Italian encroachments, they are not as safe as they might be.

There is scarcely a night without the news-criers come round the silent streets, sometimes after ten o'clock. Their voices echo and answer one another, and the wind howls in the chimneys. Things of evil omen, who ever heard of them proclaiming good tidings?

I saw a most extraordinary tricycle pass today. A bath chair made of wicker work in which reclined a smart lady, and behind, where one should push, a gentleman treadling, puffing and blowing and looking very sheepish. I wonder any one will make such an exhibition of themselves. How the bicycles swarm now, and yet a few years since, every one turned round to stare at a *velocipede*!

Monday, March 2nd. Went to Eastbourne Sat. till Mon. 2nd. Went over to Pevensey Castle, Sunday. We could not go into the Keep as 'Visitors are requested not to walk on the grass *on Sundays*'. It is most surprisingly large and interesting. I found scented violets which I never did before, and it struck me as a curious coincidence that they are supposed to have been introduced by the Romans, as also the rose.

Holman Hunt's picture of the *Flight into Egypt* is at the Fine Arts in Bond Street, creating a certain languid excitement. He has been working at the subject seven years. The first was only on calico because he had no canvas, and broke down under the weight of the paint. He says his colour-man disappointed him, they say he forgot to give the order.

He is pitied as an unsuccessful man some way. He has a very large family. I should imagine not a very cheerful disposition, and his art cannot possibly repay the time spent on it. Whatever one may think of his work, one must respect the man, amongst the crowds of painters who dish off vulgar pictures to sell – Mr Millais might well remark, here is poor Hunt been seven years at his picture, and I shall finish mine in seven weeks.

Sunday, March 15th. Saw Oscar Wilde and his wife just going into the Fine Arts to see the Holman Hunt. He is not peculiar as far as I noticed, rather a fine looking gentleman, but inclined to stoutness. The lady was strangely dressed, but I did not know her in time to see well.

Saturday, March 28th. A lamentable falling off. Had my few remaining locks clipped short at Douglas's. Draughty. My hair nearly all came off since I was ill. Now that the sheep is shorn, I may say without pride that I have seldom seen a more beautiful head of hair than mine. Last summer it was very thick and within about four inches of my knees, being more than a yard long.

There are signs that the domestic animals are revolting. From Holborn comes news that one Mr Ashton, returning home, discovered his black tom had two visitors in the passage, whom Mr

Ashton proceeded to eject, but all three set on him, and after a violent struggle Mr Ashton was driven precipitously out at the front door, and fell into the arms of two policemen who took him to the hospital.

On their return, they found old Mrs Ashton the mother had retreated into the back drawing-room badly scratched, and she also was conveyed to the hospital. The two policemen returned a second time and had a tremendous battle, in which one cat jumped on the leading policeman's helmet. However, the two strangers were killed at last. Unfortunately the blackie leader took warning and escaped through a back window, since which a large body of cats are said to have been seen moving towards Oxford Street.

I don't consider cats thoroughly domesticated animals. I have twice been attacked by two which had not kittens, when trying to turn them out of the garden. Once I retreated at full speed, the other time I had a most unpleasant fight with a heavy walking stick.

There is a story told of a well dressed woman in Paris who was summoned by her landlord on account of the mysterious disappearance of a clock. She was very indignant at the charge when before the magistrate, but the clock settled the question by suddenly striking twelve inside her bustle. There is an advertisement of a crinoline 'warranted not to waggle'.

AMBLESIDE

Saturday, April 11th. Came to Laurel Villa, Ambleside, Mrs Clark, 11th.

Thursday, April 16th. Drove up Langdale Valley. Saw Dungeon Ghyll, which is more striking than I expected. Saw also the attempted revival of linen hand-weaving at St Martin's Cottage, Elterwater, under the superintendence of old Ruskin, Fleming, and an energetic lady named Miss Twelves.

It is doubtless a great resource for poor women in the dales, and will sell as a curiosity, but the linen is infinitely coarser than that our great grandmothers wove, and its durability is more due to honest bleaching than to the hand-loom. A pretty little girl was spinning at a great rate.

The mother of Mrs Clark, of this lodging, had the farm at Rydal, and was very familiar with the Wordsworths, particularly the old lady. Wordsworth is always referred to as *the poet* in these parts, and local tradition says Dorothy Wordsworth was the greater poet of the two.

For some years before her death she was subject to fits of madness, which her brother could generally control. During these, though a pious and sensible lady, she used to swear like a dragoon. She had a craze for putting her clothes on the fire, and they at last got a fender up to the ceiling.

She left a great many of Wordsworth's furniture and odds and ends, such as a large clothes horse, to Mrs Clark's mother.

What a strange chance! a blind beggar with a very pretty wife. The autograph of Tam o'Shanter has lately been sold in London for £150.

The native manners in this village are very amusing. The volunteers went off one morning in buses to a Review, commanded by an officer in spectacles. First a sword dropped out, and one bus stopped to pick it up. Then when they were fairly started, down rushed a fat little man from the town, completing his toilet as he ran, amidst cries of 'stop for Billy'. There were numerous young women in the party. All behaved very well, but what they would do under fire is another thing. Their band practised in a lonely pasture on the previous Saturday evening with picturesque effect.

The goods of widow Gibson, grocer, were sold by auction yesterday. As it was very wet all the gossips sat in the open windows, four or five apiece to the top of the house, while the auctioneer, standing on the furniture in the road, shouted up to them. I saw him sell a black coal scuttle (one of the leading articles) and with immense gesticulation, to Mrs Short, the greengrocer, at a 4th. story window, the widow in weepers being on the first floor.

The hearse is a sight, I can say no more, a moving mausoleum with life-sized black sculptures.

Went to Ginnet's Travelling Circus. Very good, wonderful performing bull.

LONDON

Friday, May 1st. To Camfield on May Day. Oh the beautiful Spring! If one's spirit was assured to haunt birds' place, suicide in the duck pond might be worthy of consideration. Wild ducks nest.

Wednesday, May 6th. How is it these high-heeled ladies who dine out, paint and pinch their waists to deformity, can racket about all day long, while I who sleep o'nights, can turn in my stays, and dislike sweets and dinners, am so tired towards the end of the afternoon that I can scarcely keep my feet? It is very hard and strange, I wonder if it will always be so?

Friday, May 29th. I always thought I was born to be a discredit to my parents, but it was exhibited in a marked manner today. Since my hair is cut my hats won't stick on, and today being gusty, it must needs blow into the large fountain at the Exhibition,[5] and drifted off to the consternation of my father, and the immense amusement of the spectators. We had to wait some time till the gutta-percha man was fetched and waded in to his chin for it.

It was of course too wet to put on, but as it was fine I did not care, for it is one of the peculiarities of my nature that when there *is* anything to be shy about, I don't care in the least, and I caused a good deal of harmless amusement. If only I had not been with papa, he does not often take me out, and I doubt he will do it again for a time. The weather, which has been very cold, suddenly turned to hot summer.

For some time there has been a discussion of two and three columns in *The Times*, started by a *British Matron* about nude pictures. Nearly all the letters take the same sensible view, but the pepper of discussion is not necessary to keep up such a savoury subject.

I do not see the slightest objection to nude pictures as a class, nor are they necessarily in the least more indecent than clothed ones. Indeed the ostentatious covering of certain parts only, merely showing that the painter considers there is something which should be concealed, is far worse than pure unabashed nudity. The shame of nakedness is for the naked, not the observer, and the pictures cannot feel.

If there is a question, it is between the artist and his model. Some painters are much more unpleasant than others according to the realism of their art. The president is not more solid than a dream, but when Alma-Tadema[6] paints a striking portrait of Mrs Alma-Tadema which you could put your hand into, it may be getting near the line.

Saturday, May 30th. Been somewhat lively this last week. (1) Mr and Mrs Saunders went off for the Whit. week and left with the cook, a dirty doited little body, £12 to pay the books, which she put in the dresser drawer, and the *buttons* abstracted. All this is sad, but the sequel is absurd. The *buttons* became drunk, bought two revolvers, put part of the money up the pantry chimney and buried the rest in the back garden. This singular behaviour having attracted attention, he is imprisoned for six months. It is the second misfortune the Saunders have had with their servants. The wicked might say it is a reaction from the prayer meetings.

Also (2), last Saturday night, between twelve and one, being moonlight, the neighbourhood was awakened by a female who need not fear to walk the streets by night, seeing that in seven minutes she can summon as many *Bull's-eyes*[7] from a radius of half a mile.

This presumed distressed female in the back lane, suddenly set up piercing and continuous shrieking with strangely powerful lungs. My father woke suddenly, bounced out of bed to the window, and acted upon by the sudden rising and sympathetic emotion, exclaimed 'Dear me, I feel faint,' and bounced into bed again, while mamma humped out at the other side. Meanwhile the screaming was something awful, and all the windows along the row were opened, and police were hurrying up from distant beats.

They all enquired in chorus 'What's the matter, what's the matter, do be quiet and tell us my dear!' Whereat the distressed female screamed louder for the course of five minutes.

Some of the disturbed householders hadn't much sympathy for her, for the voice of Mr Benjamin H. Bounce[8] was heard from an upper chamber of Number 2, 'When are you going to take that precious woman away?' His sentiments were correct, for next morning on enquiry, she proved to be a French woman who had been visiting a sister servant at one of the houses, got drunk, been turned out and set up this noise for which she deserved the lock-up.

*

Wednesday, June 3rd. Heard Strauss' band at the Exhibition. They play most divinely. The papers do not praise them quite so strongly as they might, as there is great jealousy of a foreign band. I do not think they play the more ambitious music as well as Godfrey's band, but the dance music is perfect.

I never saw anything more amusing than Herr Eduard Strauss conducting. As the tune opens out he rises more and more on his tiptoe, and finally revolves fairly dancing, whereat I do not wonder. He is a dark, stout little man, with a large forehead, very fine mouth, curly hair, moustache and imperial. He has the most extraordinary control over his band. They say his head and hand are in direct communication with every member of the band.

They are about fifty, one being a lady, the harpist. It is a peculiar medley of violins, trumpets, harp, symbols, triangle, tambourine, drum, and the thing which makes most noise and which I supposed to be a trumpet, but is a large slab of thin iron which is struck like a gong.

Every now and then Strauss seizes the fiddle, and still dancing and occasionally waving his bow, winks over the edge at performers who are not sufficiently alive. The only fault was that the pieces were so short, but he was always called back, once three times. The reason for his great compliance was that Count Munster, and a pretty German daughter sitting in the front rank, were applauding enthusiastically, to whom Herr Strauss bowed and recommenced.

We had old Mrs Gibson of Walthamstow and her husband. Her father Mr Cogan, the Unitarian minister, kept a school to which Lord Beaconsfield went, and I believe the old lady is in the habit of telling stories about him, how he used to keep the boys awake half the night romancing.

KESWICK

Friday, July 10th. Came to Lingholm, Keswick, Cumberland, 10th July. Papa quite sorry to leave the Exhibition and *Mein lieber Eduard Strauss.*

My education finished 9th. July. Whatever moral good and general knowledge I may have got from it, I have retained no literal rules. I don't believe I can repeat a single line of any language. I have liked my last governess best on the whole – Miss Carter had her faults, and was one of the youngest people I have ever seen, but she was very good-tempered and intelligent.

I regret German very much, history I can read alone, French is still going on, the rules of geography and grammar are tiresome, there is no general word to express the feelings I have always entertained towards arithmetic.

Sunday, August 16th. August 16th. being Sunday, five Keswick men and one from Penrith went to Lodore Hotel to drink, and coming back at 8 o'clock, dusk, began fighting, upset the boat, and they were drowned. The Hotel has a very bad name. Keswick roughs have a regular habit of getting drunk there every Sunday, and Saturday too.

Those drowned were John Gill, Thomas Lightfoot, and Harry Mitchell. They belonged to the lowest set in the town, and will not be missed, but unfortunately the catastrophe has had no effect on the survivors, they were fighting in Keswick within an hour after. They and all the roughs and idle in the place have been dragging day and night since, the weather being fortunately calm, and the moon growing to the full.

One man struck the other and fell out, the other overturned the boat trying to reach him. One swam ashore, two others and the little dog got in the boat, the other three went down, and sixteen or twenty boats have been 'trolling since, but had nearly given up hope by Tuesday night, the bottom being muddy and varying suddenly from ten to twenty-four feet.

They also dived – but on Saturday night, two boys who thought they would have a try, brought up a body at the first drag. It came up like a cork, caught by the flaps of the coat. The Board of Health has taken up the matter I am glad to say. It is most horrible having those things under the water, we hardly like to go up the lake.

There have been many drownings on this lake, but invariably caused by drink. The landlord of the Derwentwater Hotel at Portinscale went out with another man, both drunk, and both drowned. Twenty-two years later to the very day, his son and one of the others went out in a similar condition, and the son fell out of the boat near Fawe Park where the butler heard a scuffle, but thought but little of it at the time. The other returned, sat down in a chair remarking casually, 'Oh me, someone was drowned.' He was too bad to say more, but people at the Inn hurried out and found the body standing where the butler heard the noise, with hardly an inch of water over the head. Bodies are always upright, on their head or feet.

Another recent misfortune was with three drunkards going to this same Lodore Hotel when it was rather rough. They rowed so hard at the waves that they filled their boat with water, but in spite of the entreaties of the steersman who was sober, they refused to land, out of bravado, so he left the boat and swam to St Herbert's Isle, whence he saw them drown. There was also a cheap tripper on a Saturday, but the list is endless.

It is a terrible place for drink, there were two in the lock-ups last Saturday, one a woman. Every fourth Saturday is the worst, when the miners are paid all their earnings and go to the gin shop.

The lake is very rough sometimes, great white waves, but one never hears of misfortunes then. Sensible people keep off it. When this happened it was a most lovely evening, warm and sultry, not a breeze of wind. The sunset was still fiery in the west and south, the moon was rising, the reflections of the great blue mountains lay broad and motionless in the water, undisturbed save now and then by the ripple of a passing boat. East, south and north, the blue mountains with their crimson crests towered up against a clear blue heaven, flecked with little white fleecy clouds. Westwards the thunder clouds came rolling across the fire; yet under such a sky, and amidst such peace and calm, one hears shouting and drunken voices singing 'hold the fort' in a variety of discords.

Next morning the boatmen are 'trolling up and down with fish hooks fast to a board, and down below the water lilies, among the greedy pike, there is a man, the highest and lowest in the scale of creation. The last body was caught on the Sunday, when was also half a pig's head which they had stolen at the Inn. The parents of one man were both drunk at the funeral.

Tuesday, August 25th. Went to Buttermere by Grange, Honister, and back by Newlands. Extraordinary and striking drive, but one to make one thankful to see a field of corn; an awful road. Never knew what jolting was before, three of party, including self, excessively ill following night; recommend said excursion as a cure for colic.

Monday, September 7th. Letter to my father from Aunt Mary announcing Kate's engagement to one Captain Crookshank, who has been in the Army, is now a Stockbroker 'by no means rich', not a word about his religion, friends, or age. One should not judge before one hears all the case, but this sounds a silly business if nothing worse. They are to marry next month, and are going to live in a furnished house in the suburbs, where, as Kate ingeniously puts it, the pleasures of town and country life will be combined.

Aunt Mary has not a particle of sense, but I can't understand the girl not having more self-pride or ambition. What would your old grandfather have said, he would have been horrified. Father is grieved and exasperated to tears. Kate and Blanche were almost like his own daughters a few years since. It was very foolish of Aunt Mary to make no fuss and stop Capt. Crookshank looking after them and taking them out. If he had a beautiful daughter like Kate there is no doubt he could marry her very well, he is intimate with all the rich and respectable Unitarians' families, or if ambitious, he could easily take her into fashionable society. I know he took Kate to Lord John Manners among other places, and she made a great impression.

Not that I in the least consider position or wealth as the great objects of life, though I am sure they are more necessary to Kate's happiness than they would be for mine. Too much money is an evil in most hands, but too little is a sore trial to one extravagantly brought up. Fortunately Kate's £10,000 was tied up by my grandfather in such a manner that her husband cannot meddle with it, but what is £350 a year to a girl who dresses as she does. Love in a cottage is sentimental, but the parties must be very pleasing to each other to make it tolerable.

I can't say that I'm surprised at this business, I thought she would marry someone fast, but this is a poor affair. If he were in the Army even, he might rise. If ghosts are disturbed by after events, grandfather will turn in his grave, he will have little rest, there is a curse on this family. If this is what beauty leads to, I am well content to have a red nose and shorn head, I may be lonely, but better that than an unhappy marriage.

LONDON

Friday, October 9th. Came home to London 9th. Papa brought Bobby the pony, my one satisfaction.

I was quite struck with the changed feeling on getting into the flat Midlands. I found myself continually looking at the sky, which happened to be particularly fine and stormy, as an old long lost friend. It is such a comfort not to be shut in with great frowning hills.

Here in London it is worse with houses, it is a horrid place. Saunders chimney afire when Elizabeth arrived, that nuisance recommencing.

Tuesday, October 13th. Went to Camfield 13th. My dear grand-mamma very lively and delighted to see us, but shrunk into a wee old woman.

When we got home 9th., letter waiting from Aunt Mary announcing Blanche's engagement to Charlie Wrigley. Quite another matter to the other. Mother is sorry that he is her cousin, and enlarges on that subject to me so continually that I begin to think she desires particularly that I should be acquainted with her views on it; an unnecessary precaution at present.

Sunday, November 15th. Mr Millais came here 15th. in the evening to get papa to photograph next morning. He seemed in good health and high spirits. 'I just want you to photograph that little boy of Effie's. I've got him you know, he's (cocking up his chin at the ceiling), he's like this, with a bowl and soap suds and all that, a pipe, it's called *A Child's World*,[9] he's looking up, and there's a beautiful soap bubble; I can't paint you know, not a bit, (with his head on one side and his eyes twinkling) not a bit! I want just to compare it, I get this little thing (the photo of the picture) and I hold it in my hand and compare it with the life, and I can see where the drawing's wrong.'

'How are you getting on with your drawing?' My certes, I was rather alarmed, but he went to another subject in a second. He is a simple person in worldly affairs, he said to papa about the election, 'I supposed we're all obliged to vote aren't we?'

He addressed some most embarrassingly personal remarks to me, but compliments from him would take longer to turn my head than from any other source. If he sees a tolerably comely girl, he cannot keep his tongue still, and I am perfectly certain that when I was a child he used to tease me in order to see me blush.

Thursday, December 10th. Muzzling of dogs 10th. December. A most blessed change. Now, when I am set upon by three collies at once in the High Street, I simply smack them with my umbrella and laugh.

Thursday, December 31st. New Years Eve, or rather the last hours of 1885. How awful it seems at the end of a year to think it has actually passed into space never to return! Gone except its memories! Much bitterness and a few peaceful summer days. Oh life, wearisome, disappointing, and yet in many shades so sweet, I wonder why one is so unwilling to let go this old year? not because it has been joyful, but because I fear its successors – I am terribly afraid of the future. Some fears will inevitably be fulfilled, and the rest is dark – Peace to the old year, may the seed sown therein bear no bitter fruit!

1886-7

'We were in a deplorable state all round'

Monday, February 1st.–30th. I went this afternoon with my mother to visit Lady Eastlake, the object of our visit being to fetch a drawing by one of her nieces which she had persuaded my father to buy.

I had never seen Lady Eastlake and had a great curiosity to do so, but must confess my expectations were rather damped beforehand by my mother's reluctance to call; according to her the old lady was a perfect dragon. I think the feeling that we were certain to find her at home may have added to it. One goes calling with much more assurance when one can reflect one's acquaintance may be out, but here, we reflected we were in for it, all the way through the old-fashioned ill-paved streets leading to Fitzroy Square.

The Square itself seemed old-fashioned, substantial and genteel, perhaps a trifle *passé* on a foggy day, but this afternoon the low winter sun slanted pleasantly between the chimney-tops, through the leafless plane trees, on the cheerful sparrows airing themselves along the grooves in the masonry, and also showed up the thick ancient dust upon the window panes.

The outside of number seven showed a solid good-sized house with a good doorway. One can generally judge a London house by the doorway. I noticed with much surprise the little green half-blinds in the dining-room windows like venetian shutters, *stood*, not *hung*. They are common in the old houses at Carlisle, but I never saw them elsewhere.

The door was opened by Lady Eastlake's old butler, not *the* old one, but one as old as one can imagine. The first thing I noticed in the hall was a piece of Italian sculpture in low relief, graceful, headless, in dark grey stone, let into a mahogany frame or stand.

The old butler hurried up the steep staircase like a beetle. He turned out his feet at right angles; they were very large, or rather his shiny shoes were, I could not make out his feet, they were all knobs. I was much impressed by them as he went up before, two steps at a time.

I also noticed there was a piece of plain crêpe stretched up against the banisters. At the time I had a misty notion it had something to do with the late President, but, on reflection, I think it is because Lady Eastlake is so very large, that when she used to go up and down stairs she caught her dresses on the banisters.

The old man knocked at a door, and opening it at the same moment announced us.

I found myself in a large, light room, with large windows and a smaller drawing-room at the back. The walls were hung with Old Masters in dusty, heavy gilt frames, other pictures and drawings stood on the chairs. The tables were crowded with books and papers, above hung a great glass chandelier in a brown holland bag. There was a very handsome white marble chimney piece, another in the back parlour. The furniture was old-fashioned and covered with a faded chintz. There were a quantity of odds and ends, and casts, ancient and modern, one a Parian bust of Her Gracious Majesty.

Lady Eastlake was sitting in an armchair at the fire, the table being beside her. On the opposite side, as if a companion, was a large picture in a sort of case on an easel. Whether it was the genial weather or what, I know not, but Lady Eastlake seemed very pleasant. Mother said she was better than she'd ever seen her before! Perhaps she was less overpowering through being seated all the time.

She was writing on some large sheets of paper closely when we went in. She had on a black woollen gown trimmed with black lace, a lace cap, and a pair of most mysterious silver pins as large as skewers, stuck into the twist of her hair above the ears. I could not help looking at them all the time, I could not think what they were stuck into. Also, on her breast, was one yellow china primrose natural size, without any stalk, same as a button.

On the table lay her black cane with a crooked handle, a silver band and a sort of Indian ribbed nose. She was very pleasant, talked about the family, the weather, old servants. 'My butler had not been so long, at least not for this house, he has been about twelve or fourteen years. My coachman has been longer' (so have the horses thought I), 'A very nice man', laid up with something and another. 'I was very much distressed a year or two since, I lost an old housekeeper. I miss her still, she was in the house before we came, she couldn't read or write. I thought that showed she had belonged to a large family and sent to work early.' 'No, she did not seem to find it inconvenient, one or two other servants would always write her book. She learnt at last after she was fifty, an old butler left and she could not bring herself to ask the next. It was like copy book but it did very well.'

She began to talk about politics, 'I am very sad about things, very.' Speaking of Gladstone with much dislike, she admitted he had the power of talking people over. 'Oh that's the worst of him, no doubt, I wouldn't trust any one with him. I don't think he has as much conceit about his personal appearance as your friend Bright. I mean Bright would never go about in such a state of old clothes. I've been told by artists that he's very particular when he's being painted, about every thing and the position. But Gladstone talks away without even looking at the picture. He would not wear such collars if he cared what he looked like.'

'I don't think I've ever met him at dinner when he had not his cuffs all frayed; that's Mrs Gladstone. Oh yes, no doubt she's a terrible slut' (said Lady Eastlake with emphasis). 'A most untidy person. I believe Hawarden is a very dirty place, no punctuality, the meals any way. Mr Gladstone would not mind it if she hadn't her stockings on!'

Speaking of the Queen and Mr Gladstone, 'I'm told she says he doesn't even treat her as a lady.'

Speaking of the Salisbury family, 'When they were poor they used to live at the other side of the square there. At that time Lord Salisbury was earning his living by writing political articles. It was his principal income. Most of the children were born there.'

Lady Eastlake did not attempt to rise from her chair or couch, I could not see which it was as her feet were under the table. I asked to be allowed to step round the room to see the pictures. She remarked they were mostly Old Masters, 'difficult to understand'. Come, that's not a dragon, thought I.

She did not *say* anything about Art. I should have rather quaked had she begun, but should have listened with the greatest interest. I was thankful at the time, but rather sorry afterwards.

'That's a beautiful picture, a sweet face,' a woman or girl in medieval Italian costume, with her head on her hand. The face was very beautiful, the tone subdued. I thought it was a copy from an ancient picture, and very quakily enquired who it was by. However, she answered with perfect composure 'By Sir Charles Eastlake, my late husband. I always have one of his pictures out. I'm very fond of that one.' I thought it very beautiful (privately) and perfect in its line of art, the only fault I could find being that it was too large for the subject, over life-size. In this particular it formed a pendant to Lady Eastlake sitting on the other side of the fire. I had thought I had seen the face before, but she said it had never been engraved. 'I think it is a lady whom he has often painted.'

We have stayed some twenty minutes. Lady Eastlake talks rather slowly and at times mumbles a little. I should think she soon gets tired. Her voice is rather deep.

I should not think she was ever handsome except from figure and carriage, and her face, sensible and strong minded, is not very pleasing, though her manner was cordial and kindly. Her hair and thick eyebrows were grey, green thoughtful eyes, and a firm mouth, a woman of strong passions and conscious of power and learning.

When we rose to go, 'Will you ring the bell, my dear? pull it out a long way.' Jonathan the little old man knocking and sticking in his head. 'Will you take two supplements from the bottom of the heap and wrap up the drawing.' John selected two whole sheets, though the drawing was small, laid them on, and, as no string appeared, held them on somewhat feebly, for *them* slipped off when he was half way down stairs. I noticed he descended two steps at a time as he had mounted.

So we departed, I much pleased with my visit.

Tuesday, February 9th. – Monday, 8th. The Riot: To think that I should live to see such a day.[1] It is most terrible and alarming, for I do not see where it is to end while we have such rulers. We narrowly missed being in it.

I went with mother to the Stores at 3 o'clock in the Haymarket. Father met us there. He said there was a large Meeting in Trafalgar

Square, and that some disturbance was feared, but we were quite comfortable and took our time.

As we went I had noticed a good many rough men and workmen going along Piccadilly, and considerable numbers were going across to go down St James's Street. I remember they kept dodging across under the horse's head.

We stayed a long time at the Stores, and started home about a quarter-to-four. At that time a few were still arriving, but a great many respectable workmen were going quietly west, home, about half smoking. Consequently the first we heard of it was *The Times* this morning.

The government of this unhappy country must be in a singular state to allow such doctrines to be openly pronounced as Messrs Hyndman and Burns addressed to a mob of some twenty-nine thousand people in Trafalgar Square yesterday. The goings-on are fully discussed in the papers, so I will record nothing but that which came to us from observation.

Reynolds said Mrs Bridgewater's brougham returned to the Mews in a battered condition during the evening. Mrs Bridgewater was unhurt, the coachman said a large stone had passed within an inch of his face. A brick had gone through the back of the carriage, another missile had struck the window-pane. They were attacked in Piccadilly, escaped into Curzon Street, and so up the Park.

The wood pavement is being mended in several places, and they used the blocks. They must have gone to the Meeting meaning mischief or they would not have had stones; there were none about, as the streets are all wood.

They did not attack the Reform, I am inclined to think this was less from favour than from their not having got to work when they passed it, as their Leaders must have known about the recent black-balling which has been much talked of. They broke the Whig Club in St James's Street indiscriminately. They have not touched Childers' windows.

Papa went to pay a bill at Swears & Wells in Regent Street this morning. There was so thick a fog that he could not see across the street and came back at once. At 1.45 he again went down in a Hansom to the Club, but returned before 3 o'clock with the news that the mob was out again.

Not a shop open East of Albert Gate. The shop-keepers in

Knightsbridge were strengthening their shutters with planks. He could hardly get through to the Club, the streets were thronged with dirty roughs. He was so alarmed that he came home at once.

Some one at the Reform said there had been another meeting in the Square. The mob were trying to get up St James's Street, but the police kept charging them. They were dodging up St James's behind the police. The old Duchess of Norfolk lies there dying. All the servants from the Reform, and many members of the Club, were on the steps watching and laughing. Unfortunately there was a Levée going on.

There were a good many carriages out, father saw Lady Salisbury getting into hers in Arlington Street. The windows of the Carlton are pierced by small stones and mended with paper. In Piccadilly they are almost all out in the ground floors, frames and all, it is incredible, are we to have something like the Gordon Riots again?

In Piccadilly many of the houses have glass flower boxes. These seem to have been special objects of attack. Papa says he never saw such a sight as in Pall Mall. The mob kept advancing, and then every now and then the police on foot and horse-back would charge, and the roughs run back helter-skelter. The cabman who brought him home remarked 'A bad job for trade sir, a pack of fools!'

Wednesday, February 10th. There were all kinds of wild rumours yesterday; that the soldiers were called out, amongst others. A meeting of the wretched shopowners in high indignation. Someone in authority will be a scapegoat, whether Childers, Broadhurst or Henderson, I know not. No one seems to lay the blame on the working men, it is the Jacobins, roughs and thieves. The papers unite in condemnation.

It is thought the shop-keepers will fail to get compensation. The authorities yesterday frankly admitted their inability to keep order, and advised the shops to close, posting extra police at some of the jewellers.

The mob were quite as badly inclined, but were kept back. There is some talk of the lady who was attacked in Piccadilly, and escaped, bidding her coachman 'drive over the dogs'. I trust she said nothing so vulgar, but she had strong provocation.

The only amusing thing I have heard of this business is that when they sacked the wine shop at the top of Piccadilly Hill, they ignorantly drunk a large amount of Janos water,[2] not knowing it from wine.

Today is again most unfortunately foggy. Father went to the city by Underground, returned by noon. Went to Mrs Bruce's in Hyde Park Square, avoiding the Park. Thick fog. Met Dr Sadler, who said they were in a great state at Hampstead. The workman's candidate, who lately got 27 votes, declared he was coming to get his revenge with 500 men. When the Sadlers left, a large number of people and police were in the roads.

It is said that the police almost outnumbered the meeting in Trafalgar Square this morning, but tonight there are rumours of a new advance from Greenwich and Deptford. The fog is most unfortunate. Numbers of rough looking men about the streets here in South Kensington, many hurrying along the High Street towards town. Considerable consternation.

Discussion as to locking front gate. The Government show no sign of moving, the House is not sitting. Old Gladstone only comes to town today instead of tomorrow from Lord Rosebery's.[3] It is scandalous.

Thursday, February 11th. There seems to have been a perfect panic yesterday. All Southwark and the East End shut up and barricaded, from the rumours of a mob of ten-thousand roughs from Greenwich and Deptford, who however, did not arrive, and the police managed the local rabble after a fashion.

The bridges were guarded, the troops held in readiness at the barracks, and a guard at the banks. The shops in the Strand and West End closed in the afternoon. The alarm spread even to this part, the shop-keepers in the Fulham Road at one time believing the Mob was coming. The police prevented the Hampstead section from getting beyond window-breaking this day.

There are an extraordinary number of rough looking men wandering about the roads. This afternoon groups of three or four kept coming west along Fulham and Bayswater Roads. Whatever may be their means, most of them are fat and well fed, a good many smoking, some in gloves, mostly addicted to bright coloured neckties. They go quietly enough.

The only time I misliked them was just as we got out at Mrs Thomas's opposite the Oratory. Five were passing west, and looked first at the Brougham, and then at Reynolds and the mare, such a scowl. I should have been terrified had they formed part of a crowd. We kept west of the Park.

A great many people are leaving town. It is again rather foggy. Father has given £30 to the Lord Mayor's fund.

In *The Times* appears Lord Fife's interesting letters. He leads the Scotch Liberals. It seems generally believed the government will collapse within a month, they are doing nothing whatever.

Father says he will be sorry if the Tories have to deal with this business, because, however wisely and well they do it, they will incur odium through prejudice. The Liberals, or rather Radicals, for it has soon to be a very different party name, having brought the country into this mess, should bring it out. Unfortunately they will not.

Friday, February 12th. The police seem to be exercising an excess of vigilance or nervousness now, but people have been so thoroughly alarmed they will believe the faintest rumour. On Wednesday the Fulham shopkeepers were reported to close on a moment's notice. The police expected the Mob along here.

It is said that one of the ill-treated jewellers is dead. People are unwilling to go into town, many are leaving. My mother is continually listening for sounds outside, particularly in the evenings. My father is becoming very yellow, and lower than ever. Had a faintness on Wednesday. Has heard something about Gladstone which he cannot mention to ladies, at the Reform Club. Talks about going to the Colonies, Edinburgh, quiet provincial towns, but he has done that occasionally for the last ten years.

Myself middling, past being low, reached the stage of indifference and morbid curiosity. Reynolds low, and I believe so are all the race of coachmen and makers. He has a policeman friend who tells him grisly things in the late evening, which when duly reported after breakfast, and together with *The Times*, give my father a turn for the day.

Policeman said the Mob were coming yesterday, that they (the police) were double on the beats, and hardly let off for an hour. I was not a little amused at the professional interest they were showing when I went to the Kensington Museum on Thursday. In one room the Riot Act was being read in a loud voice, in another it was pasted with gumpaper on a leading glass case. It is said that on Wednesday evening the police warned the houses about Grosvenor Square to put out the lights in their front windows.

The government does nothing. Reports of riots in Leicester and Nottingham. Rioters at Birmingham are going to Chamberlain. I wish he would openly take the part of Hyndman & Co and be involved in their condemnation. He is with them in spirit. Land is as much personal property as plate or carriages.

Wednesday, February 17th. Went into town for the first time. Confess I felt rather funny at Hyde Park Corner, thankful we were in a Brougham. Did not go along Piccadilly, saw only twenty-one houses having more or less broken glass, as most are mended or mending. Noticed many panes marked with chalk newly glazed. One house in Grosvenor Square, and another in North Audley Street boarded up with planks. Half the shops appear to be still perfectly empty, particularly jewellers. Many of the latter are having iron netting put over the windows.

Trial of Hyndman, Champion and Burns at Bow Street 17th. They are being treated with every consideration,[4] Counsel, adjournment, it is scandalous. Why, they ought to be hung at once like dogs. I consider they are the most dangerous kind of criminals in existence. A murderer affects but a small circle, they, if unchecked, will cause wholesale slaughter, and ruin society.

MANCHESTER

Friday, February 19th. Went to stay with Aunt Harriet at Pendleton.

Tuesday, February 23rd. Went with my mother to lunch at Aunt Sidney's. My father unfortunately could not go, only my aunt and cousin Jessie were there. My aunt who seemed in good health received us very cordially.

We began lunch at once. She sat in an old-fashioned high, green, wooden armchair, and for the first ten minutes said very little, occupying herself with her dinner and a glass of ale. As to me, I could hardly take my eyes off her, such is my respect: I felt she was listening to every word. Now and then she made a shrewd remark, tempered with her uniform kindliness.

Mamma and I conversed first about Aunt Mary having let her house to Aunt Polly. Aunt Sidney was much amused and said decidedly, 'It was because Polly couldn't bear to be behind Lucy in anything, but it was rather hard on Edwin too.' I went on speaking about Aunt Mary and then about Kate's prospects. I was surprised to find she had believed Aunt Mary's first glowing description.

Aunt Sidney offered no comments, except that so far there had been much smoke and little fire. I began to wonder, in alarm, if it required my father to make her talk, but she presently warmed up and became more delightful every minute of our stay.

We described our desolate journey to Stalybridge, 'Did you see any one that knew you at the Mill?' 'Well very few, hardly any at all. Oh yes, it was like that, I went when I was at Bolton to the Chapel – I said to my son Edmund, do find me any *one* old person that I know; but he could not, – it's very sad to have outlived one's companions, I saw more friends in Bolton churchyard than I have left alive.' A shadow passed over her peaceful face.

We gossiped of Aunt Lucy. Aunt Sidney quite admitted the hardships of Aunt Clara's being turned out of Queen's Gate. She did not begin to talk properly till wé went into the parlour, sitting bolt upright, slightly moving her rocking chair, with her hands on her lap, she settled her feet and began.

The subject which led up was not agreeable, it was Aunt Mary's paint and powder. Aunt Sidney held that powder required rouge, because it made the face lack colour. Some discussion on the manner of powdering, 'My father always powdered to the end of his life, but I don't remember what he did at night, it had to be done every morning – his shoulders were always dusted with it.' 'No, he did not wear a queue – he had his own hair – a great deal – Oh yes, I knew several old gentlemen who wore queues.'

'I wish there was some dress now for old ladies – they used to look so well,' (with animation in reply to my questions). 'They had their hair curled here' (above her forehead), 'and powdered, and all close up (round the neck) they had frills – muslin, yes, just like in Reynolds' pictures.'

'I remember a Mrs— that I used to admire so much. We met her every Sunday morning as we were going to chapel, she used to be

going to St Ann's church in the town. My father used always to be
so attentive, polite, to her, and she did look so nice,' went on my
Aunt with amusing decision, 'I made a vow when I am an old lady
I will dress like her – Well, she had a high white gown and bonnet,
and a sort of black lace shawl – they wore black mittens, their sleeves
came just below the elbow.'

'People were old much earlier then; why, we used to think when
they were sixty, they were on the verge of the grave. Why, after
fifty, they sat like this, with their hands propped on their laps for
the rest of their lives, and I suppose the young people did not go out
much. Well they had a great deal to do in the house.' (I happily said
something about the house in Ardwick.) 'Oh yes – in The Polygon[5]
– in a garden – I have a quantity of old family letters written there
about 1757', (how I listened) (Great grandmother Potter), 'Yes, she
was a Miss Moore of Lancaster, she wore her hair powdered, and
she used to go out in a Sedan. They were very convenient, if it was
wet they were just brought into the hall and you got in, you've read
Cranford? You remember Miss Matty in the Sedan?'

'Of course they would be no use now, but in those days there was
quite a society close together in Ardwick, and besides, the boys had
all two horses. You would not think it in one of those letters – I have
one inviting some one to a strawberry feast in the garden, it was
such a delightful day etc. Yes, they seem to have been funny old
ladies, three maiden sisters, Miss Allcrosses, Oh, the spelling!'
(laughing), 'yes, no doubt the fashion in spelling was different then
– some words – for instance "niece" was always spelt "neice", but
it is funny at times, one letter ends, 'I must stop now because I have
to go across (the road, I suppose) to make a *forth* at quadrille.'

We have seen old letters said I, but nothing to those you mention,
they are about a journey Grandma Leech took when she married.
'Oh yes,' said my Aunt contemptuously as if it were yesterday, 'I
remember Miss Ashton telling me about that journey.'

When we had done laughing, the talk turned to Edith and Edmund,
'And how unlike in body and character they were to poor Aunt Bessie,
and Walter too,' said my mother. 'So light hearted – and what pretty
hair he had, quite golden, I don't know who they're like.'

Aunt Sidney spoke long and lovingly of Aunt Bessie, and I have
seldom seen my mother become more animated and fluent.

The Sidney Potters seem to have been very much attached to her, and seen her almost more than any one else, after her marriage. We spoke of Mr Beard's being so much overcome at Edith's wedding.[6] Last night at the Town Hall he said 'Ay Chapel had seemed to him to be full of ghosts,' yes, he said so to us. It must have been his thoughts, not associations.

After a pause, Aunt Sidney went on warmly, 'I remember so plainly the last time she came to her chapel, she was here afterwards. Oh she was pretty, I never saw anyone like her, so sweet. I remember one evening she had bows in her hair at the back, the hair was worn low then – yes, that lilac dress was very pretty, even with the hoop.'

Mother said she thought she had been even prettier before her marriage. 'The lower part of her face went thin afterwards. I only saw her once or twice before, and she was in mourning, black did not suit so well. Still – she was very pretty afterwards. I remember at the first Exhibition, we were walking in the Park, Walter was with us, and a gentleman looked at her so, and came back and passed us twice; she was so pretty.'

We were interrupted about 3.20 to my intense disgust by the arrival of the carriage. I only had a few words more, aside, after I had on my cloak. When she had kissed me, she said, still holding my hands, some things about my grandmother. I spoke of her curls, 'She used to be such a pretty little girl with brown curls all over – what we used to call a Brutus head.'

'My dear, when shall I see you in Manchester again, you must be sure and come, you have a bright face; good bye.'

I will to my best power describe Aunt Sidney, as she jerks her rocking chair a little up and a little down, sitting bolt upright before the fire.

She has shrewd, quiet grey eyes which seem to look through one. Twice I saw them observantly fixed on me. A very peaceful firm mouth, the expression of one with strong sensibility and powers of observation, but who had come, through trouble and experience, to look calmly and peacefully on life from the outside of its strife and turmoil.

One is struck by her knowledge of character, and great wisdom, and memory. But her manner is so kindly that one feels love instead of shyness. In this respect I confess she is less constraining to a stranger than my dear grandmother. I cannot explain it, for I don't understand how anyone can fear my grandmother.

Aunt Sidney must be nearly eighty, and is rather lame, but mentally in perfect vigour. I never saw a woman except my grandmother, with such a powerful mind, or any one man or woman to equal her in story telling. Her voice is clear and pleasant, she speaks rather low, distinctly, with a slight touch of Lancashire which, however, is more apparent in the modulation and abrupt decisive way of beginning a sentence, than in pronunciation.

Her sense of humour is evident in everything she says, but how seldom do we see humour joined with so tender a sympathy with the sadder and graver side of life.

She is of middling height, erect, broad, but not exactly fat. As she sits in her chair she certainly could not see her feet. Her breast seems to come straight out under her chin. I cannot see if she has much hair, it is silver, neatly braided each side under her cap. The cap is white gauze, with broad streamers down her back.

She had a brown shawl round her shoulders loosely, a black, thick, watered silk gown, very full and plain in the skirt, trimmed with some jet on the body, the waist rather low, black mittens, a large brooch, several old-fashioned rings and a pair of near black leather shoes.

Her eyes twinkle and she looks in the fire as she speaks, and a smile, now sly, now sad, comes over her face. She became particularly clear and animated when speaking of old times, she seemed fairly to see them in the fire. Her face is quietly pleasing from expression. I should doubt if she were ever handsome, but it is character that makes the face. I never saw a kinder, sweeter old lady.

LONDON

Thursday, February 25th. Home on 25th. How amusing Aunt Harriet is, she is more like a weasel than ever, and her tongue – it exceeds all description.

Monday, March 1st. Rather heavy snow. There has been a most singular nuisance going on since Christmas about Manchester. A gang of young men calling themselves *Spring-heeled Jacks* have been going about in the dusk frightening people. They wore india-rubber dresses which would puff up at will to a great size, horns, a lantern and springs in their boots.

One jumped right over a cab in the Eccles Road, nearly frightening the gentleman inside out of his wits. One poor girl in Swinton Lane had a fit.[7] They were cowardly bullies, also thieves, for they took money. Some say they are Medical Students from Owen's College, and it is not impossible I am afraid.

They were bad to catch, but the authorities sent some detectives. One of these met a *Jack* who demanded his money or his life. The detective pretended to be frightened and get out money, but instead he produced some handcuffs and caught him. Another was captured on a Sunday evening by some young men who beat him soundly, and then discovered he was an acquaintance. One was in the next garden to Hopefield a fortnight since.

The maids durst not stir out a step in the evening, which, my Aunt remarked, was well.

Tuesday, March 30th. Went to see the Exhibition of Holman Hunt's at the Fine Arts in New Bond Street. A small collection consisting of oils and drawings, but containing as much work as three times the number of pictures by most artists.

The excitement caused by the Pre-Raphaelite revival has not as yet completely subsided, Millais having painted in every style satisfies every critic, but the Holman Hunt Exhibition has stirred up the discussion.

There is much strong individuality and persistent self-reliance in his pictures, that everyone either hates them or else admires them enthusiastically. There seems no middle opinion.

The violence of dislike is amusing, though from all accounts poor Holman Hunt does not find it so, I should have thought a man who could paint such pictures would be above caring for what the world says. He need not fear the future, real honest work will find its level in time, when the rubbish falls away and is forgotten.

There is not one picture which can be called a pot-boiler, if I may use that inelegant word, which so irritates Sir J. Millais.

I think *Strayed Sheep* and the *Hireling Shepherd* are the best pictures. *The Light of the World* is very wonderful in execution, but it seems impossible to hit the happy mean.

★

Wednesday, April 7th. Death of Mr Forster 5th.[8] A great loss to the nation at the present crisis. If the Queen has been to London once lately, she has been six or seven times, twice this week, what is coming over her? Arrival of the Abbé Liszt,[9] great enthusiasm, they say he stretches eleven notes with ease.

AMBLESIDE

Tuesday, April 20th. To Low Wood Hotel 20th. Clean and dull. Wonderful fine weather, hot in the day, 12 degrees frost at night. Enjoyed myself middling, was not in good health.

Do not care for the Peaks, a poor starved country, extraordinary number of dead sheep. Found two recently dead behind walls, and four skeletons in a single walk to Sweden Bridge, also two carcases floating in the Rothay, which is disgustingly noisome in parts. Papa drove to Keswick on a vehicle locally known as the *Cherry-bang, from the Sally!*

Extraordinary number of local curiosities. Old gentleman, blue on one side of his face, boy without a nose, extremely bandy retriever of Dr Redmayne, lady lodger with a black moustache, idiot, and Town Crier.

Tilberthwaite water works just beginning operations.[10] People in the shop say it will *not* pay. I am rather of that opinion, there is no doubt that when first proposed, the Corporation hoped to sell water at a high rate to Bury and other towns. What with this and the Canal, I think the future of Manchester is very serious.

LONDON

December 1886

Bertram came up from school on July 29th. His last term at Mr Frederick Hollins's, The Grange, Eastbourne. We being in difficulties as to where to pass the holidays, and my grandmother being quite unable to move to Camfield, it was decided we should go there, taking our own servants. This plan was not without drawbacks, but succeeded on the whole. We stopped six weeks. The weather was not however hot, for August.

Having always from childhood looked upon Camfield as a palatial residence, it was a little startling to look behind the scenes, not to mention into the drains, which were still partially open. They had been found in a shocking state, why no one ever had a fever, passes me.

For the first ten days the house was wrong side up, with plumbers and carpenters and painters. They were country workmen who laid down a London system of pipes which they apparently did not understand. I wonder why water pipes always burst on Sunday? All the time we were there, there was a periodical downpour through the ceiling of one of the closets. The plumbers returned several times and mended up the pipe with putty (!), which thawed gradually during the week and gave way at precisely half past eight on Sunday morning (one on Monday), to the extreme puzzlement of Mr Page.

When the family are away the house is looked after by Mrs Newberry, an aged woman who has someway got over my grandmother. Her dirtiness and general character were so nasty that I refrain from describing them. The first evening the maid-servants sat upon the kitchen table, the floor being in possession of inconceivable quantities of cockroaches.

During the night Cox was nearly devoured by fleas, but that was easily explained by the discovery that Mrs Newberry had used the butler's bed: but the most serious complaint was that of Jim the groom, who announced that in the small hours of the night, he had been set upon and awoke by B flats.[11] This being unfortunately true, the little room above the saddle room was sprayed with Keating's powder and shut up.

However, it is ill complaining about a house that is lent to one, and I never, all things considered, passed a pleasanter summer. We had not two wet days during the six weeks we stayed there.

On Oct. 18th. occurred the death of Poor Miss Mouse, otherwise Xarifa. I was very much distressed, because she had been so sensible about taking medicine that I thought she would get through, but the asthma got over her one night, and she laid herself out in my hand and died. Poor little thing, I thought at one time she would last as long as myself.

I believe she was a great age. Her nose and eyebrows were white, and towards the end of her life she was quite blind, but affectionate and apparently happy. I wonder if ever another dormouse had so many acquaintances, Mr Bright, Mr J. Millais, and Mr Leigh Smith had admired and stroked her, amongst others. I think she was in many respects the sweetest little animal I ever knew.

1887

Bertram back to school Jan. 27th. I to Camfield Feb. 18th. to 28th. Bertram half-term 5th. March.

8th. March my uncle Mr William Leech died at 7.30 a.m. on Monday morning. He had only taken to his bed the afternoon before, and we did not know of his illness till we had a telegram announcing his death. It was a great shock to my mother.

Friday, April 1st. Bertram taken ill with pleurisy at Charterhouse, of which it also is useless to speak more, for the thing is done and can never be undone. He was well enough to come home on April 13th. when the school broke up.

Demonstration in the Park for Home Rule, Easter Monday. Very flat. That old goose Mr Gladstone viewed the procession from a house in Piccadilly. As they passed the Carlton they stopped, and the different bands all played the *Dead March in Saul* in different keys. A great many broke off at Hyde Park Corner and did not go in at all. Said to have gone to the Beer Shop.

Bertram had not a severe attack, and mended quickly. We went to Grange-over-Sands on Morecambe Bay, April 19th. The weather was fearful, storms of sleet and snow. Poor lodgings. We naturally did not like the place, but I must say we saw it under most unfavourable circumstances. Went on to Ambleside April 25th. Weather moderate, Home 5th.

I am writing this in the end of June, having been very ill with something uncommonly like rheumatic fever.

I felt very well at first at Grange, and made great efforts to walk with Bertram. I believe I managed about a mile-and-a-half at a stretch. I found it hard work and my feet hurt, I suppose with the stones on the shore. The right foot toes hurt very badly the day before we left.

I had great pain on the journey to Ambleside, and did not once go out walking while there.

The pain went up to the middle of my foot, and then the ankle, it swelled. Dr Redmayne attentive, very nice, with a bad stammer. He tied it up comfortably, we supposing it was a sprain, but in the night it suddenly came up in my knee and was fearful. Doctor at 5.30 a.m. In bed all day, feverish.

Next day a great deal better. Dr Redmayne thought we might safely go, as papa was so anxious to, it certainly was very awkward. I rather think if I could have stopped in bed and gone on with Dr Redmayne's medicine, I might have avoided it.

May 5th. went into other knee during journey. Got up stairs with great difficulty and to bed, where I stayed nearly three weeks, if one excepts being moved on to a sofa for two hours every day during last week.

Very little fever, great deal of rheumatics. Could not be turned in bed without screaming out. Continually moving backwards and forwards, up and down each leg, never in more than one place at a time. Cotton wool and hot flannel.

Mr Mould, in whom we do not believe. It is my belief the old gentleman has but two medicines. I had first the camphor, then both mixed (!), then the quinine alone. Dressed 22nd. May. Down stairs 26th. Out 28th.

Amazed to find myself in summer, having last seen the trees in winter. I have had no spring, but no more has anyone for that matter. I have not missed much.

We were in a deplorable state all round. Mother at her wits end with me, papa exasperated with the prospect of a Chancery Suit,[12] and the question of what to do with Bertram after his illness.

In the middle of this came Uncle Willie's Sale which included grandmamma Leech's and Aunt Jane's pictures and the family silver.

In the last week of the holidays came the news, in a circular from Mr Page, that Mrs Gilbert who had nursed Bertram so kindly, the Matron, had diphtheria and is since dead. Bertram was taken from Charterhouse and sent back to Mr Hollins at Eastbourne. I believe he would not have stopped for another winter-term in any case.

My father was very unwilling to give up the Public School, but from what we have since heard of the diptheria, he is most thankful.

So am I for all reasons. Bertram was most delighted, having much disliked the Charterhouse. I do not believe in Public Schools, nor mamma. Papa is getting to the same opinion.

Monday, November 14th. Scene, at lunch. My grandmother disapproved, in a state of high and violent indignation and dispute with the rest of the family, as to the cautious pace at which the coachman drives the mares, Preston and Windermere (!) up hill. 'Eh – dear – *I* k-now, – I've, been, in, gigs, with – my fat-her – – – why – – we were – *all*, thrown, out, of, – a – gig – – at once (roars of laughter) – – I – re-mem-ber – – one day. We – were – going – – to, Preston, – what – do – you – say – Clar-a? – (overriding objections to this example of skill with much sweetness and complete deafness), Eh – dear – I know – yes (with much satisfaction and vivacity) *I* – was *right* underneath! – – – My father – al-ways – went quick-ly – to – give – them – a – *start* – at – the – bot-tom.'

1890-91

'My dear Esther . . .'

A VISIT TO THE WINTER EXHIBITION AT THE ROYAL ACADEMY

Tuesday, February 4th. Uncle Thomas, who looked apoplectic, explained fluently that his cold had left him no voice so he could not talk to us.

As to Mr and Mrs Gladstone, they came in directly after we did, and I took a good stare at the old gentleman as the rest of the company seemed to be doing so, without putting him out of countenance.

My dear Esther,[1] he really looks as if he had been put in a clothes-bag and sat upon. I never saw a person so creased. He was dressed entirely in rusty black, like a typical clergyman or a Dissenting Minister or Dominie, and has a wrinkled appearance of not filling his clothes.

His trousers particularly were too long, I did not notice his finger tips but one would expect his gloves to be the same. I forgot to look at his collar either, one accepts it as a matter of course, being Friday it may have toned down. You are probably exclaiming at my not describing himself, but indeed he seemed to be shrunk out of sight inside his clothes, in the same fashion that some grey wisps of hair straggled from under his old hat. But very waken, not to say foxy the old fellow looked, what there is of him.

As for his features, they have lent themselves with singular accuracy to the caricaturist, one villainous skit in particular recurs to me, which represented him as a callow nestling with enormous goggle eyes.

Mrs Gladstone had on a round velvet cloak edged with sable, probably an heirloom. She rushed about with voluminous skirts, and, when I first noticed her, was pawing a bishop's wife, who appeared in the seventh heaven. Very few people spoke to them. My uncle said he should have done so, and I have no doubt he would, for though his admirers approach him with fawning adulation he does not appear to inspire awe.

They made straight for his own portrait by Millais, and stood in front of it, a shocking daub it is and does not do him justice at all, for however one may dislike him, undeniably he has a face one could notice unknown in a crowd.

I'm sure there were other characters there if one had only known them. There was one lame, elderly Scotchwoman in a frayed plaid gown and old-fashioned jewellery, who must surely have been a Peeress to wear such tips to her boots. Oh, and I must not omit to mention the little man trying to look like Titian, whose appearance immediately provokes my aunt to describe his hanging pictures on a ladder at Palace Gardens.

You must not think I did not look at the pictures, but you can read the newspapers for them. I think it a good Exhibition, but not many striking. On the other hand, if we except Sidney Cooper, there are few atrocities on the line. Atrocities in subject are, however, numerous, I noticed the incidents of the deluge in one room.

If artists select such subjects they can hardly complain of their pictures remaining unsold. Who would care to live with Mr Nettleship's *The Abyss*, a sort of life-size Quintus Curtius business of a Lion and an Antelope, in which, by the way, Mr Nettleship appears to have forgotten that the lion as the heaviest body would fall undermost.

I was agreeably surprised by Mr Prinsep's and Mr Brett's pictures which had looked so glaring in the studio. I'm afraid they paint with an eye to this effect. Hook is almost the only one of the older artists who has done himself justice this year. Of the young men, Stanhope Forbes has a clever almost powerful *By Order of the Court*.

The most original picture of the year is Wyllie's *Davy Jones's Locker*, but that he is said to have painted it from a diving bell I should have held incorrect. He has painted a perspective landscape under the sea, with a Spanish galleon in the distance. It is very poetic but not equal to the Japanese method of treating the subject.

The only other very original large composition was a *Perseus and Andromeda* by Bryan Hook, in which I admired the treatment of the monster, who is depicted as a gaping spotted dog-fish. The painter has caught the rasping yet velvety-looking texture perfectly, but the flesh painting is wretched, and there is one bit of realism that could have been dispensed with – Perseus, who is rather like our fishmonger, appears to want shaving – and yet I suppose the ancients used razors if one comes to think about it?

I soon got tired of standing. We sat in the sculpture room watching the people come in. Our unknown benefactor has chosen the right year to send the tickets as far as fashions are concerned.

I suppose not since the Empire whose gigot sleeves they emulate, have the dresses been so graceful as now. I fancy with that exception, and a short dowdy interval ten years back, this is the first time since the Cavaliers that my fashionable petticoats have been innocent of the least scrap of padding or whalebone. Even Watteau's sack was worn above a hoop.

Of course the fashion is capable of ugly extremes. Some of the skirts are too skimpy and some of the peaked shoulders too high. The colours most worn are soft greys of every shade, a subdued plum colour which they call heliotrope, fawn and sage greens. They are commonly trimmed with several rows of ribbon-velvet round the bottom, either the same colour or black.

The collars are plain and high, the leg of mutton sleeves are cut tight below the elbow, often requiring to be buttoned, and although so large above, are not creased, but cut to a shape.

One reason why I give so long an account of this frivolous subject is that I think this dress, which is too pretty and simple to last, is not receiving justice from that mirror of our grandmother's foibles – *Punch*. Mr Du Maurier's taste inclines to a multitude of folds, and besides he was quite *beschwärmt* by that same dowdy Princess' robe. It may be graceful under his pencil, but it was a sad garment as I remember it, particularly when it was buttoned up the back.

There Esther, keep this silly letter – it will be amusing fifty years hence, when the Irish question is settled and the ladies wear panniers and peaked waists.

May 1890

A VISIT TO HILDESHEIMER & FAULKNER

My dear Esther, It is an odd consideration, (absit omen) that one of the first events I have to write to you about should be a stroke in humble imitation of my heroine Fanny Burney[2] – Perhaps you suspect it is no coincidence, but I assure you such was my modesty (or stupidity) that, though my little affair had reached its crisis in the very week when our correspondence commenced, I yet never noticed the likeness till yesterday, when my conscience reproached me for not having chronicled my success. So do not flatter yourself, dear Esther, that you have been evolved from the kingdom of nightcap on the wings of triumph and analogy, on the contrary were you a less obdurate correspondent I should within a week have demanded sympathy rather than congratulation.

Now in the first place, proverbs and all good sayings notwithstanding, the root of this happy business was pique and a desire for coin to the amount of £6. I should never have overcome my constitutional laziness but for Walter[3] to whom I am properly obliged – You must know we work a mutual admiration society and go *in moaning* together over the apathy of the rest of the family.

We decided that I should make a grand effort in the way of Christmas Cards, and if they fell flat, as usual, we would take the matter into our own hands. The cards were put under the plates at breakfast and proved a five minutes wonder. I referred to them the other day and found my uncle[4] had forgotten their existence, but he added with laughable inconsistency that any publisher would snap at them. All the same I might have waited till doomsday before he would have moved a finger. He is a provoking person. Also we wanted a printing machine, price £16 which he regarded with even more languid interest.

So in the beginning of February I began privately to prepare six designs, taking for my model that charming rascal Benjamin Bouncer our tame Jack Hare – I may mention (better the day better the deed) that my best designs occurred to me in chapel – I was rather impeded by the inquisitiveness of my aunt, and the idiosyncrasies of Benjamin who has an appetite for certain sorts of paint, but the cards were finished by Easter, and we provided ourselves with five publishers' addresses. I was prepared, at great expenditure of stamps, to send them all round the trade, but it was a shock, particularly to Walter, when they came back from Marcus Ward's by return of post. I had set upon Marcus Ward partly from patriotic grounds (nothing like fine motives), partly because I had toned the colours from one of their Almanacs. I said we would try Raphael Tuck last, it is such an absurd name to be under obligations to.

Walter inclined to Hildesheimer & Faulkner, so we sent them there secondly, when he passed through town for his Oxford Exam. I wrote to him on Tuesday evening, advising him to lower the price to £4 and try De La Rue, *if*, as I had a presentiment, we saw the Cards again, so you see I did not *feel my property coming*, 'like her chops'.

However, it came the following evening (May 14th.) in a fat letter, the interesting part of which I had to keep in my pocket, while my aunt discussed the remissness of Mr Scott and Walter, of whom the latter was too much excited to write anything but shop.

The envelope contained a cheque for £6 which I had to return to Walter because he had omitted to sign it, and a very civil letter under the misapprehension that I was a gentleman, requiring me to send some more sketches.

My first act was to give Bounce (what an investment that rabbit has been in spite of the hutches), a cupful of hemp seeds, the consequence being that when I wanted to draw him next morning he was partially intoxicated and wholly unmanageable.

Then I retired to bed, and lay awake chuckling till 2 in the morning, and afterwards had an impression that Bunny came to my bedside in a white cotton night cap and tickled me with his whiskers.

I put off telling my uncle and aunt until I got the cheque back, I believe I told them on Friday. To tell the truth, I was very uncertain how he would like it after the way he had snubbed Walter. However, the cheque was a great softener: I think they were much pleased.

I worked away at the Sketches much impeded by the criticisms of my relations and a severe bilious attack. I made several more in the style of the first, as we thought it probable they only wanted one or two to make up the set, as they had mentioned some were not suitable. Also two rough suggestions of more elaborate designs, but i was not at all disappointed that Mr Faulkner did not consider them, as I have some idea of working them out into a little book some time, in fact they were taken partly from the *Cinderella*.

My uncle took me to the City on Tuesday in a Fly, as I was not well enough to stand the Underground. I had never been so far along Holborn and found the drive most interesting, which was lucky, for it was just like going to the dentist. My uncle was rather excited, making little jokes 'There Moses, where Aaron?' and there it was on the opposite side of the road. As for me, I felt so miserable with the joking that I was sufficiently depressed.

We found the place without difficulty, it proved to be like the office of a warehouse, just room to get in between the door, the staircase and innumerable desks and pigeon holes and parcels. My uncle sent up his card and I sat on a bench, conscious of being peeped at with great curiosity by several clerks. (I was ornamented with a large piece of soap plaster.)

Then we stepped upstairs into a back office, more than ever like the dentist's; there were several Albums full of cards on the tables.

Presently Mr Faulkner appeared, a bald, youngish gentleman, rather quiet and abstracted and the appearance of not being strong. I thought he gazed with mild astonishment at my uncle, but I was relieved to notice that, after the first few minutes of that worthy gentleman's conversation, he quietly gave it up.

He was very civil to me, but so dry and circumspect in the way of business that I cannot think of him without laughing. Not one word did he say in praise of the cards, but he showed a mysterious desire for more. He grinned a little at some of the fresh sketches, but not much. My uncle was of opinion that he was keeping quiet. He took them out of the room once, perhaps to laugh.

He did not definitely decide on any that I had brought, indeed the most precise thing he said was that he thought we should be able to do business, but he suggested that I should go to the Zoological Gardens, which he would hardly have done had he not intended to buy.

We looked through a multitude of printed specimens. Mr Faulkner was less cautious in his comments on them, and I think I measured his taste pretty closely. One thing struck me, in the way of business (and he was so close, I had to judge by circumstantial evidence), he insists on my designs referring to the Season, whereas not one in ten of his stock do, which shows he thinks he has found some one who can invent to order.

Some of the flowers and landscapes were lovely, and they have one lady that draws animals better than I, but not humorous, most of the comic ones were poor, though my uncle observed there was nothing vulgar.

Mr Faulkner had got a child's book, not of their publication, and showed me some of the pictures with an evident ambition to possess something of the same kind.

He dwelt with peculiar fondness on some terrible cats, or rather little men with cats' heads stuck on their shoulders. His one idea seemed to me to be fiddles and trousers. Now, if there is anything hideous, it is trousers, but I have conceded them in two guinea-pig drawings.

He did not strike me as being a person with much taste, in fact he rather gave me to understand, when I objected to drawing such and such an animal, that it was the humour that signified, not the likeness.

Unfinished

1891

IMPRESSIONS OF MRS HUGH BLACKBURN[5]

Friday, June 5th. Went to Putney Park this morning, and was very much interested to meet Mrs Hugh Blackburn – she was apparently on a few days' visit, and leaving this afternoon, so her sketch book was unluckily packed up. However, I don't know that I altogether regretted it as she may possibly be getting old as regards her drawing, and her personality was quite sufficiently amusing.

I have not been so much struck with anyone for a long time. I was of course strongly prepossessed and curious to make her acquaintance, but she is undoubtedly a character, apart from her skill – unless indeed there is anything in a theory I have seen – that genius – like murder – will out – its bent being simply a matter of circumstance.

I remember so clearly – as clearly as the brightness of rich Scotch sunshine on the threadbare carpet – the morning I was ten years old

– and my father gave me Mrs Blackburn's book of birds, drawn from nature,[6] for my birthday present.

I remember the dancing expectation and knocking at their bedroom door, it was a Sunday morning, before breakfast.

I kept it in the drawing room cupboard, only to be taken out after I had washed my grimy little hands under that wonderful curved brass tap, which, being lifted, let loose the full force of ice-cold amber-water from the hills.

The book was bound in scarlet with a gilt edge. I danced about the house with pride, never palled.

I consider that Mrs Blackburn's birds do not on the average stand on their legs so well as Bewick's, but he is her only possible rival. Certain plates, notably the young Herring Gull and the Hoody Crow, are worthy of the Japanese.

Mrs Blackburn's family have an old acquaintance, if not connection, with the Huttons. She is a lady of apparently over sixty, not tall, but with a very sturdy, upright presence, and rather striking features. In fact, in spite of the disadvantage of an ancient billy-cock hat and a certain pasty whiteness of complexion suggestive of ill-health, I thought her a handsome lady.

Her hair was becoming noticeably white, particularly the eyebrows, her nose aquiline, sharp black eyes, a firm mouth with thin lips, and strong hands. Her voice was clear and pleasant, she spoke with a Scotch accent, and with just sufficient Scotch assurance and abruptness to be quaint without being harsh.

Her manner was very alert and noticing, well assured, but in no wise aggressive (she made no direct reference to her drawings). She gave me the impression of a shrewd, practical woman, able and accustomed to take the lead in managing a family estate.

She appeared to have experience of farming, and got into a lively argument with Mr Stamford,[7] of the building of hay-stacks.

She is extremely fond of animals and flowers, and I could hardly have seen her in a more convenient place for airing her tastes than round the Putney stables and gardens. 'That is a fine beast, I like the colour of that cow, it is very pretty,' and then she went off into a disquisition on the anatomy of tadpoles, and the two species of water lilies in the duck pond.

They are very delicate when they are changing. I've had one, only that became a frog, it was delicate, it had fits. And then when we were talking about their food she said comically, it was not good to give them bread, I have known them to burst, it is disagreeable.

In the farm yard nothing escaped her, from the great pig 'wallowing' in a mud-hole, to a little white pullet with its comb in its eyes. The ricks particularly attracted her notice. They are very large and the strong coarse hay is such a contrast to the feathery greenish product of the north. No doubt it is also heavier in the bulk of each cartload, which may be the reason why it was 'perfectly well pressed' by its own weight alone, as she admitted to Mr Stamford during the argument on *trampling*.

'No, no, *no*, we do nothing of the sort, nothing of the sort!' Mr Stammy became quite testy on the subject of 'putting up persons just to walk up and down all day', not to mention a horse in Norfolk, which he obviously didn't believe in. However, he was appeased when she said fervently, regarding the great stacks, with her head on one side, that it 'was a beautiful sight'.

The stacks are the especial pride of Mr Stamford, next to an interminable (and very dirty) Chopper in the barn, where there was another argument as to whether a certain substance was grains or peasemeal. – I thought it well that the party came away with a full complement of fingers.

They have a splendid breed of black Berkshire pigs at Putney Park, long-backed, crisp, short in the ears and deep in the chops, and with that elegance of carriage and gait which in a horse is known as *action*.

There was one little animal in particular which a less appreciative eye than Mrs Blackburn's might have judged *a picture*. Mr Stamford, who, for an excessively bashful man, is the most queer individual I ever met with, got into a very domestic disquisition upon the old sow, who being too fat, on giving birth to a family of thirteen, did not find herself in a state of health – in short had no milk for them, and they all died within twenty-four hours to Mr Stammy's great grief, the sow, however, I saw sitting up to the ears in the horsepond, with a placid expression.

'Did we have them on a dish!' said the matter of fact Mrs Blackburn, 'Oh – I think that would be a horrid looking dish – only a day old – just like babies,' said Mr Stamford, highly scandalized. He departed to town immediately afterwards, having taking affectionate and old-fashioned leave of her, with much courteous inquiry about her health, to which she replied that she trusted she had not got the influenza, she felt 'but squashy'.

It must be understood that I do not in the least mean to imply that Mrs Blackburn is all matter-of-fact without sentiment. She is a broad, intelligent observer with a keen eye for the beautiful in nature, particularly in plant-world life, as well as for the humorous, indeed I see no reason why common-sense should not foster a healthier appreciation of beauty than morbid sentimentality, in instance of which, I was not a little amused, when we paused to examine a clump of wild hyacinths in the shrubbery, to hear that scraggy and precise person Miss Annie Hutton[8] say, that a great bed of hyacinths is like 'a bit of the sky come down, and something hazy – a blur of colour – '.

Mrs Blackburn described with poetic feeling an island in the sea opposite her home, which in spring was covered with hyacinths and primroses (her love of nature expressed in sweet homely Scotch made one think of Burns).

She spoke with great affection of her beautiful Argyllshire home, where the mild Trade Wind blows all winter, and 'the sea is never *cauld*'.

To me personally, she condescended to talk in very friendly kind style, asking me about my pets and relating little anecdotes and observations on her own. The only touch of pedantry I observed in her conversation was her pointing to a little bird on the railings – 'That is a *Muscicapa striata striata*, – or common Fly-Catcher, I know it by the shape of the head!'

Altogether I carried away the impression of a kindly, chatty old lady, with keen common-sense and a large fund of humour, capable of deep feeling, but in the meantime heartily enjoying an encounter with an enraged muscovy duck.

1892

'They are the most odd specimens . . .'

FALMOUTH

We came to Falmouth on 31st. of March 92 for our Easter holiday.[1] It is a tremendous long journey, perhaps seeming longer than it is because one is less conversant with the route than with either of the lines to the North. We started at 10.15 stopping only twice (Swindon and Taunton) before reaching Exeter, and got in at six.

I may mention we came on the Broad Gauge. An ordinary width of carriage but the wheels projecting *almost* outside it. I understand it is to be finally abolished in May.[2]

It was a cloudless day, but a cold east wind in town. As we got west the sun became more powerful, and by the time we reached Exeter people were walking along the dusty roads with umbrellas.

The spring growth is far more advanced here, green leaves burst on hawthorn and some sycamores, where in London are bare sticks. On the whole the spring is late, however, doubtless from want of rain, for it has been as hot as mid-summer and smothered with dust. This dry dustiness is a little unlucky for seeing the famed Falmouth Tropical Gardens, but one cannot have everything, and we never before had such a glory for weather, cloudless days, burning sun, and an air so pure that it transmits every smell within twenty yards, from wall-flowers to fish and manure.

We have had only two cloudy days out of twelve, on one of which were a few drops of rain. On many nights it was so warm that one could sit out till nine o'clock watching the waves in the moonlight. It is a peculiarity of this climate, that, apart from actual sunshine, the night feels scarcely colder than the day, which happens because a great proportion of the warmth comes from the sea.

As to this county of Cornwall, the part which most surprised me was Liskeard and Bodmin roads, on the backbone of the county as it were. It reminded me of Wales. Great plantations, very remote and uninhabited, with the evening light striking sideways through the gaps in the hills, and a beautiful bright stream, the Fowey, sparkling under the oak trees. I thought there were no trees in Cornwall.

After Lostwithiel, we got into a district which realized my expectation of a Cornish wilderness. Such a nasty place, not a town nor even a straggling line like the Welsh miners' villages, but about one cottage to every two fields, scattered evenly over the whole landscape without visual thoroughfares, but that matters the least as there are no gates to the gaps in the stone dykes.

There is a mine on the average to every hundred acres, and deserted shafts, usually unprotected, as common as rabbit holes, and a sprinkling of china-clay all over the county.

The latter in itself is rather a beautiful substance, though it is said to infect and ruin the rivers. I saw it stored (in blocks rather larger than salt) in St Austell, in a long range of sheds beside the line. It is of a softer and more pleasing colour and consistency than chalk.

To the north over above this interesting landscape, one could see the skirts of Dartmoor forming a howling wilderness, once inhabited by a race appropriately named the Gubbins.

On the left the railway skirted the coast, alternately looking down now and then on little creeks and harbours deep below, where the china clay was being loaded in Brigs, and we got our first sight of the green Cornish sea, and cutting across further inland, the creeks running up into deep combes, over which we passed, a single line of rails on perfectly frightful white wooden bridges.

One is apt to smile at the descriptions in old county histories of terrific cliffs and horrid gorges, where real nature on enquiry presents very ordinary rocks, but I wonder what Gilpin Esq. would have said to those bridges.[3] When it comes to green flags and a wobbling motion, it is quite time they were rebuilt of stone. We must have crossed at least twenty.

The combes themselves seen from this giddy height were very pretty, the steep sides clothed with hanging woods of stunted oak and fine wild hollies, and down below in the distance a glimpse of brilliant sea. On the uplands between them more tin mines, of forlorn appearance.

The industry is said to be in a bad way at present, but I imagine it always presents rather a scaly aspect, having all the ugliness without the size and importance of a coal or iron foundry.

Falmouth, or rather Penryn, though not over promising, is most disfigured by a foreground of this unpleasing character. I believe there are no active mines actually near the town.

The railway takes a sweep to the left and comes round above the south beach, the terminus being on the Isthmus at the back of Pendennis Castle. The harbour and town on the left, the hotel and the commencement of villas on the right above the beach, and the railway cuts through some delightful little old houses and gardens.

How can one complain of a line that has palms planted along its embankments? They are the first thing that strikes a new arrived. I do not admire them myself, but they are perfectly well-grown specimens of their kind, i.e. they have no stunted or starved appearance of exotics out of place.

There are very fine evergreen oaks, bay tree, aloes and hollies. One eucalyptus tree about thirty-five feet high in the old Killigrew Garden, but it has been touched by the wind. In the same garden of the quaint old manor house, Arwenack, now Lord Kimberley's estate office, is a red camellia in full flower, and the children offer camellias and rhododendrons in the market quite commonly.

This old-fashioned residential end of the town is very pretty. We walk about and peep wistfully over the garden walls of the Foxes.[4] They are garnished with barbed wire, and I have even observed broken glass, but inside the sacred precincts all is exceedingly peaceful and sunny. So much so that my father the day after our arrival expressed a strong wish to turn Friend.

One garden at Penjerrick, the residence of Miss Fox, who with her nephew Mr Robert Fox, seems to be the head of the family – is thrown open to visitors twice a week. It is a rambling old house full of aviaries and pets, doves cooing, and beautiful Persian cats walking about under the rookery on the lawn.

The house stands at the very head of a straight narrow combe, with trees shutting in either side, a tropical garden in the steep trough of the ravine, and a little patch of blue sea far below in the distance. It is the most successful and striking piece of landscape-gardening I ever met with, but struck me as being almost too picturesque. It must be extremely beautiful in summer, but after all, tree ferns and feathery canes are rather out of place in an old

English garden. There is nothing like a box-border and the scent of wall-flower and polyanthus over a snug brick wall.

One thing at Penjerrick amused us, an ingenious arrangement of cord and pulley, whereby the old dame at the Lodge was able to open the gate without leaving the porch of her Cottage, a charming example of that union of kindly comfort and successful usefulness in which Quakers excel.

Those of this town have fixed their dwellings in pleasant places, but do not seem over-burdened with wealth. Perhaps the property of the Foxes has decreased through sub-division. They seem very numerous. Mr R. Fox and his aunt are said to be the only members of the family who are well-off.

The name appears constantly in the town, intermingled with the Cornish Tre, Pol, and Pen, also Hodgekins and Peases intermarried. St Mawes also is said to be full of Quakers, but I do not see that they have any Meeting House on that side of the bay.

They are not recognizable in the streets, having altogether dropped the Quaker costume, but I fancy they have retained more of the old-fashioned enthusiasm and simplicity than the Friends in London. All the same, it does not strike me as a strong Congregation, this point of vitality, exceedingly earnest, and the building almost full, but would not hold above fifty or sixty persons. So many were old men.

But indeed these interesting people are almost certain to dwindle out of existence in time. They are too good for this world, even for this cloudless beautiful Land's End.

The Chapel is a good modern building, but from its small size, I doubt if the Quakers are really so numerous in this town as one had supposed. They seem however, to be much respected, and presumably a power in the place. Whether it be owing to their influence or a characteristic of Cornwall.

This is a quiet, well-conducted town, which is the more remarkable owing to the number of British and foreign seamen loitering about. It forms a great contrast to Devonshire towns, particularly Ilfracombe, but it may be the Welsh who upset the latter place.

I have seen only one man drunk since we have been here, and observed no fighting or roughness of any sort amongst the sailors. They loll about in the main street, spitting on the pavement, their only objectionable habit; shake hands with one another in an elaborate manner, and stare unmercifully for the first week. Indeed all the people do that, and appear inquisitive, and if you look back they pass the time of day amiably.

The foreign sailors stare impartially at everything in a fidgety inquisitive fashion. Some of them are very picturesque. I saw one leaning against a post on the quay for hours, in a scarlet woollen cap, bright blue jersey, and great sea-boots, others with sashes round their middles, and one old Frenchman in sabots. They appear on their good behaviour and attract no attention amongst the natives.

The town is cosmopolitan, one sees five languages on the window of the barber's shop. Everything has a nautical flavour, the baker sells *ship bread*, the grocer calls himself a ship's chandler, the ironmonger's window is full of binnacles, pulleys and lanterns, sail cloth is the leading article at the drapers, and in one shop they announce fresh water on sale. Also, every mortal shop sells Valencia oranges, such bad ones too.

It is a poor town for shops, except one or two connected with the shipping, and the streets very narrow and steep. They are not over-clean either, and in the morning every householder sets out a pail or wooden box of refuse, right out on the pavement, and there is a smell of rotten fish.

Burton's old curiosity shop which makes the greatest display is quite a museum, crammed from floor to garret with odds and ends, but the great part absolute rubbish. The foreign things, which form the greater part of the stock, struck me as not so much bona-fide curios bought from sailors, as an inferior class of article imported wholesale. Perhaps the oddest part of this collection was a great quantity of French cavalry sabres, pistols, helmets and bayonets from German battlefields and the surrender of Metz.

How he got them I know not, but they were certainly genuine, any quantity of sabres at five shillings apiece and holster pistols, said to be Waterloo, and rusty enough for Blenheim, at about the same price. There were hideous African idols and weapons labelled 'poisoned' in large letters, which is a novel way of attracting purchasers, but indeed it seemed more of a museum than a shop.

Mr Burton, a stout grey gentleman in spectacles reading a paper, would hardly answer enquiries lest he should appear to press one, and his trust and confidence were really charming. Ladies and gentlemen were requested to walk up into twelve rooms including the garrets, and on the stairs tumble over several large ships' bells which they may ring if they want an attendant.

Little Miss Burton, who explained from a long way off that I had not broken some dancing Japanese pottery, which was true, but she could not possibly see. I bought a white pot-head of bone which was one of the few English curios of any antiquity, excepting a man-trap and sundry small cannon-balls.

Outside the shop on a plank were some old books at twopence each, which was not so cheap as appears at sight, for they were mostly second volumes of sermons, also one Latin Boethius of great size bound in calf, all at twopence.

I am afraid old books are at a discount down here, my father gave us an absurd account of a book sale he attended at Truro, to pass the time, with a little old auctioneer, 'Do I see a Penbury? seventeen volumes for ten-pence – do I see a rise of suspense?', pointing with a pencil, and knocking down the lots therewith. Somebody *On the Atonement* and three other works thrown in, for which a curate offered five-pence but was cut out by another bid of eightpence. The volume *The Odyssey* of Homer four-pence, so Mr Burton may make a profit after all.

As to his trust and confidence, I fancy it is justified by the conduct of the town. There are three policemen – I have seen one of them at the Barbers. They have a Hutch no larger than the Tub of Diogenes, at the back of Custom House Quay, with a great flag-staff and a very little garden.

They are the most odd specimens, just ordinary natives dressed up in blue clothes, and all seem to have bunions, or very mis-fitting boots. They are on friendly conversational terms with the other sailors, and I have seen one of them having eggs at a Butchers.

The people here are all singularly alike, and one can well believe the statement that they are the purest bred race in Britain. I am only surprised that the old Cornish dialect has died out earlier than several others, for they are extremely isolated in situation, and if one or two persons whom I have talked to were fair examples, they are naïve and unspoiled to an amusing degree. Very friendly, kindly, cheerful, healthy, long-lived, and the numerous old people very merry, which speaks well for a race.

The children are extremely pretty, but like the Welsh, it goes off.

The women certainly are not on the whole, though intelligent and fresh-complexioned. The universal type is black or rusty, with crisp hair, women more black than men, and blue eyes very common with both shades.

An ordinary type with the men, (the young men especially, are so like as to be twins), is a short thick neck, slump in the chops, short straight nose, (with the women very commonly turns up, which is a reason why they are the less good looking), and in both sexes a straight narrow forehead, eyebrows strongly marked and deep-set.

As the men's faces become thinner through age, it is apparent that they have high cheek-bones. I notice with the red type, the nose is occasionally less straight, but always short. The women have singularly oval faces.

The town men, though their hair is very strong, are neatly trimmed. Our driver has a head like a dagger, (he was particularly Cornish, very civil, but with a certain naïve dignity or reserve. I was shocked to discover that this man was Scotch), but the quarry-men and farm-labourers look veritable ancient Britons, with their wild black locks and light blue eyes. All the same I fancy they are very mild.

There is another type I notice occasionally, favouring the Chinese, and joined to an apparent imbecility. I fancy it is *lusus naturae*, and does not count.

I should not say they were an intellectual race, though their bright eyes and straight foreheads give them a thoughtful look. They take a great interest in religion however, great Chapel and Church goers, and keep holiday to welcome the Bishop of Truro. They are exercised at present by a storm raised by the Bishop of Exeter, through holding a Confirmation at a lunatic asylum.

My observations do not, of course, apply to the Cornish miners. I have seen nothing of them.

One thing that lends animation to this town is the presence of the *Ganges* boys. Lads mostly between fifteen and seventeen, from the training ship *Ganges*, which is moored high up in the Carrick Roads. They are sent here when first recruited, rag, tag, and bobtail, to learn the first rudiments of drill and discipline, (there are only dummy guns on board), and their spirits can really be only compared to ginger beer. They are somewhat noisy but always in charge of a superior officer when on shore, and their healthiness and clean merry faces make them a pleasure to look at.

My father was photographing at Mylor, where there is a naval yard or store. A boatload of these boys arrived at the quay, and having spied him, began to whistle and arranged themselves in an elaborate group. He took off his hat to them when he had finished, and to his surprise and confusion they raised a cheer.

They look the picture of health, but I am surprised to hear there have been one or two epidemics of diphtheria on the *Ganges*. Perhaps it is too full, five-hundred on board, and it is not large for an old three-decker. It looks beautifully clean, and a little garden in one of the galleries at the stern. They set the sails occasionally, but the ship has only twice been moved from her moorings in the last twenty years.

Possibly the diphtheria may have come in with some fresh boy, but it is mysterious how epidemics can spread, even in this pure air (though it occurs to me that may account for it, I never observed such an air for transmitting smells). They have had influenza very generally at Lizard Town, which is separated from every where by ten miles of moor.

There are a number of blue-jackets about, as well as the *Ganges* people, (who are dressed in white), possibly Coastguards. They are extremely orderly and have a great objection to getting their feet wet, if crossing in the rear of a certain lumbering wooden box which the Corporation call a water-cart. Also the Militia in training at the Castle. I never knew before what frightful sounds can be produced from a bugle.

We went over St Mawes on a gloriously sunshining April morning, walking up from the little quay, where we had landed from the ferry steamer *Roseland*, the garrison consisting of one amusing Irish sergeant, one soldier and a decent wife, were sitting in a row on the bench in the sun, in a corner of a steep little garden laid out with wall-flowers and cabbages on what had once been the Moat, the only sign of war being the neat pile of empty bombs beside the Battery below, and sundry ancient stone balls set up as ornaments in available corners.

My father asked the sergeant what effect they could have had on the stone walls of the Fort, in parts solid rock, whereupon he screwed up his face into convulsions of silent laughter.

Everything is clean in St Mawes now, as whitewash will make it. They have even whitewashed the font. The sergeant told us with pride it had been begged for Truro Cathedral, but the authorities could not part with it. It seemed to me more like a stone coffin.

There were several dated handsome chimney-pieces, one of which had had an inscription, but the sergeant had filled the holes up with whitewash because they were chipped and looked untidy! but I dare say it was illegible, as it was not mentioned in the guide-book.

But enough remains to make it a model show-place, with winding stairs, condemned cell (?) and a dungeon like a bottle, under a trap door. Not the least interesting was the view from the windy battlements, where asphalt has been laid over the crumbling lead, and numerous little garments were hanging up to dry on strings.

Our Irish friend became eloquent, and proudly excited on the subject of range-finders, submarine mines and great guns. The battery below was old-fashioned, built low to hide under the swell of the sea, but they had consequently to raise the muzzles of the guns when firing, which caused an unsafe pressure on the breech.

He seemed very cheerful nevertheless, and in spite of his sins with the whitewash, I hope the young man will survive to command the two great guns which are to be set in the crest of the hill above, to carry as far as Westland Point. When they are in position the beautiful harbour will be as safe as modern science can make it, but the earthwork has to stand empty for a twelve-month to allow of the earth settling, and old Gladdy may come in before then and the French shortly after.

Not that an enemy would find too safe a landing-place even now, but it will be a sad day for old England when they have come near enough in to pass the submarine mines.

We did not find time to go to the Lighthouse on a Point corresponding to St Mawes, but further out to sea. It has a revolving light, apparently electric.

I do not know much about the sea, but nothing has surprised me more than to hear that there are shipwrecks in a harbour which is almost land-locked, and one of the finest in the world. I thought what constituted the value of a harbour was the smoothness of the water inside, and consequent safety of shipping, but one of the saddest shipwrecks on record, that of the *Queen* transport returning with invalided troops from the Peninsular, took place on Trefusis

Bertram and Beatrix Potter

Number Two, Bolton Gardens, October 1889

Hill Top Farm, Sawrey

In Sawrey Village

View from Sawrey towards the Langdale Pikes

Beatrix Potter in the porch at Hill Top

Point, right in the middle of the Roads. The victims, soldiers, women and children are buried in the neighbouring churchyards.

The land-breeze is the roughest, the steam Ferries *Roseland* and *Wotten* are sometimes unable to cross for days in the winter, to the great inconvenience of the inhabitants of the little fishing villages in the creeks.

There was an east wind while we were there, steady and safe, but decidedly choppy in Carrick Roads. My father took great credit for not being seasick, and I think I may do the same, having had the subject so persistently presented to me. I had never been on the sea before, and I can honestly say I thought the swinging motion agreeable; but in every instance it was from the stern, or what a cockney tourist called the *boughs*, moved sideways.

We went several times on the *Roseland* and one afternoon all by ourselves in a little tug, the *Sylph*, black with a yellow cornucopia and a gigantic pineapple falling out of it by way of figure head, and a crew of three, and the property of Williams late Co. Ship's Chandlers.

It was a brisk little craft but bad to get hold of, having fled to parts unknown on two days when we wanted it, and when finally chartered, was discovered rushing about the harbour, with us at the extreme end of the wrong jetty, my father blowing a whistle in the teeth of the wind, to the amusement of the natives, and my brother in an extremely bad temper, and the whole party laden with cameras.

My mother turned back on account of the wind, but the experience proved very enjoyable in spite of its commencement. I don't know whether this thirty-shilling trip was proportionately better than the six-penny ones on the *Roseland*, except for the honour and glory of commanding a whole tug, which gave papa unbounded gratification, but we had no choice if we wanted to go up the river, as the public boats do not run in winter.

The harbour is certainly the great attraction at Falmouth, each voyage more beautiful than the last. I do not think we saw half of it. The peculiarity of it is the extremely sudden turns in the creeks, so that you imagine you have come to the end of the water, as at Malpas (or Malpa), but a reference to the map shows that there are miles of winding river round the corner.

The river was as smooth as a lake, about the width, for the greater part, of the bottom end of Windermere, but more beautiful. The steep sides mostly wooded, stunted oaks and wild hollies, with here and there a little whitewashed thatched Cornish cottage, hanging right over the water.

There are several beautiful houses in good positions, particularly Tregothnan, the property of Lord Falmouth. One pleasing feature of the landscape is the number and tameness of the birds, a heron, numerous gulls, cormorants, sea ducks or guillemots, and one flock of wild geese. I suppose there are stringent laws against their being molested. The cormorants fish inside the harbour along the boats, where there was also a porpoise one day.

We saw some large dog-fish go past outside the Castle, their back fins cutting through the waves. They are said to pursue the pilchards. I did not see any pilchards, or much signs of fishing. The Falmouth boatmen say it does not pay. Some go out from St Mawes where they also catch lobsters.

I saw a red-headed sailor there, and his son, taking up their pots, and another time unloading a motley collection of fish at the bottom of the steps, where a demure tortoise-shell cat presently came down to search for bits, peering cautiously into the water.

The steamer stays a little while there (at St Mawes – the early afternoon), under shelter of the jetty, and the captain cooks his lunch and cold tea, brought to him by a particularly sweet little girl, to whom he gives two-pence and a kiss.

The children are certainly remarkably pretty. I cannot imagine why they do not fall into the water, or get caught by receding waves. It is not a safe coast for children. On each of the two occasions we were loitering for the boat, we were amused to see a seafaring man cuffing a fat little son for going too near the edge, but he was again hanging over the edge the moment his father's back was turned, fishing out drift-wood with a string.

The boys handle a boat at a very early age, cleverly paddling about with a single oar over the stern. All alike use a most unintelligible language, but it is especially puzzling among the children, owing to their rapid talking.

I did not discover that it was anything particular as to dialect, but arose from clipping the consonants or even syllables – not vowels – thus, a 'bad bot', then 'comform'l', (a very common word, at all events in the quest of lodgings, the 'ladies' being neighbourly)=comfortable, but the palm for compression must be awarded to an odoriferous person who hawked mackerels in a little ship's wheel barrow without legs, and shouted 'ker mack, ker mack, *ker*!' This man and the Town Crier made the principal hustle as regarded trade, except on the market day, Saturday, when the town was crowded and lively.

By land the country folks arrived in numberless little donkey carts, drawn by charming donkeys, and the ferry steamer was laden with passengers' parcels of vegetables and baskets of farm produce.

Going back in the afternoon the load consisted of more solid provisions, flour, bread, meat and groceries, virtually the food for the ensuing week, for the people of St Anthony seem to depend almost entirely on their Saturday marketing for supplies. I thought the Saturday company on the steamer was exceedingly amusing, if one could stand the tobacco.

It is between seventeen and twenty miles to Lizard Town from Falmouth, but a most excellent road, genuine macadam, and for the most part bordered by a dyke of gigantic blocks of granite neatly fitted together. We had a wretched looking pair of nags, but they did the distance coming back in an hour and three-quarters, which seems hardly credible. I may remark that we found the posting charges extremely reasonable, half-a-crown an hour the usual charge.

This long drive to the Lizard took place as usual in cloudless sunshine, and such dust that the hedges looked as if powdered with snow or blackthorn blossom. There are not many hedges, however, and when you get fairly on to the tableland, sometimes but one clump of trees, sure to be inhabited by rooks, is visible over a landscape of many square miles.

It is extremely rough desolate land, and odd as it may read, gains a certain imposing character from the immense size of the blocks which form the multitudinous dykes round the little pastures. There is scarcely a living soul to five square miles, and like the stone walls in the north, one feels inclined to regard these erections as the totally useless work of an extinct race of giants, till one remembers that they are in reality built less to enclose the fields than to rid them of boulders.

The low places and tops of the hills were unreclaimed, the one marshes of peat and rushes, the latter picturesquely heaped with boulders, and in summer overgrown with fern and the rare Cornish heath. But nature while providing the agriculturalist with abundant material for fences, has totally neglected wood for gates. Accordingly we did not see half a dozen in the twenty miles.

The usual course is to drive in the sheep or cattle and build up the gap with large stones. In the case of milk-cows or cart-horses this is inconvenient and the strangest and most rickety makeshifts are piled up. The oddest I saw was a fire grate.

The cottages about Mabe and Constantine are most substantially built like the dykes of granite blocks, but nearer the Lizard I saw some wretched hovels of mud. Not that there was less stone, but it was out of the region of quarries.

The dykes which are such a notable feature of the landscape are almost invariably tipped with gorse bushes, now in full blaze of colour. The glorious expanse of gorse and wide open swelling landscape reminded me a good deal of Anglesey, but I think the latter has much the advantage in beauty, all sand, which gives it a softer aspect than granite, besides here the doubtful details of distant quarries like white scars in the hill sides, and further south an occasional distant chimney or deserted shaft. It must be an awful place in driving sleet and wind. By a merciful providence they have little snow.

Another thing which I should not expect to have observed is the narrowness between the two seas, a small peninsula, a small thing, but in this great arm of land it is a very curious sensation. I do not think the sea on the north was ever visible, but the lay of the land and the low sea clouds on left and right distinctly were.

The construction of the country westward prevents one from having the further sensation of approaching Land's End, we turned off too soon.

We met scarcely any vehicles on the road, poor road. I reflected once or twice rather uneasily on an accident which occurred many years ago in the rather similar wilds between Ilfracombe and Morthoe. The wheel of the Fly came off, and the old fellow had to run a mile-and-a-half to borrow a screw driver. However, we went the whole distance at a hard trot, with one pause to *water* the horses.

The local farm carts are very odd. A cross between a lorry and a timber-wain, very long with a peaked hay-rail back and front, and no sides except a low planking over against the hind wheels. To add to the length, they usually harness three horses in single file, the middle horse being frequently a young, raw beast in training.

With regard to the farm animals, the cows are awful, though very possibly they swell when there is anything to eat. When we were there, there was literally nothing on the fields. I should be puzzled to define the breed of cattle, a streak of Devonshire red and brindle, an occasional black or piebald smooth-coated animal, something like the Dutch, a frequent cross of inferior beasts, and many white-faced Herefords amongst the stock cattle. Which their bulls are, I cannot imagine, they are not let out. I rather fancy the black is the original one.

The sheep and lambs are the best of the farm stock, no peculiar breed but fine large-grown animals, singularly free from rot. The pigs are black and lanky, principally remarkable for an air of humour.

The cart-horses are very tolerable, though light, and there are signs of the farmers taking some trouble in horse-breeding. Comfortably-fed brood-mares in comparison to their starved cows, and many young cart-horses. We saw one of their stallions in the road, low at the tail, high on the shoulder, springy legs, particularly the ankle joints, high crest with a mop of hair over its ears and a tapering neck. Too young-looking a horse to have made its mark, but a type which seemed generally aimed at amongst the young cart-horses. Doubtless a light type of horse is more suitable to the steep but good roads and abrupt turnings.

The local gentry do not seem to do much driving. We saw one or two good horses, but from the nature of the country there is no hunting whatever, and the gentlemen's seats are mostly near the water, and probably yachts are more in fashion than thoroughbreds.

The local ponies are miserable, Exmoor does not penetrate so far. The donkeys small and sturdy. I saw no mules. Lastly their poultry is excellent and often pure strains. From the frequent sale advertisements of prize sittings of eggs in the local paper, I opine that prize poultry is rather a hobby in the west. I certainly saw the very largest Cochin cock I ever set eyes on in a backyard at Penryn.

Of dogs we noted the great number of clumber spaniels, but I think these good-tempered animals are kept for the pleasure of their company, for there is no game. I saw not a single rabbit on the drive to the Lizard, though some burrows in the dykes, usually with signs of recent spade grubbing, so I suppose poor bunny is treated as vermin.

The cats: anyone who notices animals will be aware that they differ greatly in different parts of the country, are here very fine, and many Persians in unlikely places.

With regard to farming, the thing that strikes one is the sparsity of population and farm steadings. I wish I had counted how many we passed in that drive of twenty miles. I fancy a good many of the laboriously enclosed meadows are almost worthless, there seemed to be a very small head of cattle and sheep on a great expanse of country.

Certain parts like the Goonhilly Moors, a great tract between Helstone and the Lizard, are absolutely worthless, miles of gorse and Cornish heath, and one vast track, burnt black either in mischief or some faint hope of grass.

It is said in the guide-book that wonderful crops of barley are grown near the Lizard. I saw no such signs whatever, but perhaps the moist steamy summer climate produces wonders. That the soil is not so good as it looks, I judged decidedly from the great numbers of rooks. Also the cottages in that part are heavily thatched.

They have an awful habit at Lizard Town of making footpaths along the tops of the dykes about a foot wide. I don't know what happens if two people meet, or there is a gale. The only thing I liked about them was the multitude of daisies on the sunny side of the wall as one looked down. Also a yellow clover twining between the locks with a deep red spot on its trefoil.

Lizard head is worth having seen (I should not care about a second visit). The most curious thing about it is the stream of vessels passing. They run up a string of flags to signal to the Lighthouse and Telegraph Station, and for this purpose, come in much closer than one would have expected considering the nature of the coast.

The rocks themselves are not to compare with Holyhead for grandeur, and my father and I not having steady heads, found the place extremely unpleasant. I should not think the actual height equals two-thirds compared to the cliffs at the Stack lighthouse, but there you go uphill to the very edge, which together with a good railing – gives a much greater feeling of security, and at the same time a finer effect than a slope of burnt grass at an angle of 45.

For the most part there is no foliage at all here, the Coastguard's path winding like a steep track along the slope, which with sudden drops and ruts, falls into a chaos of jagged black rocks. It is a most cruel-looking coast, horrid black teeth sticking up three-quarters of a mile from land. There is a Lifeboat Station close below the Lighthouse. I wonder how they can ever pilot it out between the rocks.

It is said there have been no shipwrecks at the Lizard for two years, since they have had a good fog-horn, as I understand the great danger of this coast arises as much from fogs as rocks, the damp heat causing sea mists.

The only story of shipwrecks which I gathered, was more curious than frightful, as reported by Mrs Bulley, a respectable woman at one of the stonecutter's yards.

She said when she lived at Cadgwith, once she saw a brig early in the morning, which had come too near in shore just before dawn. It was such a day as this said she, cloudless blue sky and not a ripple. All the country people were on the cliffs watching.

The crew had rowed away in their boat, the beautiful ship had every sail set but there was not a breath of wind, and she came drifting on with the tide right into the cove, and then all at once without a sign of warning, went down in deep water close to the shore on a hidden rock. There was no one on board.

The Lighthouse which is a large barrack-like place, the Signal Station and stone cutting, seem to form the staple of Lizard Town; a somewhat dreary collection of cottages, of course utterly bare of trees.

There are nine or ten little booths for the sale of Serpentine goods, all very moderate in price, honest in workmanship and bad in pattern. They have one design, the old Cornish water jar, which they repeat over and over again, but unluckily without any true comprehension of its really elegant shape.

I never was more painfully struck with the complete absence of *Eye* in the average English workman, but these good people take such an honest conscientious pride in their work that it is quite ungracious to criticize it, and after all, this spontaneous village industry is far healthier and more vital than certain that could be named in the north, which carry out handsome foreign patterns from extraneous sources, as a parrot might repeat the alphabet.

The best piece of work I saw was an inlaid table slat, I consider stone mosaic is hideous perversion and chopping up of a naturally harmonious and beautiful substance, one pattern sins as much as another, and with this reservation, the work in question was well done.

I was amused to enquire after Mr Brett, who is well remembered at Lizard Town, though he has not been there of late years. One old stone-cutter told us with pride that Mr Brett had sat for hours in his shed on Saturday afternoons, painting a *stuffed* cormorant.

We did not go to Kynance, perhaps we should have found it more interesting than the Lizard. We only saw one hawk, a sparrow hawk, during this long expedition. They seem singularly scarce, and perhaps for that reason, little birds are proportionately numerous. I think it is one of the pleasantest features of Falmouth to hear them singing in the thick vegetation close to the sea. The blackbirds woke us up in the hotel garden, and we were favoured with the autumn song of the robin – in April.

There is much thick brushwood on the slopes of Pendennis (part of it was unluckily burnt one night). It affords secure nesting places for a great variety of birds; thrushes, sand-larks and pipits, wagtails, yellow-hammer, green and brown linnets, chaffinches, warblers, and prettiest of all, the little wheatear.

Below the Castle on the slope of shingle and sand amongst the rocks, another branch of natural history absorbs attention, for the beach in parts is literally composed of shells.

Their variety is doubtless due to the warm sea. I don't know if we found any that were really rare, but some of the commonest sorts are the prettiest, and I know no objects whose beauties are more truly a joy for ever. I picked up such a large bag full, I was quite ashamed of myself, but there was a gentleman in spectacles to keep me in countenance. Also a decent old man who came down and ate dulse like a cow, looking much confused when observed. There were seldom above a dozen people on the whole stretch of beach. I may here repeat that I think it unsafe for children or bathing, it shelves so suddenly.

One or two windy nights threw us more and more shells and strange seaweed. I found forty-nine cowries and four little blue-caps in an hour the last morning; and then on April 12th., as if we were not sufficiently comfortable, we went off like fools to Plymouth.

★

The weather turned cold the very day, which may have aggravated the change which came over the spirit of our dream. The dirtiness of the Grand Hotel at Plymouth was however distinctly tangible, and the waiters only exceeded in nastiness by the recollection of a nightmare in Wales.

EXETER

We hurried away next morning to Exeter, so it is hardly fair to record an unfavourable impression of Plymouth, except I may safely say I was disappointed with the Hoe. It is exactly like the grounds of the Naval Exhibition, broad asphalt promenades, cigar kiosks, and even the Lighthouse all complete.

I believe the latter is really the old Eddystone, not a sham, but it looks one, stuck on a grass-plot. At the foot of the Hoe is a frightful iron pier covered with advertisements of soap.[5]

The Sound, though doubtless wider, is not to compare with Falmouth Roads, which had spoiled us for beauty, and I could not realize the distance and consequent length of the Breakwater. I think we ought to have gone out to it and round to Devonport by water, but we could *not* stand the hotel.

The natives are rough, and there is a superabundance of new brick streets and repellent granite forts about the Hoe. We went out in a row-boat after tea, with a tired boatman who had been up the river on a job with *dynamite*. I don't know how many tons, but I remember he had caught two tons of herring in one night, and seventeen dozen of mackerel close to the steps, and a Conger eel that weighed 148 lb.!

The sun went down before we got round Drake's Island; the moon came up over one of the Hill Batteries and in the other direction we could see the occasional twinkle of the revolving Eddystone light. The water was of oily smoothness and reflected the ship's lights red and green, in long wavering streaks. It was very cold and I wondered if my bed was clean, what do chamber maids do with a dry mangle in the kitchen closet? I have a not unmixed memory of Plymouth.

I am very fond of Exeter. Even on a great Railway like the Great Western, it retains its primitive self-contained air of importance.

Macaulay never bestowed a more appropriate epitaph than the 'Metropolis of the West'. The lower parts of the town are somewhat squalid, but the High Street and adjacent neighbourhoods are animated in the extreme, and display most excellent shops.

The Cathedral Towers rise solemn and peacefully, casting a shadow of respectable antiquity over the bustling town. (I regret to state they light bonfires in the Close on the 5th. November, the Exeter rabble are notorious.)

In the Close are many gabled old houses, with quaint sundials and carving. We strolled about peeping down the entries into little pebbled garden courts, a patch of sunlight framed in an ancient doorway. The sun came out again while we were at Exeter, and the world looked fresher for the rain. Flower-women were selling Lent-lilies at every corner, and the prettiest Italian girl I ever saw going about with a tambourine, while her dusky companion ground a jingling piano organ, somewhat incongruous with cathedral bells.

The pear trees were white as snow in the Deanery garden, the lilac touched with green, and the air full of the smell of hyacinths, blowing to the pious and immortal memory of Dutch William of Orange who came in triumph into this sweet old-fashioned capital of the West more than two-hundred years ago.

We came home on April 14th. through a snowstorm, and our old Spot died two days later – Sic transit.

HEATH PARK, BIRNAM, PERTHSHIRE

Tuesday, July 26th. Left London with East Coast and Forth Bridge, 7.30, King's Cross. Stopped only at Grantham, York, Newcastle, Berwick (?), and a wayside station before reaching Edinburgh, at a repulsively chilly unearthly hour.

I am not sentimental, but I know no view more weird and beautiful than that from the high-level bridge over the Tyne in the night. The red lights on Bamburgh and the Farne Islands, and the first tinge of dawn on the steep little flagged roofs of Durham equally striking, are seen in the same night journey, but going south.

The light came in this instance near Berwick and was broad daylight, but cold and damp when we stopped through some delay near Dunbar, opposite a sleeping station garden full of rose bushes weighed down with wet.

The Bass and North Berwick Bay presented a curious and beautiful effect through layers of cloud against a silver sea and sky, but by the time we crossed the Forth Bridge the clouds had spread into a mist, hiding the view down the Forth. The bridge itself lost nothing in height, enveloped in shifting fog.

I kept awake for the cold, flat expanse of Loch Leven with its strange heavy hills, and then slept till Perth. I did not see an interesting hedgehog near Cockburnspath. Last time we passed in the early morning it was gobbling up little spring cabbages in a promising little railway garden. I could not help laughing at the business-like manner in which it was hurrying from cabbage to cabbage, a mouthful in each, quite close to a signal box.

Benjamin Bunny travelled in a covered basket in the wash-place; took him out of the basket near Dunbar, but proved scared and bit the family. Not such a philosophical traveller as poor Spot. It is the first time for ten years we have travelled without him, and coming back to the district where we had him first, I thought it rather pathetic.

He used to be very much in evidence – it would be unkind to say in the way, – just before starting, jumping about the carpetless floors with his heavy chain and getting between the men's legs until safely hoisted on to the top of the railway bus in front of the luggage. He smiled benignly between his curls, and usually captivated the driver. He had a passion for carriage exercise. I suppose it was the dignity of the thing which pleased him, for he looked profoundly miserable after the first half hour. The difficulty was to prevent his riding off in omnibuses, like any other gentleman.

His funniest exploit occurred once when he was in the High Street with Cox, when, seeing a footman throw open the door of a carriage, he jumped in with great presence of mind in front of some ladies.

Wednesday, July 27th. Reached Perth about seven o'clock in the morning, and washed in uncommonly cold water. Got the *Scotsman* and also copy of preceding day's issue with caustic comments on Carnegie's strike.

Scotch papers are refreshingly acrimonious and spiteful provided you agree with them. I sometimes wonder, considering the metaphysical abstruse turn of Scotch intellect, that the articles provided by their political journalists should be brilliant rather than profound. They make *The Times* leaders appear ponderous in comparison. Exceedingly well written and doubtless well informed, or they could not be so versatile in argument, but they concern themselves more with the cut and thrust arguments of party politics, than with fundamental principles and the evolution of politics. They reserve their powers of metaphysical dissection for philosophy and the Kirk, wherein perhaps they are wise, certainly practical, but it leaves the Scotch open to the accusation of being politicians first and patriots afterwards.

I believe setting aside the great question of religion, the Scotch people as a mass (that is to say Low-landers and Towns-people, as distinguished from the Celtic Highlanders), have never been seriously moved by any political wave since the days of Bruce. Scotch history as written, is a record of intrigue and party politics, creditable or the reverse when the Union was bought and sold.

Conspiracies and rebellions, Darien, Glencoe and the Porteous riots, make lively reading and doubtless all things work together for a result and end, but the only two important factors in Scotch history have been religion and money – (in the sense of commercial growth since the Union). Even in religion they are highly aggressive, in fact ill-natured sceptics might suppose it is the life of the Kirk.

I believe if the Ulster convention had been Sectarian instead of comprehensive, it would have gained rather than lost weight as a case in Scotch opinion, where every fighting man is either Free Church, Established or Roman Catholic. The moral of this is that it is important that Mr Gladstone should continue to put his foot in it, with regard to Disestablishment. It does not much matter which side he takes provided he is irritating his opponents and transparently dishonest.

There was an extraordinary miscellaneous scramble in the first-class restaurant-room at Perth. A hard, hairy Scotcher opposite doing it thoroughly in five courses, porridge, salmon-cutlets, chops, ham and eggs and marmalade. Under my chair a black retriever and on my left a large man in knickerbockers, facing a particularly repulsive Scotch mother and young baby feeding on sops. All the company extremely dirty and the attendants inattentive.

I don't think the new station at Perth is an improvement at all, except in handsomeness. I remember the old first-class waiting room with a rather greedy relish as a child. It was one of the rare occasions when one was allowed to eat ham and eggs. From the arrangement of the local trains in those days, we had several hours in Perth, a leisurely interval in the middle of the re-move.

There used to be a large dingy-coloured panel of the Royal Arms, in the old refreshment room which I looked upon with awe. The company was quaint and highly flavoured. I remember one objec-tionable old gentleman with a bald head and greasy wisps of hair, tied on the top thereof in a knot. The only familiar survival in the new station is little Martin.

Arrived at Birnam station about eight. We took possession of Heath Park, which in spite of its fine name, is a Villa,[6] well-built, but in disrepair, standing in one acre of ground.

It is situated at what an auctioneer's clerk would call 'a convenient remove' from the station, mainly up a steep bank and over a hedge. There is a fine view, however, over the top of the station. The trains prove to be a source of constant amusement. Papa is constantly running out, and looks out of the bedroom window in the night.

Thursday, July 28th. Finished unpacking and settled into the Villa. I think myself that a house that is too small is more comfortable than one a great deal too large. The stables are minute.

There is a lane at the back, and a group of cottages and sheds, tenanted by Miss Hutton, her ancient brother Willy Hutton the joiner, who is said to be a reprobate but stone deaf, numerous lodgers, a scrambling family, two cows and a tame jackdaw. Where they all pack away I don't know. The jackdaw comes to us.

The villas on either hand are discreetly hidden by trees. On the left there are English lodgers, on the right Mr McInroy of Lude, a fine old gentleman in a kilt, whom we can hear through the bushes scolding his family.

Sunday, July 31st. Went to Cathedral and heard Mr Rutherford, his doctrine is barbarous, but a good fluent speaker for those that agree with him. The Precentor is a curiosity.

★

Monday, August 1st. Went out with the pony, first to see Kitty MacDonald, our old washerwoman, afterwards up the Braan road. Kitty is eighty-three, but waken, and delightfully merry.

She became confidential and told me the history which I already knew, of her reasons for leaving Kincraigie. She lived there for sixteen years after her Dalguise cottage fell in, but last summer an old man of equally discreet years settled in the other end of the bigging[7] and she would not stay!

She did not tell me two other circumstances, that her neighbours teased her for a witch, nor about the immense fires which she kept up day and night for the last few weeks. She had got the attics quite full of sticks, and did not want to leave them for the old man. She is a comical, round little old woman, as brown as a berry and wears a multitude of petticoats and a white mutch.[8] Her memory goes back for seventy years and I really believe she is prepared to enumerate the articles of her first wash in the year 71.[9]

Thursday, August 4th. I may say that I lost half a day. The hen-quail got out of the window which was unsettling, besides that, I had eaten too many gooseberries the previous day. The cock is certainly tamer without her, a startling little fat bird, but I was disturbed to think of cats. There is a black one in particular belonging to Miss Hutton, which brought in three rabbits on one evening. She is afraid it will end in a rabbit-snare, which is rather rich. It has been seen on its hind legs peeping in at the rabbit hutch, also dogs.

It is not a safe place for Benjamin Bouncer. I walk him about with a leather strap. He is the object of many odd comments from that amusing person McDougall,[10] 'Eh, see him, he's basking!' (on his back in the sand), 'Are you aware that rabbit will eat sweeties? see how busy he is!' He is constantly giving it peppermints which I suspect are pilfered from his sister-in-law Miss Duff.

Friday, August 5th. Pony to Inver, mamma and I went to pay Kitty 7/6 for knitting stockings. I never saw any one so delighted with the possession of coin. She shook it up in her hand and fairly chuckled.

I afterwards went a bit along the Stanley road. Afternoon, mamma and I went to tea at Mrs Culbard's, the doctor's, through a pouring shower.

Mrs Culbard is a somewhat elegant, slight, elderly lady, of plaintively amiable friendliness, but perfectly incoherent in her conversation. She is very chatty, but her anecdotes have neither head nor tail. Miss Culbard I like, she is a practical stout person, with rather a sweet quiet Scotch face. Goes about with a stick, slightly lame, in consequence of a terrible accident eight years ago, when she went through the ice on Polney Loch, [11] and held on for an incredible time while they fetched ropes from Dunkeld.

Her brother is just like her, but even more stout, a good tempered but curious object in knickerbockers. His wife was rather a nightmare, looks older than he, much powdered, and high heeled shoes, I should imagine American, or a mésalliance.

There were five or six other ladies, but they came in late. Miss Culbard told a good story, the talk being on the absurd names of flowers, about an old Scotch lady who was putting up her roses against a flower shop. Her friends made kind enquiries and she replied in great distress that 'Sir Gordon Richardson had got the mildew, and Mrs George Dickson was covered with little beasties!' (meaning green flies).

Monday, August 8th. Hopelessly wet, which was the more provoking as Bostock & Wombwell's Menagerie was advertised to be at Dunkeld for one day only. I had no desire to see the performance because of the lion-taming, which I object to, but if there is any show I like, it is a circus. We went down in the wet in the evening and found the thirteen or fourteen vans drawn up in the town square, and covered with a tarpaulin, with several satellite peep shows. In front of one, a vulgar, noisy proprietor was inviting the public to pay tuppence and see the man with a beard six yards long. I had rather not. There was a considerable crowd of dirty natives outside, but having mounted a step ladder on to a pasteboard stage, we found there was no other audience but ourselves.

The animals were splendid, so much healthier and fresher looking than most at the Gardens; Bertram thought the lions, twelve in number, were rather light in the limbs, doubtless by being tame bred, but in my opinion their sleekness made up for it. There was a magnificent lion in a division by himself, and divided by a partition, a lioness and two very little cubs, playing like kittens.

At either end of the small van, a polar and a brown bear. They had a very complete variety of beasts, and the only single animal which looked out of condition or unhappy, was one of the pair of performing elephants, who was deplorably ill with a cold. The keeper, a big black-haired fellow seemed much concerned, and invited her 'Nancy, poor old girl,' to take part of his supper, but she dropped it and stood with her trunk crumpled up on the bar 'like a sick worm'. The poor thing died three days later at Coupar Angus. They are hopeless if they receive the slightest injury or illness, as they simply mope till they die.

In ridiculous contrast was a little Jack donkey of the very smallest proportions, who was marching about loose under the noses of the lions, stealing hay.

Tuesday, August 9th. Drove round by Stenton and Caputh Bridge with the pony. Murthly Castle in spite of its magnificent appearance has never been inhabited. It was left unfinished by a former Laird, and when the late Sir Douglas Stewart succeeded, the old sinner cut out every beam which was to support the floors and sold them. It would be a puzzle to get out the ends which remain in the walls, and still a worse one to get in fresh ones.

There are innumerable stories of his meanness, he was absolutely impecunious when he came into the estate, but he left scrapings to the amount of £250,000. He made a rule to add five shillings to his income every day, mostly by squeezing the coppers. It is said he once went to a shoemaker with two very old pairs of boots, the worst pair of the two was to be cut up and used to patch the other pair.

Mr Stewart Fotheringham is unmarried, an object of interest to the titled families of the county. The next laird is a shoemaker or baker, I forget which, in Aberfeldy.

Wednesday, August 10th. Photographed in the morning, with the assistance of McDougall, who distinguished himself by chivvying up 'wee duckies', but on putting on his spectacles to inspect the result, unkindly said he couldn't make head or tail o't, there were eight duckies instead of just seven. However, he said it was splendid, and said 'gosh' in a low tone at appropriate intervals, which is almost as mysterious as the 'seelah' of Mr Peter Marshall.

He told papa when he was a little boy (his father was Lord Fife's head forester), he was following the plough when the share turned up a nest of four little black things, to the terror of the ploughman who exclaimed 'Eh laddie what are they?' McDougall being an observant little boy, replied that he had seen a picture of them in a book, and they were called rabbits.

Donald McLeish the gamekeeper at Kinnaird can remember the first that appeared in this neighbourhood, they turned up on St Comb's farm. [12] The peculiar thing in McDougall's story was the alarm of the ploughman, for they cannot have been so utterly unlike the familiar hare, which, at all events the blue one, is indigenous in the Highlands.

He told another curious story of a fox which he trapped in a snare. When he came in sight of it, it was sitting up with the wire round its neck, but on his going round behind it with the intention of shooting it, it flopped down 'dead'. It actually allowed him to open its eyes and mouth with his fingers, pull it about and carry it home in his game-bag, only dropping the disguise when shut up in an empty room.

It lived six years in a kennel and fed upon porridge. It was so sly, it had a habit of saving a portion of porridge within reach of his chain, then pretending sleep, and pouncing on the hens, which it took into the kennel 'feathers and all'. Lord Fife allowed it to catch as many as it could.

Tuesday, August 16th. Went to see Mrs McIntosh[13] in the afternoon, much amused with the old mother, stone deaf and unable to leave her chair, but very affable and merry. She sat in her arm-chair beside the kitchen fire, and opposite on the other side the hearth sat two black and tan dachshunds belonging to Miss Grace, very precious and tied to the dresser with a bit of string.

Afterwards went along with the pony nearly to Guay. Met the Tinker caravans with baskets as we came back. What dirty shock-headed little rascals, but as merry as grigs on a fine day.

As to the lowest stratum of tinkers and tramps they are perfect savages, mean spirited and trembling in sight of the county policeman. You see very old ones, and when once seasoned, they are tough.

I met a fine looking old woman on the Stanley road the other day whom I remember, not changed in the slightest during the last fifteen years, but the younger members of the gangs are much thinner by comparison, which prevents their increasing to the proportion of a plague, although prolific.

I should think they are very seldom tamed off the tramp. I remember one instance. I wonder what was the result of that little idyll, perhaps as well we do not know. There used to be a rather pretty modest-spoken girl who came round every summer with a company who sold baskets, her granny was blind. One year she did not appear with them, and we were told she had married a young fisherman on the west coast, and settled down.

I remember one set who possessed a *cuddy* [14] which attracted almost as much attention as an elephant with a travelling circus.

When we got our 'Benny' from Lancashire (!) in 73, there were many persons in the village who had never seen one before, and regarded her with as much curiosity as their fathers had bestowed on the other long-eared gentry. I read a story once that a certain arab setting eyes for the first time on an ass, exclaimed, 'Behold the father of all hares!'

Wednesday, August 17th. Photographed the rabbits and the tame gulls with much trouble.

Thursday, August 18th. It did rain.

Friday, August 19th. Drove as far as the Inch farm, morning. Afternoon laid up, sick headache.

Saturday, August 20th. Still somewhat indisposed. After breakfast taking Mr Benjamin Bunny to pasture at the edge of the cabbage bed with his leather dog-lead, I heard a rustling, and out came a little wild rabbit to talk to him, it crept half across the cabbage bed and then sat up on its hind legs, apparently grunting. I replied, but the stupid Benjamin did nothing but stuff cabbage. The little animal evidently a female, and of a shabby appearance, nibbling, advanced to about three straps length on the other side of my rabbit, its face twitching with excitement and admiration for the beautiful Benjamin, who at length caught sight of it round a cabbage, and immediately bolted. He probably took it for Miss Hutton's cat.

It would certainly have come up and smelt him had he sat still, and his behaviour was the more provoking because he had been walking about on his hind legs the previous day begging for two nasty dead ones on the kitchen door. It was one of the most curious performances I ever saw, the rabbit was undoubtedly wild when the stampede took place, and I was not in the least concealed.

After lunch went to the flower-show which was flat. It was held in what the Scotch call a Marquee. I understand that on the previous night they danced. McDougall said because they were just moribund, a curious reason for dancing.

The show-season is so much overdone now that they cannot get a paying attendance. It was very dull after the crowded noisy show in the Town Hall in the old times, with Charlie Macintosh and another fiddler knitting their brows and fiddling as if for dear life on a ricketty planking over the staircase.

Neither was there any poultry, nor butter, nor honey, afterwards I went back to the house. Been rather exhausted with strong medicine.

Mamma went into Dunkeld with the pony, and, coming out of Miss Anderson's shop, caught her heel and came down. She cut her elbow badly, to the bone. Went with her to Dr Culbard,[15] who was kind and very fat and snuffy. I did not distinguish myself, indeed retired precipitately into the garden, and had some difficulty in avoiding whisky. However, we all had tea by the way of a compromise, Dr Culbard tucking in his table-napkin by way of a bib, and cutting a great slice of bread and apple jelly.

I felt much ashamed of myself, but upon my word I felt faint at the flower show; we will put it down to castor oil and seidlitz powder. How mamma managed to cut open her arm without even scrubbing her dress sleeve I cannot imagine.

Sunday, August 21st. Went into garden immediately after breakfast, but saw nothing of the wild rabbit except its tracks. Benjamin's mind has at last comprehended gooseberries, he stands up and picks them off the bush, but has such a comical little mouth, it is a sort of bob cherry business.

Wrote picture-letters to the little Moores. There was a squirrel in the laburnum under the window mobbed by about thirty sparrows and some chaffinches, its fierce excited little movements reminded me of a monkey, but it did not get a spring at them.

Mamma's arm sore and uncomfortable, but not bruised. Her arms are very fat, and I incline to think the sharp blow between the edge of the step and the elbow bone caused the flesh to crack as it were.

Monday, August 22nd. Drove to Guay with the pony. Saw a beautiful cock capercailzie in the top of a fir tree.

Tuesday, August 23rd. Very hot. Went to Mrs McIntosh's to try and photograph Charlie Lumm's fox at Calley, but with very little advantage except that I was touched with the kindness of Mrs McIntosh. She let the pony stand in their stall, gave me a glass of milk, and tramped up the wood with me to the under-keeper's cottage.

The wood is very beautiful at the bottom of Craigie-Barns, such tall Scotch firs, and the game keeper's cottage with its bright old-fashioned flowers and a row of bee hives. The fox proved a tyke, tearing round and round the tree, in the absence of Charlie Lumm, but as things turned out, it did not signify.

Coming down we passed the Eel Stew, with high post railings where her Grace's supply of eels are preserved, having been trapped in the Lochs. Her Grace will have two or three cooked for supper every evening almost, when she is at home, at which information I was much amazed. How the sprightly yet dignified Anne Atholl has survived to be an old lady on such a diet I cannot think, and in this one (solitary) instance there can be no question of Deguillies[16] eating up her substance, for as Mrs McIntosh said, one would as soon eat a serpent.

I was able, being of catholic opinion in such matters, (though I would not go the length of my great grandfather old Abraham Crompton, who used to pick off live snails along a certain ivy wall), I was able to candidly agree to this widespread Scotch prejudice – indeed I should rather prefer the serpent if it is correct that the kitchen-maid has to drive a nail through the eel's head into the dresser before she can skin it.

Down in the meadow we passed the pretty dappled Ayrshire, and came upon the truant Charlie Lumm sitting on a railing with two others smoking their pipes. In the kitchen the old granny was safely sitting in her chair, a little weary of being left alone. She was feeling the heat, poor old granny, perfectly deaf but placid and patient. The two little bitches Diana and Dora lay in their box beside the hearth. Mrs McIntosh is getting stout and old herself, her hair much grizzled, but still abundant and wavy. She must have been a handsome woman in her youth, of a masculine type of beauty. Mr McIntosh too, though fast turning into a little old man with a stoop, was, as I first remember him, a singularly beautiful type of highlander, small of stature, but lithe and active as a deer, with eyes like a hawk's. The intense sharpness of his glance is still striking, although the left eye is discoloured; I have sometimes thought it is partly caused by something almost amounting to a cast, due to much looking along the barrel of his gun. McIntosh's scrutiny, though probably keen, is in no wise inquisitive in appearance. He is a shy reserved man, with the unsettled wildish look of one who has lived much in the woods.

His wife must be a head taller than he, a great big woman, yet I believe she has never been well since the first year of her marriage. In the same way though, they have always been well to pass, and Robert McIntosh respected, and a man of mark and authority all over the district, yet some people think she has not been happy. There is a pathetic trace of tears amidst her affection for old friends, mingling oddly with strong-minded common sense. For the rest, an upright patient character, self-contained and self-reliant in homely wisdom, and kind and very motherly towards young people, albeit she hath one son, Johnny, and he a pickle run to seed. I shall be sorry for Mrs McIntosh when the old mother dies.

Thursday, August 25th. Birnam Games. I did not go. Spent great part of the day standing on two garden benches and a buffet, all three of us, and McDougall looking over the yew hedge. It is an enviable and interesting point of view.

It came to a large proportion of the seven thousand spectators poking away through the small railway station, stragglers getting over the white station palings, seven feet high. Mr Kinnaird told papa privately he hoped it would be wet, however they were got off safely. It was a gloriously fine day between wet ones.

Watching the people go away there were very few intoxicated, but

I was sorry to see three-quarters of those few, wee young boys. The games are singularly more decently conducted than formerly, when drink was sold in the grounds, and great Highlanders were brawling and lying about by the dozen. I remember a long red knife and two savages washing their bloody heads in the river, but no one paid any particular heed. The police body were only needed to prevent the *laddies* from dodging through the railings.

These McInroys of Lude next door are rather an entertainment, they are so mortally afraid of making our acquaintance. Now we ourselves are most standoffish and unsociable amongst promiscuous neighbours, 'wouldn't speak to them for words', so that this turn of the tables is an acceptable joke.

Old Mr McInroy became insolvent, under Trust, as the Scotch say, for several years back, and presumably receives a very small proportion of the £1,500 which represents three months Let of Lude. There are five daughters, a terrier, a younger son in retirement, and the eldest son and heir, a morose red-haired person in white flannel trousers, who has 'let it be known' – I do not exactly know how, except that everybody knows everything here – that he intends to do nothing. He spends the whole day wandering to and from the Recreation Ground with a tennis racquet, doesn't play, but sits on a bank, visibly waiting for his father's demise. He is a great nuisance to meet round corners, but reduces the embarrassment to a minimum by scowling constantly at his toes.

As to Mrs McInroy, a slim, tall old lady in a crinoline and profuse ringlets, her demeanour, when unfortunately clashing with mamma in the green-grocer's shop, resembles that of a startled hen.

Old Mr McInroy in a kilt, constantly scolding and 'never ask you to do anything again as long as I live' – presents an appearance of greater vitality than his expectant heir. I suspect him of setting the terrier at Brass Bands.

Monday, August 29th. Drove as far as Dalmarnock, meeting the train at startling close quarters near the Toll Bar.

Papa and McDougall went to Killiecrankie. Another of the latter's anecdotes – this time on digestive power of birds. He saw a heron catch four large trout, and shot it while the tail of the last fish still protruded from its mouth. He opened it at once and found that the three first fish were already messed up and unrecognisable, as was also the head of the fourth fish, though its tail had not had time to be swallowed. I can believe a good deal as to the gastric juices of a heron, I once had the misfortune to participate in the skinning of a fine specimen.

The weather for the last few days was cold with a bitterly keen wind. I suffered much from pains in my head. I felt it when in the hotel in June. The air is rather too fresh for me.

Wednesday, August 31st. Wet in the morning but cleared. Drove out with the pony, who was rather over-fresh having been in since Monday morning.

Went to see old Kitty with some worsted. Perhaps the Kincraigie folk had some ground for saying she was a witch, for, when we came up to her little cottage, there was a little toad sitting in the middle of the little flat, grey stone inside the doorsill. When we knocked it hopped away under the closet door, and the little old body came out in her light slippers, winking and blinking.

She had been taking a nap after dinner, empty bowls which had apparently contained porridge or potatoes and milk on a chair, and her big Bible on the table her elbow 'Ou, aye, its a lang waak to the Kirk, hutzle, hutzle.'

Afterwards we drove up to the Rumbling Bridge, which was a fine sight, the water thundering down and foam splashing on to the bridge like heavy rain.

As we returned we overtook about fifty dogs, the property of Barclay Field,[17] dragging six keepers, in straps preceded by a cart. The pony flatly refused to pass them, I rather sympathised with him. I do not on the average care for dogs – especially other peoples. What can be the pleasure of owning fifty brutes, kept in a pen, fed upon porridge, and walked out by a drove with a long whip. I think a well-bred pointer is one of the most repulsive looking animals in existence.

Thursday, September 1st. Again showery. Saw Bessie Cleghorn at the station, and was amused to ask after her mother, who, when lately here, took leave elaborately because she was going to Stirling to stay with her son George – if she was spared. She insisted so much on the latter proviso that we were profanely amused, but it seems she was right, for when she got as far as Perth, she did not feel 'at all the thing' 'in her stomach', to be precise, also 'missed the connection', which I took for a complication of the disorder, but referred to trains, so she came back.

I should like to hear Cleghorn's comments after having taken leave of 'mother' for three weeks. Bessie stumping about on her one leg and crutches, always smiling and never feels the cold nor nothing. I remember when she was growing up and had ten toes, she used to keep company with the son of old David Wood, shoemaker and entomologist. However, she may not have missed much, for, though still a bachelor, he is the grumpiest man in the parish.

I shall never forget old Mr Wood coming to Dalguise one hot Monday afternoon in search of 'worms', and producing a present out of his hat of about two dozen buff-tip caterpillars, collected on the road. They ought to have been in a red cotton pocket handkerchief, but they had got loose amongst his venerable grey locks. He is still living and much the same to look at, but what McDougall calls 'a wee bit dumpy', rather past.

So is the Birnam post-master, Mr Lowe, whose name affords an exquisite pun to the little boys, chalking up an 'S' before it. He actually objected to take a half-crown the other day in payment of one shilling and seven-pence, because the change, which he counts on his fingers, 'is such a bother'.

There have been a family of tinkers about, in the most *dégagé* costume which can be imagined possible in a civilized country, the infants were dressed in shawls and pocket handkerchiefs. They appeared very cheerful.

Saturday, September 3rd. Drove round Loch of the Lowes in a gale of wind, but must be very sweet on a summer day. How partial rain is amongst the hills! The farmers between Craiglush and Butterstone were piling their hay into the comical tall cocks of the country, quite dry, but at Birnam we had been soaked.

Tuesday, September 6th. A lovely hot autumn day, burning sun and heavy dew on the grass in the shadows. The bracken and potatoes are nipped in exposed situations. A day like this somewhat reconciles one to the climate, which I had begun to misdoubt. A strong admonition to chilblains on the 1st. Sept. is no joke.

There was a streak of dappled white clouds right across from east to west, from hill to hill, mare's tail, Mother Holda's yarn hung out to bleach in the sun and wind; McDougall said they call it Aaron's beard, it means a shower – but the *carry*[18] very high.

I went to Inver to photograph old Kitty and that graceless person Tomby the dog. I don't know when I laughed so, and Kitty nearly rocked off her stone. Her great anxiety was to properly arrange the *soke*[19] sideways, to display the shape. By good luck it was finished except about three rows.

Another old neighbour came past whom she totally ignored, but gave me her history in an undertone before she was fairly passed. Also the story of the governess at Kinnaird 'from Roosha', who drew her picture, 'was it like', she never saw it, which puzzled me, but she persisted; and explanation was quaint, she drew the old woman's back, looking out at a window, so that Kitty, who properly considers a portrait should concern itself with the front side, does not know whether the face is like or not! A *Through the Looking Glass* fashion of considering a picture.

I herewith at 10.45 p.m. enter a formal protest against old Mr Willy Hutton in the lane. By daylight he is a charming old fellow, stone-deaf and speaks close to you in a whisper, with his head on side, emphasising his remarks with the forefinger. But when it comes to locking out the old reprobate in the middle of the night, I feel inclined to throw my boots at him. He addresses in a tone of hilarity which subsides into a child-like protest and implory to 'let me in'. 'Open that door', repeated at long intervals, like waiting for the next crow of the midnight cock. Then the rain commences, the storms arise, and the old villain begins to howl. He finally catches it.

Friday, September 9th. Went to Mrs McIntosh's again and took six photographs of the fox, and also her Grace's dachshunds, which behaved as badly as plebeian dogs. On the previous day Bertram had gone to Dalguise with McIntosh who allowed him to pull out a salmon to his great delight. On the same day Barclay Field was reported to take fifteen at Stobhall. They post down from Drumour in state, changing their horses at Birnam, but on Wednesday came into collision with Mr Reid, the baker's cart, at Ladywell.

Now the moral of this incident is the small amount of damage produced by an apparently frightful carriage accident. My private experienced opinion is that the great point to be remembered is that a vehicle really tilts over comparatively slowly, and that instead of trying to save yourself by spreading your hands, you should twist round and throw up your feet. This theory, however, rather implies a top position. I have not the very slightest desire to try it a second time from underneath!

The Drumour *Pole* caught Reid's ancient bay, which bolted down the hill towards home, took the curves successfully, but jumped into the hedge at the bottom, where the Amulree road joins the main road at right angles.

There was a spray of lentil beans and green sugar-bottle glass, and a great scatter of tin canisters at the catastrophe. The harness came to pieces, but Sam'le was only slightly cut. How the youth kept his seat down the steep cutting under the railway is a mystery, and shows the unexpectedly mild results which sometimes attend accidents.

It was as well he happened to carry no passengers, (no, he had two, but they fell off early in the proceedings). Reid's cart is generally a cross between a Noah's Ark and a basket-caravan.

Our somewhat morbid interest in this accident arises from the flighty disposition of our black mare, a most beautiful animal without a single spot of white, no vice, but irrepressible spirits. She is perfectly quiet in London, but in the country takes intense interest in the most unlikely and commonplace objects such as mile-stones, and the square ends of walls. When fresh, her progress is a course of bob-curtseys from side to side of the road.

The paving of the main roads here is the best I ever saw, real macadam, laid with a steam-roller. We have unluckily a very steep narrow lane to get down first, under the railway, and hanging over the Inchewan Burn. To make matters worse, the Burn is the favourite playing ground of the whole population of children.

They are delightful little people except the large size of small boy, who invented a charming game of 'bolting the pony' under the railway arch. Considering the nature of the ground, I cannot imagine a more diabolical proceeding. We invited the police, a mild yellow-haired person, who carries a pair of white cotton gloves which he never puts on. He failed to catch 'the laddies', who replied to the defiance with tin cans; but a judicious application of the whip had most salutary effect, and they now sit in a row on the new railings singing a sort of chorus like little cock robins 'Dirty horse, dirty horse.'

Sunday, September 11th. Went to Cathedral. Met old Kitty toddling along by herself to Little Dunkeld with Bible and Hymn-book, wrapped up in a piece of white paper. She was neatly dressed in black, with a crêpe bonnet. Doubtless ancient mourning bought at great cost for some bygone funeral, for she is the last of her race since 76, a quaint mortification that her *dress-clothes* should be black.

Heard a long, very long, but able discussion from Mr Rutherford, on the promise to Abraham (Genesis 15), and by deduction, faith. I listened with considerable interest, not to the matter, which was worthy, but to the line of thought, a frank admission of the almost staggering difficulty of accepting many Articles of the Creed which embraces the latter-day Christian, and exhorted his hearers to close their eyes and have faith.

He took up his text ingeniously, and I thought in the hands of a more powerful preacher it would have been a very beautiful illustration. The Patriarch Abraham exhorted to consider the mystery of the stars, everything is a mystery, O Lord increase our faith. I should think the absorbing task of a Scotch minister is to keep his congregation out of metaphysics.

I was a little surprised to hear such an admission in a Scotch pulpit, but five minutes later the discourse was old-fashioned enough, quaintly discussing chapter and text in the most literate historical sense. It is interesting and curious to note the continuous old-world line of thought in the Presbyterian church.

If the fierceness of the persecuted covenanters has evolved into rather spiteful personalities and disputes, somewhat trivial to an outsider, they still love the old stern texts. If you borrow a Bible, it falls open at Isaiah, and one must remember the covenanters fought not so much for doctrine as Church Government, and there remains a certain 'dourness' which suggests that the principal change in the situation is simply the absence of that persecution which maketh a wise man mad – and leads to retaliation.

The Scotch Hymnal is a colourless medley. The real national church music is the metrical versions of the psalms. Southern taste pronounces it utterly barbarous, and it must be admitted that the sweet rhythm of the authorised translation[20] has been eradicated with something like intentional spite, but I cannot bring myself to look with completely cold disrespect on the verses which Scott preferred on his death bed, and which strengthened the covenanters to meet victory or death at Drumclog[21] and Rullion Green.[22]

The portion of the Cathedral where public worship is held is walled out of the old building in an arbitrary ugly fashion. It is very plain inside, and down below intensely cold. We generally sit in the west gallery, the high old pews distressingly covered with hieroglyphics. They are open under the seat, and *non non quam* descends a peppermint, hop, hop, hop, from tier to tier.

One looks down on the dusty tops of the sounding board, a rickety canopy carved somewhat to resemble the crown of St Giles Cathedral,[23] but its effect is marred by being tipped forward as though it might fall on Mr Rutherford, earnest, pale and foxy-haired, with a pointed beard and decent Geneva bands.

Perched just below him (the pulpit is very high), is the Precentor, a fine big man with a bullet-head, chubby red face, retroussé nose and a voice like a bull. He is the Birnam schoolmaster. He pitches all the tunes too high, and it seems the etiquette that he begins a note before the congregation, and prolongs the last note after them in a long buzz.

Facing the pulpit is the Duchess's pew, covered in a way that always reminds me inappositely of a grand-stand. The Duchess is away from home, but the servants are ranged in order. Over the front stands the Atholl coat of arms, its two wild men and savage feudal motto – 'Forth, Fortune, and fill the Fetters' – about as appropriate in a modern Kirk as the gigantic broken figure of the black wolf of Badenoch in the vestibule.

They keep up one old custom, I mean locking the doors during service. One may hear the rasping of the key during the final prayer. I wonder what happens if anyone faints, not that I imagine a native capable of such an indiscretion.

The bottle-nosed Dr Dickson was down below in staring plaid trousers, and a perfectly new pair of tan driving gloves.

Monday, September 12th. Drove round the Loch of the Lowes with the pony in drizzling rain. There was a great flock of mallards on

Butterstone, I should think fifty. They come out at night into the barley, and they must eat eighteen shillings worth a night.

Ducks and fallow deer are the most mischievous game for crops (rabbits I confess reluctantly, strengthened by observation of the revered Benjamin, are not game at all, but absolute vermin as regards eating). I remember Robert Low, a farmer at Dalguise, shooting a fallow in a fit of exasperation. He came and told, and there was the beast like a dead calf amongst the oats. They have been at a patch of potatoes close to the line between here and Inver.

Before the railway was made, people said it would frighten all game out of the valley, but it has not the slightest effect upon it, except that extinct animal the brown hare, which had a trick of using the line as a highway like the other natives, and when it met a train sometimes lost its life through indecision, as cats do in London.

I remember a partridge's nest with an incredible number of eggs, in the hollow between the two sleepers in the goods siding at Dalguise, where trucks were constantly shunted over the bird's head. It is common to see roe deer from the train, they lift their heads and then go on feeding. There are many in the wood at the back judging by the tracks, and yesterday I flushed a pair of beautiful woodcocks on the spring head where we get our water at the edge of the wood.

Now there is a public path up this wood which people trek up to the top of Birnam Hill, and they trespass everywhere, which leads me to doubt whether, if the new ideas of access to mountains become law, whether they will after all do much harm in the way of scaring game. I consider it an unjust intrusion, of course, and will give a great handle to poachers. Its direct interference with sportsmen would be packing the grouse and making deer-stalking very exasperating, but as far as miscellaneous game is concerned, the tourists here go practically wherever they like now, and the wild life becomes tamer through familiarity.

Tuesday, September 13th. To Perth with papa, the first time I have been on the railway since we have been here, which I consider shabby. I enjoyed it extremely. It was very showery and the corn all drowned, a sad sight on the fine rolling land about Luncarty and Strathord.

I notice how much the practice of dishorning cattle has come on of late years. There has been some litigation about it. I fancy there is as much to be said for and against, and liable to abuse as many other customs.

From an aesthetic point of view, not obvious to farmers, it is perfectly frightful when applied to anything cross-bred with Ayrshire, as are most of the local cattle.

A natural *hummel* as are all the best bred *Doddies*[24] has an immensely heavy broad head, so much so that a stranger will constantly mistake a *Doddy* cow couchant for a young bull – but the Ayrshire has a high narrow forehead, which in old cows gives a scared wild appearance, even when garnished with long sharp horns. But remove the horns, and the result is an idiotic beast with great flapping ears, and much the same silly type of countenance as that ugliest of animals, the red deer hind.

I wonder where these good Ayrshire cows come from, for the bulls which are turned out are all Polled Angus or short-horn, and the cows all Ayrshire. The bulls swarm and have battles royal. Every farmer has one even if he hath but six cows. I cannot think it a good plan, for a small farmer cannot afford a good bull. He keeps it till it is as big as the other bullocks, kills it and rears another.

Perth was uncommonly cold and draggled. My new boots which hurt, conveniently got wet through shortly, and papa stood me another pair, two pairs in one year, 'Oh Gemini,' but this latest pair are very comfortable.

Had a large lunch for ten-pence, 'Cookies', 'Bridies'[25] and lemonade at Woods, two nice merry lasses, who advised us to the shoemakers, whose name by a coincidence was also Wood. I was looking at the younger one's hair, how quickly fashions spread, the loose mane and the side-wisps coiled on the top of the head instead of tied with a ribbon or plaited.

I did not hear one whistle of that odious song, there is just one boy has it at Birnam, Glasgow is badly infected, fashion and habit is as curious in contagion as the influenza.

Perth in the new parts is a well-built town, plenty of good reddish stone, and the side streets very wide and deserted, paved with cobbles, and much grass grown like the streets of Edinburgh.

We went along the North Inch, admiring the little gardens full of flowers. Passed a very large hideous new Free Church, a barbarous mixture of gothic and castellated architecture. We saw a second large Free Church.

The shops are good, especially the drapers. There are a great many cats. The wynds and lower back parts of the city are most noisome, indeed the Scotch are a filthy people, their main idea of the use of a running stream is to carry off what they call *refuse*.

Every burn that passes a farm has its jaw-hole, serving as an ashpit. At Dunkeld the town-rubbish is shot below the Bridge, and at Perth we were shocked at the volume of black fluid pouring out of several large sewer arches.

The beautiful white gulls pounce on the garbage and are remarkably tame. An old man was throwing them bits of bread for which they darted, screaming, dropping it and soaring again.

The railings are extremely rickety, people are constantly drowned, but there is a sluttish carelessness of life. Witness the universal habit of walking on the line. There have been two run over between here and Blair this summer, but the Fiscal looks at them and they are put underground without more ado.

From Perth Bridge we looked over at the river coming down in spate, at the corner of the South Inch below us, a knot of men and a brown and white dog pulled out a dead sheep, but, upon consideration, launched it again with a boat-hook.

The Museum was shut. I looked in at the shop windows at the photographs of Perth. Miss Julia Neilson,[26] probably on tour, Mr Balfour,[27] sundry Law Lords, and often the Duke of Clarence with poor Princess May.[28] Poor lady, an attractive face, but I doubt if very correct features, the eyes and nose too sharp, the mouth large, not so pretty as her mother is represented to have been, and with the same tendency to stoutness, but her photographs do not do her appearance justice.

Thursday, September 15th. Being too showery to photograph, papa went to Perth again, picked up the China and called on the Millais', encamped with old Mrs Gray. Their house is rebuilt.

There happened the same day to come out 'An Interview' with Sir John in *Black and White*.[29] I have read several such. It strikes me they must give rather an erroneous idea of the victim, I do not

believe he could say all that fine language on end to save his life. It
is just possible the sentiments might have been extracted piecemeal
with a corkscrew. I should think he is a character who will be
described in some future day by biographers in puzzling contra-
diction, like Dr Johnson.[30] Some looking only at the noisy, coarse,
selfish side, which I am afraid exists, and others who have received
real kindness from him, will go to the other extreme.

He made a rather touching remark accompanied by strong
language, that he could not bear to go near Birnam for the same
reason that we felt about Dalguise, he was so distressed at having to
leave Murthly.

Wednesday, September 21st. Papa and McDougall to Killin. A
cloudless, frosty autumn day. Drove with the pony after breakfast
to Bally Cock Farm. We waded up the sandy track behind Mr Peter
Stewart with a load of corn, and when we got up found I had come
to the wrong house, and had to send the pony down to the bottom
to climb the corresponding knoll, I, getting across a back way
through middens, piloted by Mr Peter who had by this time
recognized me.

He turned back at a broken dyke, but I was guided by shrieks in
advance, and presently round one of the cottages appeared a tabby
cat in full flight with a rabbit skin, and Bella, head-over-heels in
pursuit, armed with a mop. She did not see me, but presently
coming back in triumph, broke out into a splutter of welcome using
my christian name in her excitement. Very much amused I was, and
nearly bitten by a prospective victim of the camera.

The pony carriage at this moment emerged from the opposite
side of the Steading, calling forth another torrent of broad Scotch,
which so bewildered the groom that instead of putting the pony
into the byre, he took the concern up an inclined plane of an
archaeological character, landing on a level with the chimneys,
whence it was got down with some difficulty. I was relieved to see
it stowed away in the byre where Mr Pulinger remained peeping
out in a state of surprise.

Except for its peculiar position perched on the sand-hill, there is
nothing very remarkable about Bally Cock Farm, though very old.
It is a nice old kitchen with some modern conveniences added.

Miss May Stewart was making scones on a girdle at the great open fire, with half a tree at the back of the logs. Dusting and turning the big round flags, talking all the time in a loud clear voice and using the rolling-pin with such pretty slim hands for a farmer's daughter, I might have photographed her for the *Queen of Hearts* had there been more light.

The fire had burnt for four and twenty years. The old brown cupboard had stood in yon corner for one hundred and fifty years. Her father, old Bally Cock, was born in the adjoining cottage, he was a fine-looking old man.

Miss Stewart's hair is very grey, prematurely like her brother Peter, but still very good looking and vivacious. They are a remarkably handsome family except the red-haired Bella. Here were two more Marjories, a little child Madge, and another cousin Marjorie Stewart. Black eyes, black hair, a white skin, short petticoats, very tall, a little stiff, the finest looking young woman I have seen for a long time.

She was working in the farm and came up with one of the horses. I think I understand the feeling of that common person Mr Pepys, it gives me a thorough pleasure of a platonic kind to consider a beautiful face. I took two photographs of Miss Stewart with the dog Jocky and little Madge. She abandoned the scones and was determined to 'brush her hair', which being explained was a brooch made of a white Ptarmigan's foot mounted with silver.

Then Bella took me back to the other farm, dragging little Madge in one hand, and the *machine*[31] in the other, talking all the time at express speed. Her uncle Jack began in Gaelic, but pulled up and shook hands as did Mr Peter formally, whom I had already seen. The people here when you say 'how do you do', work out the question and return it in an old-fashioned honest manner, you have to allow for it before tumbling into general conversation. I took two carts and horses and numerous people in a state of giggle, who came out better than might have been expected. There was some competition, little Madge wanted to be taken with a 'piggy', but was reminded that she had been 'done once'. I was vexed to spoil a plate which I had meant to devote to the pretty Marjorie, but she deserves a better workman.

Miss Stewart's scones were very good and the company very

merry. The visit was a great success but I was a little huffed afterwards to find out that both Bella and her Auntie May are likely to be soon married from the old house.

As for Bella who has been engaged a long time, it is a good match, and the man who gets her will be lucky, red hair, thumping boots, good tempered, cracking laugh and all – but it does seem rather an unkind irony of fate that the lassie who is admitted to make the best butter in the district, should go to live in Clerkenwell. He is an Inspector of Police who has got on, and is considered very promising. I wonder if she will lose her freshness, and forget how to say *Rohallion*[32] with several Q's in it and two syllables.

As to Miss May's sweetheart, I was too much disgusted to ask, but the only wonder is how she has contrived to remain so long single. Her brother Mr John Stewart who has grown stout, and explained more than once that he had a cold in his head, certainly appeared a 'wee bit dumpie'; but one would have thought that having got past an age when she would be likely to have children, and being the mistress of a prosperous home, she might as well keep home for Mr Peter as any other man.

This tirade reads rather spiteful, and completely ignores the romance of affection, but it has spoilt a pretty picture. I should think Mr John and Peter Stewart's view of the situation is equally prosaic, two elderly obstinate bachelors exceedingly shy: they may search the country before they find another such pretty, brisk housekeeper.

Thursday, September 22nd. Very fine harvest-day again in the afternoon. Drove with the mare up the Braan valley, past Drumour, in beautiful mellow sunlight slanting against the hill-sides and stooks of corn. Already in the middle of September the sun reaches a very slight elevation over the level of the hill-tops, so that the western slopes of the valleys are chilly and damp. The leaves are beginning to turn.

Friday, September 23rd. Drive up the Braan again with the pony and camera, intending to take General Wade's Bridge above Kennacoil. The morning began with frost and white mist, which gradually rolled up the slopes, the sun blinking out over the beautiful valley amongst the hills, but the vapours were too heavy, and towards night closed into heavy rain.

Monday, September 26th. Drove in the afternoon with the pony to Butterglen, then turned to the left towards Riechip under the impression the road was flat, whereas it goes over the hill at the back of Cardney. There is a farm right on the top, and little fields of oats.

I got out when the pull began, but the road went up and up. Could not see Loch Ordie. Went up a slight hill on the left, and should have had a splendid view but for dull clouds of rain over the Carse of Gowrie. The pony was in a lather but came down the hill in fine style, and only moderately apprehensive, the road being very soft with mud. It is surprising how well he has kept on his feet this year.

Last night, between eleven and twelve, we thought we heard the special train taking the Duke of Sutherland on his long, last journey.[33] Some people can see no sentiment or beauty in a railway, simply a monstrosity and a matter of dividends. To my mind there is scarcely a more splendid beast in the world than a large locomotive: if it loses something of mystery through being the work of man, it surely gains in a corresponding degree the pride of possession. I cannot imagine a finer sight than the Express, with two engines, rushing down this incline at the edge of dusk.

The strongly marked character and peculiarities of the Iron Duke will make him remembered in social history. Reading the interesting obituary notice in the *Scotsman*, I was struck with the mingling of the old and the new.

As his career as a public spirited generous autocrat has been a success, it is emphatically an exception which proves the new rule. No landowner without great extraneous resources could carry out beneficence on this vast scale, for it brings in neither a reasonable percentage nor very sincere gratitude. The days of a successful patriotic undertaking like the Bridgewater Canal are out of date.

The Scotch dote upon funerals and mourning, but I have not seen a scrap of crêpe about the Highland Railway. The unfortunate ending of the Duke's life would probably make little difference in Scotland in the way of dropping him out of favour. It is my opinion that, under a thin veneer of intelligence and gentility, they are all savages, highly descended of course, and the more savage the more hoity-toity, but, making certain slight allowance for circumstances, there are no Class divisions whatever.

I suppose the future *Deus ex machina* is the County Council. There was another death in the same number of the *Scotsman*, which snaps an almost incredible line with the past. Lady Elphinstone, a daughter of Johnson's 'Queenie Thrale'.

Thursday, September 29th. Drove up the Braan to the sixth milestone. A very beautiful valley to my mind. I prefer a pastoral landscape backed by mountains. I have often been laughed at for thinking Esthwaite Water the most beautiful of the Lakes. It really stikes me that some scenery is almost theatrical, or ultra-romantic.

Saturday, October 1st. I feel obliged to rest the Grey, but it was an aggravatingly fine morning compared with the preceding. I trudged up the road at the back with the hand camera, in hopes of getting a harmless shot at the pretty roe-deer.

The previous Thursday afternoon, being unprovided with the machine, I saw first a buck which bounced out of the fern 'cursing and swearing' as the local report hath it, like a collie dog with a sore throat. It walked leisurely up the road grunting and repeatedly uttering its hoarse indignant bark.

I thought it had not gone far, and following cautiously, got another sight of it when it ran off. It had but poor horns and was as red as a fox.

Finding this deer-stalking a pleasing excitement, I went on up the road, stepping from clump to clump of moss, and taking an observation with every step. I was rewarded by the sight of the hind quarters of a roe feeding in a patch where the fern had been cut. It was a good way up on my left, but its head behind a tree.

I stalked it with delightful success, getting across a hollow and up again, when suddenly I trod upon a stick: the roe's head being behind a tree I had time to become rigid before it looked up, and out came two hinds, lippity, lippity, like rabbits, startled by the noise, but not much frightened, and completely vague as to the point whence it came.

They came straight at me and stopped in full view. The front one, perhaps in the line of the wind, walked up the wood suspiciously, though without seeing me.

It is singular how defective the eyes, or more probably the minds of wild animals are for a stationary object. The slightest movement – but if you are motionless they will come close up, certainly not without seeing, but perhaps without focusing their observer.

I often consider what an important factor the arrangement of the eyes must be in determining the amount of intellect in different animals. If a man examines any object intently, he stares straight at it, seeing it at once, and equally (as regards scope), with both eyes, but in a considerable proportion of animals, the two spheres of sight do not overlap at all, and in certain species, such as bats and rabbits, there is an absolute gap between the two planes of vision.

Such a state of affairs would be a strain upon a human intellect, and, unless animal minds are more comprehensive than ours, they must either concentrate their attention on one eye at a time, or get a very superficial impression from both, the latter is probably the case. When preoccupied with feeding, they rely on their ears. It would follow logically that those whose eyes are most sideways would rely most on their ears, an interesting subject to work out. The overlapping in human sight is say $15° + 15°$ out of $60°$.

Whatever may have been the explanation of its behaviour, the hind was very pretty and curious, running about in the fern like a rabbit. It was much plagued with midges, (so was I), totally unprovided with tail which the fallows are always wagging. It flapped its ears and scratched itself with its tiny hind feet.

When it went back to feed I crept up nearer, but overdid it at last, and it looked up, with a mouthful of wild sage. The plant hung out like a lettuce-leaf in a rabbit's mouth, and it would munch a moment and then stare, and munch again. When its mouthful was finished, it stretched its neck straight out and uttered a long single bleat, which it repeated presently, pumping up the sound from its flanks to judge by the way it heaved, then it took a header over the bank of fern disappearing into the wood with a twinkle of red and white.

In the afternoon I went with mamma to Craiglush and Polney, but it was dull.

Sunday, October 2nd. Wet, very *weet*. Much concerned with the toothache and swollen face of Benjamin Bouncer, whose mouth is so small I cannot see in, but as far as I can feel there is no breakage. This comes of peppermints and comfits.

I have been quite indignant with papa and McDougall, though to be sure he is a fascinating little beggar, but unfortunately has not the sense to suck the *minties* when obtained.

Monday, October 3rd. In the afternoon mamma and I drove all the way to Tullypowrie to see Sarah McDonald,[34] through showers and wind, over roads cut and dappled with footmarks of hundreds of Highland sheep.

We met three great flocks of the little creatures, woolly white, freshly washed, bleating and pressing to the side of the road, where they snatch a mouthful as they pass. They are coming down from the hills, already for a week past capped with snow, pacing towards the great sheep-fair at Perth on Wednesday and Thursday, where they will sell at the ruinous price of five and three pence apiece.

Behind these walks the shepherd in his best clothes, or the farmer himself, slow work. A flock we meet at Ballinluig at two o'clock is turned on to the warren near St Comb's when we come back at five. The sagacity of the collies in sorting out their property is marvellously reliable. I saw a large flock turned into the same field with the butcher's sheep for the night. Vast numbers have gone down by train. They are not much bigger than rabbits.

Hereabouts there are a good many cross-bred, very ugly, having all the ungainliness of Leicesters, without much of their imposing size.

We had a weary-looking thin pair of post-horses, but they proved fresh, and went, one ambling at a butcher's trot and the other cantering. We went to Guay and Ballinluig, but came back by Grandtully Bridge and Kinnaird, to the obvious mystification of the poor nags, who lost their points in the confused cross-roads near the Bridge, and by their sulky ears and shuffling gait, showed they were of opinion that we had not turned home. I was quite sorry for them. The white, who was more intelligent, took an observation on the high ground near Balnaguard and set off, but the other did not recognize the road till we had passed Kinnaird. They showed a certain discrimination in their mistake, for the girder bridges at Ballinluig and Grandtully are almost similar.

The Tay was in flood, lying out on the meadows where the herds of dappled cattle were reflected in the shallow water. The corn all out, a sad sight to see. It is a beautiful Strath between Logierait and

Aberfeldy, more so than the narrow valley below, with its almost artificially beautiful woods and excellent deserted roads. Rich land, scattered clumps of fine timber and a fringe of natural wood at the edge of the moor, if less romantic, is more pleasing in the long run.

We passed Duncan clipping a hedge just before we turned in at the steep sandy drive to Pitleoch, and he did not put in a further opinion, which I did not regret having observed him adequately in June, for he is deaf. He is still very tall but has gone into an old man, thin, wiry and silent, pleasantly civil in manner, but deaf. He was a queer old object in June, in a flannel shirt, queer loose short knickerbockers, more like drawers, worsted stockings drawn up over his knees and brogues, low shoes with the upper leather cut all in a piece and fastened over his instep with two buckle straps. He looked as if he were half-dressed, a mild inoffensive old savage.

Sarah was flitting in and out of the cottage a long way up, taking observations with an old brass telescope. There is one little bit of road she watches for hours for the baker's cart.

Truly a habitation in the mountains of the moon. It is an exquisite view, closed in the distant west by the snowy point of Ben Lawers. We had to intrude close past the back of Pitleoch House, coming to a standstill at the stable, the end of all things, where a good-tempered stable boy was bribed to smuggle away the lean horses in the rambling old buildings, once tenanted by ten potter's pigs.

Sarah was fiddling about in the wet grass, very tall and upright, showing a worn and eager face at one end, and a pair of buttoned town boots at the other. She always reminds me somehow of a broom stick, a very pathetic one, poor Sarah.

She was in much better spirits than last time, when she seemed so overcome with the unaccustomed sight that she could only stare at us and mop her face. She explained naïvely that she had thought of so many things after we had gone, and proceeded to put questions again, which already she had unconsciously heard answered.

She had had some lodgers from Fife, an absorbing event in their little world, and of no slight importance financially. I am afraid Duncan can earn very little now, and it is a poor cottage, and there is a certain soreness in having had to leave Tullymet.

Sarah is not so much altered, but very old. The same blinking eyes looking over her chin, and the same tone of voice, especially when she manages a laugh. There was a Scotch clip here and there, but the accent was English, and Lancashire at that, over the hills at the edge of the Derbyshire peak.

She has never been home or seen a relation since she married Duncan in 72, and when we came to her in June, we were the first visible travellers from her old outside world that had reached her since our other visit eight years ago – 'when you have a house there would be nobody to look after Duncan – and the hens' – there will be few left to visit if the delay lasts much longer.

Her sister, old Hannah is still alive, but must be very old. She was like a mumbling shrivelled old mummy when my grandmother died. Betty was the eldest sister, they must have been connected with the Leeches in service for a great while back, but I don't think they ever worked in Leech's Mill.

Sarah was kitchen maid, and then my mother's cook. We were at Tullymet for one summer 70, and she came back from London to marry the gamekeeper. I remember being taken up into the attic as a child to finger her lilac silk dress. He was a fine looking man, and she had £200 of savings. I am glad to say she has this yet, my father being one trustee, but I should think the income is very bare.

I never heard anything unsatisfactory of the gracious Duncan, but he has become slow, and he looks like a tough sort of old man who might last for ever on a little meal. They have no family. She became a Catholic, after a fashion, when she married him.

If Sarah ever showed any reserve when she was gamekeeper's wife at Tullymet, it is visited on her now in her inferior rank, but the situation has probably always been beyond her control. The Scotch are friendly to a friendly English family with ready money, but an unprotected stranger is a stranger to the bitter end – although they take him in. The loneliness must be all the more appalling when every one is cousins and a Clan.

Thursday, October 6th. What an aggravating old person Mr Lowe the post master is! You go down in a hurry with two or three small affairs, say a postal order and three stamps. He says in a forbidding manner 'Let us do one thing first; *haveyougotapenny*?' He works out the change on his fingers, and after all has to carry on the halfpence to the next transaction, which you work out for him as he has collapsed into a state of imbecility. 'I *think* that's right' says he, regarding you sideways with evident suspicion.

He is a fat, hunched old fellow, with little piggy eyes, a thick voice and wears a smoking-cap with a yellow tassel, and he has immense hands with which he slowly fumbles about for the stamps, which he keeps amongst the stationery in empty writing-paper boxes. He puts on wrong postage 'Shall we say tuppence?' (!) and will sauce anybody who is unprovided with small change; he wants reporting.

I drove to Inver in the morning to see old Kitty. I felt a little self-reproachful when she said 'I was yearnin to see ye.' To tell the truth I wanted the photograph to blow over. We avoided the subject successfully. I had a great laugh with Mrs McDougall before going up. 'There's a poke here' indicating the front of her bodice, 'and a poke here (at the back) and a lump o'hair. Oh thooms wrang. Neist time I'm hae on a wrapped, th'face is no clean. Oo aye it'll be,' I don't know whether it would be in the fire, but I durst hardly look round the shelves, the old woman is so sharp.

It is a peculiarity of amateur portraits that they always enrage the victims. I have known people to cease to be on speaking terms!

Old Kitty bore no malice, but was most gossipy when she had got over a regret that the house was no weel redd up.

We talked about the worsted she was knitting and hand-spinning. She rolled off her chair and began to search high and low, finding it finally in the bed, whence she seems to produce most of her little property. It was a bag containing balls of wool, one of them, of course, unbleached yellow, spun by her more than forty years ago. It was of two strands and not bad for evenness, and very tough. I broke off a bit and kept it, whereat she laughed like a child. She 'turnt' the wheel, a very large two-handed, like the Irish still use, I fancy.

After another search she brought out a linen garment. Her mother she said with evident pride, was an excellent spinner and taught her to work well, they bought forty pounds (?) o'tow, it was very dear. This was part of the piece they spun together sixty years since. I did not like to ask whether the thing, a chemise, had been in use ever since, but it is likely, and seemed not worn in the slightest.

This hand-woven unbleached (for linen is linen, I believe the bleaching chemicals are the mischief), will last for ever. There were some lumps, but on the whole fine, strong cloth, infinitely superior to anything they make in Langdale. People will not, cannot settle down to waste their eyes on such work now. Old Kitty was strongly of this opinion 'we could not sell it under six shillings a yard' and six shillings then meant the worth of sixteen shillings nowadays.

I told her about our linen napkins with Prince Charlie's initials, but could not get a rise. Either Kitty is no Jacobite, or will not let on before an Englisher. She has a wonderful memory and declares she remembers things that happened when she was between three and four years old. Very quiet things I should fancy, up in the hills at the back of Ballinloan.

She evidently has lively recollection of the old crofter farms which clustered round the heads of the glens amongst the hills. There is only one modern cottage, standing on the site of the hamlet where she was born, which is a typical example of the places you come upon at the edge of the hill.

Generally, near the head of a large burn, a few mounds of large stones overgrown with nettles (there may not be another nettle for miles round, it must be a toughly ancestral plant, witness the Roman of the camps)[35] – enclosing patches of vivid green, and on the neighbouring slopes strange ridges like wave-marks, where the turf and stout heather has grown over what was once ploughed land.

There is sometimes a solitary robin haunting the dwarfed thorns, and nearly always an uncanny blue hare on the lone hearthstone. Such silent mournful spots have appealed to the sentimental and unreasoning susceptibilities of poets since the time when Goldsmith wrote his pensive 'Lament', and on the nerves of Radical politicians they are as red was to a bull.

I thought old Kitty's shrewd sentence was worth the whole blather of a crofter delegation – 'There was less tea drunk then.'

The simple fact is that people, even the Scotch who are still tolerable savages, (witness one of the football team on Saturday, who being objected to in hobnailed boots, offered to play in his stockings), cannot with the modern ideas of decency and comfort subsist like rabbits.

This old woman living all alone, the last of her race, might be expected to look back with sentimental love to the past, but the circumstance most insistent in her memory appeared to be 'the stinting' which she endured and which stunted her growth as a girl.

Her father had a small croft at Easter Dalguise, *Swans House*, which stands on the corner of our potato patch. She had five brothers and two sisters, she being the youngest. Her father died soon after she was born. When she was seven years old she went to 'my uncle Prince', who had a farm a mile up the water from Ballinloan, as a herd, and remained with him eight years, herding the cattle on the hills.

The crofters appear to have had the right to herd their cattle and sheep on the hills at the back of the valleys. (How did that right disappear, by the way?)

As I understand, they did not graze in common, but had their own marches.

Kitty must have had a frugal life always, but she dwelt on this early part as a time of positive privation. Apart from the hardship, she spoke with affection of the idyllic shepherd life in summer on the hills. They milked the ewes then, a thing a crofter would hardly condescend to now.

What did they live on?, just meat and a little milk. 'Aye thae were potaties but no mony; aye neeps' (rather doubtful). The staple evidently porridge. 'They wad kill a sheep sometimes, or a stirk'[36] (impassively), one of the events she has remembered for eighty years. She mentioned pigs as a source of satisfactory profit.

They were content to wear the coarse worsted of their own flocks, their scanty stock of hand-spun linen lasted practically a lifetime, and there was less tea drunk then! Plenty of whisky probably, but there was a reason for its being cheap at the back of Ballinloan.

I remember another deserted village higher up the Pitleoch Burn that we used to walk to from Dalguise, where there was an immense still like a stone bottle or oven, the neck level with the surface of the ground. For the matter of that, I believe something stronger than water came out of the burn above Easter Dalguise. There was a very large still discovered at Balnaguard thirty years ago perhaps, the entrance under the hearthstone of a cottage.

According to old Kitty, Strath Braan was populous once, 'hundreds'. I could not get an exact idea, but they emigrated in a covey as McDougall would say, to North America, 'My uncle Prince's descendants are prosperous in California', she had had a letter last week. One old cousin survives in Edinburgh, ninety-four and deaf, and failed, but cherished by the Minister's family whom she has served for forty-six years. You will scarcely find a single family in this neighbourhood who have not relations over the sea.

The old crofter farms will never return. When one considers the scanty, draggled crops grown in the bottoms of the windy valleys, it is madness to dream of ploughing up the heather. 'Then there'll be some bad meal,' said Kitty, when I told her Duncan Cameron had run up his kit-rigs regardless of the rain.[37]

That farming does not pay is a platitude. Bella Dewar informed me they had got a substantial reduction of rent from the impecunious Mr Durrent Stuart. We could not live, we made no profit, and Mabel putting to it (from capital) to pay the rent? As to allotments, they were a matter of course when we went to Dalguise twenty years ago, and nearly everybody has a cow.

In the matter of small farms, there is the case of Robert Love, who has the fourth farm at Dalguise, I don't know the acreage, but three cows, a 'two-horse farm' and mares out even then with carting coals. He is giving up next year when the lease runs out. He endeavoured once to borrow £40 from my farm I remember.

As far as I have discovered there is no soreness about the emigration, but the pride and pleasure over sons and cousins who have 'done weel' and remembered the old folks at home.

Friday, October 7th. News in the *Scotsman* of Lord Tennyson's death,[38] a truly great patriot when treason is little thought of. What a pity it was not Mr Gladstone. In the same copy of *The Times* appeared the last of the Duke of Argyll's trenchant letters.

Before the King is buried there is talk of his successor. I should say Mr Lewis Morris[39] has not improved his chances by the wretched stuff he has contributed to *The Times*, though he has contrived to publish the fact of his intimacy with Lord Tennyson. Whether he gets it or not, I expect to hear some echoes of a lively storm, my father being intimate with the choleric Welshman. Imagine the spiteful wrath of 'that beast' George Saintsbury[40] and the *Saturday Review*.

Alfred Austin's 'Ode' is very fine, but if anything, almost annoying in the success of his Imitation.[41] The 16th. stanza contradicts the first, and yet it is only plagiarism after all. Coventry Patmore[42] and Locker[43] are the only poets who are not mentioned in the running. Swinburne[44] is the man if it were not for certain unfortunate circumstances.

If they cannot give it to the only poet who is a personality, not an echo, I hope it will go to a literateur rather than a poetaster. I think Sir Theodore Martin is the likeliest.[45] Another way out of the difficulty would be to give it to Miss Ingelow[46] or Miss Rossetti,[47] which would be comparative peace between two competitors instead of a crowd, and not altogether inappropriate at the end of our good Queen's reign.

Wednesday, October 12th. I went to see Miss Jessie Anderson, which I should have done before, and sat three-quarters-of-an-hour, and see no reason why I might not have sat indefinitely had she not got a choking in her throat.

There was very little in the shop compared to old times, in fact she only opens it irregularly as an excuse for seeing old friends. I was ushered into the back parlour over a hot fire, and hospitably pressed to take a cup of tea at 11.20, but well meant.

My views on Scotch education will always be clouded with the recollection of a flock of white pigeons on a balcony half seen half hidden with flapping sheets and clothes lines, and the usual obstructions of a little back window. In the same way shall I associate Lord Rosebery with a glow of heat and a painted feather fan.

Now Miss Anderson is a singular character, considerably beyond me when it comes to analysis. I consider she is mad, at all events very flighty since the influenza. At the same time if she can be kept off metaphysics (she had just got to the dangerous word 'psychological' when her cough began), she is a person of observation and intellect, and stored with anecdote, but her stories come tumbling out in such a muddle of broad Scotch and theology, that one feels as if one was standing on one's head.

The poor thing has been much troubled by ill-health and the loss of her dear sister Mary, a very charming person, with more firmness, and a convinced Unitarian, which is the reason of her surviving sister's real affection for us. Now religion, more especially doctrinal, is a subject I will not and cannot discuss: and such a mixture, the most advanced rational views held conjointly with a beautiful childlike piety and a personal belief in visions.

I have an unconquerable aversion to listening to accounts in the first person of supposed supernatural visitations. I didn't enjoy my visit to Miss Anderson in June. It annoys me from the opposite ends of my character at the same time.

But keep Miss Anderson from this twilight land and her views of earthly life and politics are both amusing and clever, and I have also heard her tell a good ghost story, not in the first person. I should not like to accuse her of inventing it, though it is of rather a conventional type, and it is odd no one was unkind enough to whisper it when we lived at Tullymet.

Many years ago the family of Dick had an old attached servant named Mistress McNaughten, who was left in charge at Tullymet, Sir Robert Dick, the then proprietor, being with his regiment in India. The housekeeper sitting by herself sewing in the little room between the dining-room and the room at the back of the hall (I remember the room well, a horse-hair sofa that I used to crawl underneath), heard one of the doors open, and saw her master come in and slowly cross the room.

She spoke to him in great surprise, but he only looked at her mournfully after the manner of a ghost, and went out at the other door. In due time came the news that Sir Robert Dick had fallen in battle. Poor Mistress McNaughten, surely with some confusion of cause and effect, was never 'settled in her mind' after the shock.

According to the terms of her master's will she was never to be turned away, but she did not get on comfortably with his successor, and, after haunting the house like a ghost herself for several years, she went over to her relations in New Zealand. Her fate pursued her, she wandered into the Bush where her body was found after many days. Such was the sad end of Mistress McNaughten.

In the matter of politics, Miss Anderson opined that Mr Gladstone is a Jesuit, which I was able to say I had heard before! She has no belief in that over-rated young man Lord Rosebery, and gave some anecdote which I will not set down, being vague, of shabbiness on his part to the navvies at the Forth Bridge, when they wanted a cricket ground.

She detests Lord Rosebery because of his behaviour to Mr Duncan's daughter. When old Mrs Duncan was at Kinnaird she was very intimate with Miss Anderson. I remember the nice old lady, always bundled up in a white china crêpe shawl, giving me, a very small child unable to read, a copy of 'The Lady of the Lake' in polished wooden binding.[48] She thought everything of Lord Rosebery, she used to quote Tennyson because of his reading it, 'Oh, Miss Anderson,' she would say, 'you should hear Lord Rosebery recite *The Grandmother*,' and then she would walk about the shop saying pieces – 'and he was staying there, he was engaged to her' – the story as I have heard it, and do not in the least doubt, was that his precious Lordship broke the matter short when Miss Duncan's father refused to settle £400,000 on his daughter.

He had private reasons for not being able to do that as he failed disgracefully within a few months, but it is distinctly to be understood that Lord Rosebery, at the time of breaking off, was not aware of this approaching fraudulent bankruptcy as an excuse for declining to ally himself with the Duncans.

According to Miss Anderson, the Rothschilds were staying at Fisher's Hotel at that time, and he never left the neighbourhood till he had engaged himself to Miss Hannah Rothschild. I can indistinctly remember Miss Duncan, she was a tall, beautiful girl with light hair.

I was able to assure Miss Anderson that papa also detested Lord Rosebery. One ground of his dislike rather comical. Now, if my papa has a fault, he is rather voluble in conversation, and though not such a dragon as Edwin Lawrence, he is oppressively well informed. One day at Sir John Millais', my father being photographing, overheard Lord Rosebery and another gentleman, whom he afterwards learnt to be Mr Buckle, Editor of *The Times*, in the course of conversation make some glaring mis-statement, not of a controversial nature, but of fact.

My father could not stand it and set them right. He has something in common with his hero Lord Macaulay, for whom Sydney Smith suggested a purgatory of dumbness while someone shouted wrong historical dates into his ear. I don't know whether Mr Buckle said anything, but Lord Rosebery, supposing my father to be an ordinary working photographer, received the correction as a positive insult, and there was a scrimmage.

In excuse of his rudeness I am afraid it must be admitted that photographers are a low class. Did not Charlie Lamm mention with surprise that he had seen McDougall of Inver walking with one? Perhaps in consequence, and also on account of his intimacy with the Duncans, papa was not favourably impressed with the Countess either, when he afterwards saw her at the Studio.

Miss Anderson's family belonged to the Congregationalists I think, or Baptists, staid Sectarians who tolerated no inquiry of thought. One Sunday when reading their Church Magazine, which contained a list of persons expelled for heresy, she saw at the bottom, Jessy Anderson 'for gross heresy'. She had never heard the word before, and looked it up in the dictionary. I asked her if she was at all reflected on in Dunkeld, and was sorry as soon as said, but she was much amused and said her neighbours had found she was harmless, and kind to the poor.

She takes worthy interest in the ploughman and gives indiscriminately to tinkers, so we leave her with the gypsy's benison, well earned – 'May God bless ye – and the de'il miss ye!'

Thursday, October 13th. Account of Lord Tennyson's funeral. I should think no man ever had a more beautifully complete end. It has made a deep impression. There is only one person living whose death would cause the same universal, uncontradicted grief, may it be long distant, I mean the Queen. Or in a less degree, the Princess of Wales or Princess May.

Mr James Payne[49] touching the subject with questioning taste in the *Illustrated*, says Tennyson was one of the three greatest men, the other two being Bismarck and Gladstone. I once in print read a statement of the same sort which had the advantage of not being contradictable, namely, that these three were the only celebrities surviving whose obituary notices would overflow a page of *The Times*. I suppose new stars will arise.

Sunday, October 16th. Up the road some flakes of snow, much crackling of withered leaves, no deer. Gathering moss on the way down did hear a noise which on a lawful day I should have attributed to the Gas Works, but being the Sabbath, concluded it must be the Red King or a rabbit snoring.

Monday, October 17th. Up above Ballinloan to photograph. Clear blue sky, cold wind and frost. Tried 'east the burn', like the side of a house, gates and the back buildings of a farm. Went in cautiously being afraid of collies, but could find no soul 'forbye baudrons'.[50]

Knocking at the kitchen door interrupted the clatter of forks, and brought out a girl with ringlets and a dirty face. A conversation with 'Wully' invisible in the inner kitchen, in which the carriage was referred to as 'the machine', led to a determination to turn back if possible. I prudently went down on foot, that pony is an admirable person, and met the farmer coming up, a tall, sandy, toothless old fellow with a broad grin, riding a hay-cart mare with a halter and no saddle.

He advised 'west the burn'. I drove half a mile up to the Ford, and then walked on a good way through the heather, within sight of the old ruins at Salachill.[51] The road is a mere track now, with enormously deep ruts, but from the indication of large stones and some cutting, I take it to be the actual old road made by General Wade.[52]

I had a most enjoyable walk, disturbing many grouse. Saw two shepherds as I came back, dodged the burn till they were well up the hill. Singular how blind people are if they are not expecting to see anything. The sun was burning hot, and coming home a wind like ice, which is the way to get a splitting headache.

Saturday, October 29th. Was warmer and much rain, the paths washed out and great puddles of transparent water on the platform, splashing over one's heels if one stepped in it. The ditch at the edge of the wood turning into a torrent choked with fallen leaves, rushed across the road and down into Miss Carrington's front door.

Old Willie Hutton was to be seen scraping and puddling with a shovel. It is convenient if he happens to be all right when wanted, for the last fortnight he had been almost continually all wrong. I suppose people away have given him money. Papa refused to pay him on account, leaving it with Mr Kinnaird to be paid when he was sober.

He makes such a fool of himself, taking off his hat and bowing to the ground, it is a wonder he has not been run over before now. At times I suspect he is locked up to judge by the noise and the epitaphs he bestows on his sister.

He must be an aggravating relation to own. He is said to have been perverted by some English workmen who were employed some years ago building at Miss Carrington's. The idea of Englishmen teaching a Scotchman to drink whisky struck me as rather rich.

The Chapel in Miss Carrington's house is a secret known to every single person in the place. I don't know why I'm sure. I think my gossip must have been under a misapprehension.

The priest sleeps in the Chapel because it is not lawful to have a regular chapel in the house, which I don't believe, but it is such a small house it may well be convenient to keep both in one room.

There are a good few Catholics scattered about the countryside, considered in proportion to the other inhabitants. They are much apart, and the priests looked on askance as Jesuits.

Miss Carrington, who is described as being much under the control of the priest and a Catholic maid-servant, wanted to hire a room in Dunkeld but was refused by the Duchess, her object being to provide a meeting-place for the priests, savage Irish from Perth and Glasgow, who camp in the oak woods and peel the bark from the saplings for tan.

The youngest Miss Carrington I suppose is not a Catholic, as she plays the organ at the English Church. There was another who is silly, so since her parent's death she has been retired into an asylum, and her sisters are building the chapel with her money according to current report.

Went down to Mr Mackenzie's to see some splendid photographs taken by Mr Sutcliffe of Whitby. He sent up a book for us to look at, of dried ferns and moss ingeniously arranged by Charlie Macintosh, the postman.[53] I have been trying all summer to speak with that learned but extremely shy man, it seemed stupid to take home the drawings without having shown them to him.

Accordingly by appointment he came, with his soft hat, a walking stick, a little bundle, and very dirty boots, at five o'clock to the minute. He was quite painfully shy and uncouth at first, as though he was trying to swallow a muffin, and rolling his eyes about and mumbling.

He was certainly pleased with my drawings, and his judgement speaking to their accuracy in minute botanical points gave me infinitely more pleasure than that of critics who assume more, and know less than poor Charlie. He is a perfect dragon of erudition, and not gardener's Latin either.

He had not been doing much amongst the moss lately he said

modestly, he was 'studying slimes', fresh water algae. I asked him to sit down, his head being somewhere in the chandelier. I would not make fun of him for worlds, but he reminded me so much of a damaged lamp post. He warmed up to his favourite subject, his comments terse and to the point, and conscientiously accurate as befitted a correspondent of the scholarly Mr Barclay of Glamis.

When we discussed funguses he became quite excited and spoke with quite poetical feeling about their exquisite colours. He promised to send me some through the post, though I very much fear he will never have sufficient assurance to post them, but his mouth evidently watered at the chance of securing drawings, he had even tried himself in a small way, also drawing them, and dived into the hall abruptly, bringing back a sort of pocket-book tied up with string.

Now of all hopeless things to draw, I should think the very worst is a fine fat fungus, and of course they had lost their colour, but by dint of slicing, scraping and sections, they were surprisingly passable, and as the work of a one-handed man, a real monument of perseverance.

I happened by lucky intuition to have drawn several rare species. One with white spikes on the lower side he had discovered this summer for the first time in a wood at Murthly, and another, like a spluttered candle, he had found just once in the grass at the road-side near Inver tunnel. He had had opportunity of study without end in his long, damp walks. I suppose when no one was in sight, which would be the case in four-fifths of his fifteen daily miles.

When one met him, a more scared startled scarecrow it would be difficult to imagine. Very tall and thin, stooping with a weak chest, one arm swinging and the walking-stick much too short, hanging to the stump with a loop, a long wisp of whisker blowing over either shoulder, a drip from his hat and his nose, watery eyes fixed on the puddles or anywhere, rather than any other traveller's face.

He was sometimes overheard to whistle, but never could be induced to say more than 'humph' as to the weather. There were times alas of cloudiness, but that you may say about ninety-nine out of the hundred inhabitants of any Highland Parish, and old hundredth, John the Minister.

It used to be an amusement to hop from puddle to puddle on the strides of Charlie's hob-nailed boots. I forget how many thousand miles he walked, some mathematical person reckoned it up. His successor has a tricycle: it will save his legs, but modern habits and machines are not calculated to bring out individuality or the study of Natural History.

Country postmen, at all events in Scotland, are almost always men of intelligence with some special study. Probably the result of much solitary thinking and observation. David Wood, Charlie's successor, is an entomologist and grows pansies.

Sunday, October 30th. I am ashamed to say I photographed in the wood. Perhaps it may have been atoned by an act of mercy after breakfast. When I was walking out Benjamin I saw Miss Hutton's black cat jumping on something up the wood. I thought it was too far off to interfere, but as it seemed leisurely I went up in time to rescue a poor little rabbit, fast in a snare.

The cat had not hurt it, but I had great difficulty in slackening the noose round its neck. I warmed it at the fire, relieved it from a number of fleas, and it came round. It was such a little poor creature compared to mine. They are regular vermin, but one cannot stand by to see a thing mauled about from one's friendship for the race. Papa in his indignation pulled up the snare. I fancy our actions were much more illegal than Miss Hutton's.

After dinner I was half amused, half shocked, to see her little niece Maggie hunting everywhere for the wire. I just had enough sense not to show the stranger to Benjamin Bounce, but the smell of its fur on my dress was quite enough to upset the ill-regulated passions of that excitable buck rabbit.

Whether he thought I had a rival in my pocket, or like a princess in a fairy tale was myself metamorphosed into a white rabbit I cannot say, but I had to lock him up.

Rabbits are creatures of warm volatile temperament but shallow and absurdly transparent. It is this naturalness, one touch of nature, that I find so delightful in Mr Benjamin Bunny, though I frankly admit his vulgarity. At one moment amiably sentimental to the verge of silliness, at the next, the upsetting of a jug or tea-cup which he immediately takes upon himself, will convert him into a demon, throwing himself on his back, scratching and spluttering.

If I can lay hold of him without being bitten, within half a minute he is licking my hands as though nothing has happened.

He is an abject coward, but believes in bluster, could stare our old dog out of countenance, chase a cat that has turned tail.

Benjamin once fell into an aquarium head first, and sat in the water which he could not get out of, pretending to eat a piece of string. Nothing like putting a face upon circumstances.

Monday, October 31st. Coming up by the coach-builder and under the railway for the last time, I watched a dipper or water-ousel diving in the stream. A handsome fellow, and curious to see a bird apparently of the thrush tribe and with unwebbed feet, take to the water like a diving duck.

It dived always up-stream in a rapid pool, did not use wings or feet as paddles, but I thought remained in the water as long as the force of its jump, opposed to the current, kept it suspended in one place. I dare say in a still pool it might have run on the bottom, I saw it bring out a worm. They have a sweet, low song and are said to poach much fish-spawn.

1893

'I don't know when I laughed so'

LONDON

Positively I will again keep a diary, I foresee larks, contingent on the opening of Parliament.

Tuesday, January 31st. A procession of unemployed, dogged and chivied by the police on the Embankment. Mr Gladstone drove to the House in an open carriage with Mrs Gladstone. What a vain old bird he is, and with what an appetite for tickling the Mob (as long as they are not in a procession).

One cannot imagine Lord Salisbury showing himself off. He carries a proper self-respect to rather the other extreme. His cold indifference to mere vulgar popularity is set down as cynicism to a greater extent than is deserved, for he is a kind and just Landlord in Hertfordshire.

Sunday, February 5th. I went to the Pagets somewhat guilty. This comes of borrowing other people's pets. Miss Paget has an infinite number of guinea-pigs. First I borrowed and drew Mr Chopps. I returned him safely. Then in an evil hour I borrowed a very particular guinea-pig with a long white ruff, known as Queen Elizabeth. This PIG – offspring of Titwillow the Second, descendant of the Sultan of Zanzibar, and distantly related to a still more illustrious animal named the Light of Asia – this wretched pig took to eating blotting paper, pasteboard, string and other curious substances, and expired in the night.

I suspected something was wrong and intended to take it back. My feelings may be imagined when I found it extended a damp – very damp disagreeable body. Miss Paget proved peaceable, I gave her the drawing.

Miss Rosalind Paget is something of a ghoul, in fact very much. After the cholera scare she had her box packed awaiting a telegram from the London Hospital where one-thousand isolated beds were prepared. It was very brave and noble, but she is quite candidly disappointed.

She and another nurse went to see *King Lear* and were edified and excited. They said it was such an 'admirable study of senile paralysis'. It made Miss Nina Paget nearly ill, which in a devout disciple I thought was a warning to a nervous person like myself.

Irving made some people laugh.[1] The Shakespearian Miss Rosalind is a comical example of a misfitting name, except that to be sure she would make a very passable gentleman.

Friday, March 3rd. I was at the Paget's one day last week. There was a stately lady calling, with polished manners. Lady Bligh (?), with a stately inclination of the head and surprise that anyone should take the trouble to 'dress' – did not Fanny Burney slip out of the parlour because she was not 'dressed' – in order to be presented to Princess Christian.[2]

Passing to politics, Lady Bligh admitted she was in low spirits, but – 'I am *told* that is unnecessary.' Mrs Paget who appeared to be slightly flighty that afternoon on the subject of Mr Gladstone, launched into a discussion as to what would have happened if Mrs Gladstone had not got over the influenza, and being further excited by strong tea, such sentences as 'a young man with whom my father would not have allowed me to dance' etc., but having heard scandal of that sort before, I thought it prudent to retire to the guinea-pigs.

There are not wanting persons who doubt whether the apostle of the Nonconformist conscience has always been respectable himself. Lady Bligh (?) honoured me with a bow as she went out. I was rather pleased with her, it does one good to see such old-fashioned *ton* and withal she seemed a sensible person.

Miss Paget mentioned a curious thing in connection with the newest fad of the County Council – Model Lodging Houses for men, where free breakfasts are provided, and all the newest conveniences, for a nominal rent. She says the charity organization East End Branches have actually thirty cases of deserted wives and families whose husbands had gone to live in the model dwellings.

I think there may be some exaggeration about the round number – thirty – but it may have a tithe of that number.

It is a curious commentary on the Council's political economy, Miss Paget is a member of the Hammersmith Branch, likely to be well informed, though not impartial to the two Councils.

TORQUAY

Tuesday, March 14th. We set off to Devonshire and Cornwall, the Osborne Hotel, Torquay. I didn't much want to go. I did not take to what I had seen of Torquay, and it is possible to see too much of Ada Smallfield.

I sniffed my bedroom on arrival, and for a few hours felt a certain grim satisfaction when my forebodings were maintained, but it is possible to have too much Natural History in a bed.

I did not undress after the first night, but I was obliged to lie on it because there were only two chairs and one of them was broken. It is very uncomfortable to sleep with Keating's powder in the hair. What is to be thought of people who recommend near relations to an hotel where there are bugs?

I also saw a very extraordinary creature for all the world like a hairy caterpillar but it hopped, perhaps it had some connection with a fine Tom cat which – but let us draw a veil under the soothing influence of these nocturnal discoveries, plus a very dirty table-cloth and insufficient food (always excepting the smell thereof which was super-abundant).

I listened to the voluminous local information of Miss Ada Smallfield with ill-disguised acerbity. She has a bowl of sea anemones nearly all of which she has *got* at Torquay. I found out afterwards she had bought them at the fishmongers. It is very indiscreet to act the cicerone so industriously.

I would not, flatly, go to the top of Dedry's Gap, and I didn't. There are only three almond trees in Torquay, I have seen them all and they are small ones. It is a very large town and of no interest as such. The suburbs of villas and gardens are pretty, but not so much so as Roehampton, and very steep walking.

I went one singular suburban drive with mamma, Miss Harrison and Miss Smallfield, past Anstey's Cove, curiously pretty but rather

too much of a show place, and through a most dreary suburb named
St Mary Church to Babbacombe whence there is a wonderful coast
view like a balloon or the top of the Monument, the leading interest
down below being the site of the Babbacombe murder.

I was so disgusted with my drive that I privately incited papa to
going into Kent's Hole next morning by way of a reviver. We slunk
out after breakfast, Miss Smallfield who was not an early bird was
seen to throw open a window on the third floor, but we got away
through the bushes.

We afterwards lost our way which was a judgement. Indeed, I can
imagine no more unlikely or unromantic situation for a cavern. It
is in a suburb of Torquay, half way up a tangled bluff, with villas
and gardens overhanging the top of a muddy orchard and some
filthily dirty cows in the ravine below. I was pretty much exhausted
when we found it, but by dint of eating cinnamon and the
excitement of going into a cave, recovered. We had walked over-
fast for fear of pursuit.

The dilapidated wooden door was flush into the bank. Outside an
artificial plateau or spoil-bank of slate, overgrown. A donkey-cart
was encamped and the donkey grazing, the owner a mild, light-
haired young man was sawing planks.

Papa inquired if there was anybody here? to which he replied
with asperity '*I* am,' put on his coat and prepared to unlock the
cavern. The donkey was apparently trustworthy, at least it was there
when we came out.

The proprietor (I have already forgotten his name, which I regret,
for he amused me), hung a notice-board on a nail outside the door,
to the effect that the guide is at present inside the cavern, and
scrubbed out certain derisive remarks which had been scratched on
the portal during his last descent.

He locked again as soon as we were inside. His act of possession
was very funny. I implored him to take a good supply of matches.
There was a quantity of gingerbeer in a nice cool place, also an
umbrella stand. I shall not go into details about the cave, which is
well described in a pamphlet, and only remark it is very easy to
explore and only moderately damp. Papa got dirty enough in all
conscience, slipping off a board into the sticky red clay. I was
puzzled by one feature which I took to be geological, but was in fact
the dripping of innumerable candles.

When we had done the longest branch, perhaps one-eighth of a mile into the hill, and came back in sight of the door up above us, there was a shuffling of feet and voices audible, and the guide admitted another party, a lady and some children and a spaniel like Spot.

I don't know when I laughed so. The children were bad enough, but the dog was an anxiety, nothing but 'Jack, Jack, Jack.' At one point it disappeared and was presently heard to sneeze feebly in the hyaena's den. Considering the existence of trap doors to a lower cavern, I hope that nice dog did not come to a bad end.

It was a funny sight to see the little old-fashioned boy and his sister, each with a dripping candle, on tip-toe on a block of stalagmite, solemnly examining the skull of a cave-bear embedded in the low roof.

Papa who had been in the Peak Cavern was not much impressed, but I who had never been in a cave was extremely interested. I was surprised afterwards to have been so little awestruck. I expected to have met the ghost of a hippopotamus, but felt no creepiness at all.

The age of the cavern is so vast that it passes the comprehension of an ordinary mind, and I brought away a less vivid impression of geological antiquity than that of historical, dating back to the insignificant period of 1690, when O. F. Ireland chipped his name. There it stands, sharply cut and apparently scarcely coated with glaze, and within a few yards is a stalagmite, five feet high. The cave then came before the stalagmite.

FALMOUTH

Friday, March 17th. to the end of April. Went to Falmouth on 17th. Comfort to get a clean bed, and the people civil, remembering us from last year, including Mr Winter the head waiter who was endeavouring to rear the very smallest size of *buttons*, 'Where is that boy?' I distinctly saw him with his fingers in the marmalade one night after tea, also standing on one leg examining his shoe over his back during table d'hôte.

Mr Smith, the driver, was also obliging, and we had some delightful drives and steamer trips. The weather was splendid, and some of us were tempted to do more than we could manage. The sea was rather rough at first and broke the shells, but I got some I had not found before.

The queerest aquatic thing I saw was a submarine perambulator. We were photographing at the Helford river when up came a little stumpy boy and said 'Hullo!' Papa made a suitable reply, and the youth announced 'My name is John William Wandle.' He went on to talk very fast and thick. The children speak a dialect not understandable of strangers.

Five or six of them, the eldest not above ten, had let a bassinette perambulator over a steep bank into the sea, and there it stood naturally on its wheels amongst the sea weed down below the clear green water. We could not make out what had become of the baby, but it was not in the perambulator. There seemed to be no excitement, so I suppose it would be left when the tide receded, but it would be damp sitting.

1894

'. . . we got dirty to our heart's content'

HARESCOMBE GRANGE, STROUD[1]

I went to Harescombe on Tuesday the 12th. of June. I used to go
to my grandmother's, and once I went for a week to Manchester,
but I had not been away independently for five years. It was an
event.

It was so much of an event in the eyes of my relations that they
made it appear an undertaking to me, and I began to think I would
rather not go. I had a sick headache most inopportunely, though
whether cause or effect I could not say, but it would have decided
the fate of my invitation but for Caroline, who carried me off.[2]

I travelled with her from Paddington. She had a second-class
return. There was no one else in the compartment. There was dust
and a smell of beanfields. She had a cough, we talked. We ranged
over universal subjects and became indiscreet before reaching
Swindon, also very hoarse, and had several flat differences of
opinion.

She had on a hat with rosebuds in it, and a benevolent elderly
guard took a most kindly interest in her. I thought she had seen him
before, but she hadn't.

We tumbled out at Stroud with our parcels. Caroline's luggage
was found to comprehend numerous bandboxes, big and bulged.
She resigned them to fate, but judiciously distributed sixpences,
and we got into a very large open fly, after she had examined the
horse, a black hearse horse with a tail, very slow but fat. Caroline
disapproved of starved horses.

Stroud is all up and down hill, a straggling country town, devoted
to brewers and some dye works. We soon got out on to a steep
country road, pervaded by a smell of beanfields and mown hay.

Down in the valley we saw several grey stone mills with gables and little round windows, the mark of the Flemish weavers who settled here in the days of the Duke of Alva. Few, if any, are working now, unless as saw-mills, but in some there is the mark of the machinery and there is Sam Fluck in Harescombe.

Caroline jumped out at the beginning of the hill up to Pitch-combe, I was not sorry to sit still and watch her walk. She had on a dark-red dress which never appeared again, with rather a neat jacket and a skirt not too long. How she did walk up the hill! As upright as a bolt, with longish firm steps, and yet within the length like a soldier who has been drilled. She questioned the driver about his horse half way up the long hill, and jumped in again at the top without stopping the carriage.

They were carting hay in a queer long cart at the farm below Edge Common, then there were roses and gardens, and all at once the view.

The house is just over the top of the hill, and we were at the lodge as I was just beginning to grow uncomfortable. There was no one at the door, Caroline out at the wrong side in a minute, and directly afterwards Mrs Hutton.

I think we looked at each other with some curiosity: I can only say I liked her so well from the first, I can only hope she was pleased. She is like Caroline without the Hutton part of Caroline's nature, to put it the wrong way round. I don't think I ever became so completely fond of any one in so short a time.

An extremely sweet, placid temper, incapable of being ruffled, rather silent or shyly reserved, but with a most merry enjoyment at anything humorous, observant of things in general, and apparently very learned in her own lines, with tact amongst her own family and benevolent interest towards strangers. Capable of directing, yet unquestioning under direction, able to talk and able to be silent, always amiable and never dull. I cannot imagine a disposition more sweet.

It is well in this world to discover there can exist a young woman, clever, brilliantly attractive and perfectly well principled, although knowing her own mind, but I cannot help thinking I would sink the whole lump of independence to have anyone so deservedly fond of me as Mr Hutton is of *Sophy*.

When I have said that I have spoken of the only flaw that I can find in Caroline. Latter day fate ordains that many women shall be unmarried and self-contained, nor should I personally dream to complain, but I hold an old-fashioned notion that a happy marriage is the crown of a woman's life, and that it is unwise on the part of a nice-looking young lady to proclaim a pronounced dislike of babies and all child cousins. Almost as unadvised as the remark of Miss Ida Webb, overheard at a garden party, who hoped she would have a large family, it would be so interesting to bring them up.

Altogether I share the curiosity of Mr Knightley in wondering what will become of 'Emma'. It would seem unlikely that she could escape matrimony. Did she not belong to a family of old maids: mankind may be thankful that she is too honest to make them her game. She is so completely self-possessed as to be a little unobservant of feeling in others, and may do mischief unwittingly like a kitten. It will be an amusing spectacle if she should be lured herself. I shall then remember with even more amusement, the little jump and merry 'me thank goodness,' when I wound up an analytical discussion of the passions, by suggesting that Caroline had clearly never been caught.

There was a neighbour, a Mrs Lucy, came to tea, rather a handsome old lady with a deep voice and very deaf. She was taking leave of the neighbourhood, and gave a humourous account of her future residence in Tunbridge Wells, very waggish, but probably forced. She had just sold her Brougham to an inn-keeper at Gloucester who said it would do for a Mourning-coach if it were done up.

Mr Hutton came in and embraced Caroline, and regarded me critically through his spectacles. He had on large gaiters and seemed hungry. He addressed monosyllables to Mrs Lucy, and gave evidence of deafness.

I had heard of him by universal report as an austere man. I had to take his arm in to dinner, not much encouraged by his scrutiny of my puff-sleeves. His quizzical habit is made more noticeable by the little wrinkles round his eyes and frowning through his spectacles, but it is not apparent only; for next day there came to tea a Mrs Dickinson, rather nice looking, of whom he did not take especial notice, but after she left described everything she had on.

I was luckily prepared for his saying grace. Caroline flopped down, one of those things which Mrs Hutton does not observe. I was a little shocked with Caroline, but on one night Mr Hutton,

being in conversation, sat down himself and suddenly remembered
during the gravy. He says grace only at dinner, and prayers only on
Sunday night. Goes to church once on Sunday, reads the lessons
and sleeps regularly during the sermon, and afterwards discusses
the historical aspects of the Athanasian Creed with an open mind.

Whether Mrs Hutton's placidity is so deep-seated as to enable her
to listen with inward as well as outward composure I could not
quite determine. She is Church, very mildly so, but devout. Poor
Mary is next in piety, alternatively shaken up by Caroline, and
falling back upon Kingdom Come. There is no kindness in putting
doubts in the mind of one who is for this world unfortunate.

Mr Hutton is, I imagine, entirely unemotional, utilitarian and
practical in his religion. He considers the Creed of St Athanasius
was an admirable fighting invention and is now a document of
historical interest.

I never talked about religion before, and have too little command
of English to make much of an argument. Caroline kept returning
to the charge, and got more courage when I discovered that with all
her cleverness she could not understand why I enjoyed the service
in Gloucester Cathedral.

I did not profess to care about music, and I did not believe in the
Church service, and I could not hear a word they said, and why was
I uncomfortable in the crypt?, and there was Caroline on into the
night in her dressing-gown with her hair about her ears, her honest
grey eyes round in the candle light, all in a splutter, with metaphysics, political economy, and trying to understand. I don't
understand metaphysics, but I thought Caroline was transparent.

Then we got under the venetian blind to watch the fires in the
forest, coal villages amongst the woods, and then looked across to
Stockend Woods under the shadow of Haresfield Beacon. Caroline
talked of labourers, their miserable wages of eleven shillings a week,
their unsanitary cottages, their appalling families and improvidence.
All with feeling and sense, and a refreshing unconsciousness of the
world's obstinacy and difficulties, always with common sense and
courage. Such a funny mixture of old-fashioned wisdom and the
unreasoning fearlessness of a child, 'like one that in a lonely road
doth walk in fear and dread'.

Caroline is the very anti of that: on the solitary green roads over
the hills, or in the London streets, she is absolutely fearless, strong

in innocence as in triple-mail. She is perhaps rather young in experience, twenty-three, to be trusted so much alone, but she has in many respects a strong self-reliant disposition and plenty of commonsense, and certainly in the neighbourhood of Stroud, 'Hutton of Harescombe' backed by the Police, may well be a name to inspire respect.

Mr Hutton spent the following day, Wed. 13th., in chivying a family of gypsies, females, assisted by a constable named Dobbs, and communicating by telegraph with other policemen.

I should think he knows the name of every policeman in the county. One named Curley was highly commended for the capture of a male gypsy, whom he was taking for seven days at Gloucester Jail for begging. The offence of present interlopers was refusing to show Hawker's Licences, refusal to tell their name *Biron Royal*, and one stout female standing against the shaft to conceal the same, but Mr Hutton riding round astutely from behind the cart read it. Also they had three pups eight months old without a licence, and defiantly refused to buy one.

Dobbs suggested the Summons might be taken out and be ready for them when next they came on their round. 'We know your Common, we shan't go to your Common.' All of which Mr Hutton described at lunch with much dry complacency, and went to the Common, at the edge of dark, and seemed quite disappointed that they were not there. The very mention of gypsies excited him.

One day certain black objects appeared on the crest of the opposite hill, but proved to be cattle. I was reminded of Miss Copperfield and the donkey-boys.

A day or two later there was a diversion, Mr Seddon reported that certain squatters had had a drinking bout on Sunday in a cottage at Stockend. It was a question whether coin had passed and whether it could be proved. Even Mr Hutton's ingenuity was baffled.

In spite of this general supervision he is not a very active magistrate, it is more a matter of meddling in small things. Called in one day to whip a naughty boy at the request of the youth's father, he whipped him on the legs, but at the third cut he unluckily wriggled away. He extracts shillings from boys who set fire to the Common, and hands the money over to Mr Seddon the clergyman.[3]

He is much in the habit of telling stories in a deliciously dry manner of the county-court judge days. 'The scripture saith that all things have an end, but I was beginning to doubt it during Mr so and so's speech.' His family laugh dutifully at his jokes, and the girls take him to task for carving badly, and contradict him unmercifully.

Mrs Hutton listens most affectionately, and drinks Lithia water at dinner. Mr Hutton takes magnesia. Sometimes Jones gets the bottles mixed, then Mr Hutton gets up cautiously to exchange the bottles, and he removes his plate and the dishes, and in every way spares the stout red-faced Jones.

He will not ring for a servant in any consideration. He is indulgent to his tenants and very affectionate in a way amongst his family. Testy occasionally over small matters, but a kind master.

I began by being much afraid of him, and was under cross-examination the whole time, but I soon came to the conclusion he is one of the kindest of old gentlemen, and certainly a character. He called me 'my dear' on Friday, and kissed me with the rest of the family when he went away.

I could not help speculating how many lies I had told him, for he required sudden answers to unexpected questions, and moreover they had to be shouted. He was, I suppose from habit, exceedingly inquisitive. One question which nearly overset me was whether my mother brushed her own hair. This was levied at her servants, Lancashire servants, the history and duties of each of our domestics, and had we a maid? Now I fortunately did not say so, but my mother's hair takes off.

He is much in the habit of quoting Shakespeare, and expects people to be acquainted with what he quotes, also sentimental poetry, and law. It is not very respectful to dissect one's host, but I certainly think he applied the process to me.

I went out in the morning with Caroline into the copse at the back of the house, a steep wooded bank. It had been wet overnight and we got dirty to our heart's content.

I was extremely interested with the badger's marks and their claw-walks, worn bare and slippery underneath the nettles and brush, but could judge they were made by a large stumpy animal, and the size of their footsteps is quite startling in an English wood.

Caroline said that she had never succeeded in seeing one during the fifteen years that they have lived at Harescombe, yet we saw their tracks in a lane a mile from the Earths. The latter are curious, struck out by the hind legs like a rabbit's hole, but a square piled-up bank like the spoil-banks in front of a coalpit. We found some curious snails, and poked about delightfully.

After tea we went down to Harescombe, down some very steep fields, so steep that Caroline pulled me up again with a walking stick. There is a very little old church at the bottom with a curious belfry and a handsome Saxon font, rescued from a ditch.

The thing that struck me most was the number of elaborately carved gravestones in the long grass, and the little scratched figure of a Jackman in trunk hose with a halberd, which some idle person had scratched on the door lintel, and on the opposite stone the head and long neck of a medieval lady with her hair in side-cushions like Cinderella's proud sister.

There was a great iron sanctuary-ring on the oak door. A few yards further on in an orchard, under gigantic Perry pear trees, were some mounds in the deep green turf, all that is left of a stronghold of the de Bohuns. There was the remains of a moat, but we could not go into the meadow because of a great roan bull feeding quietly with some fine cows.

We passed one of the old mills where the wheel is still standing, passed the honeysuckle and rose-covered cottage of Sam Fluck the descendant of the Flemish weavers, up a muddy lane under high hedges and elm trees, where little Perry pears fall off into the black mud, and pretty cottage children ducked sudden curtseys to Miss Hutton, past two cross-beamed cottages, to a large farm where there were turkey-poults, and a lean cat who made friends with Caroline to the amusement of two of the farm labourers straggling home.

I thought the young men were rather fine looking, and some of the young women pretty, but they wear badly, poor wages, and I should say unhealthy in the combes. Cases of goitre occur.

We got as far as Hayes Farm the object of our walk, a very large old gabled limestone building, with stone mullioned windows and picturesque chimneys.

The farmhouses in this neighbourhood seem all to have been built about the same time, the latter part of the sixteenth century, and are surprisingly large. Many of them have the feature of a terrace, or at all events a terrace-wall with steps to the gate in the centre.

At Hayes Farm there were red snapdragons growing up the side between the stones. There was a striking scathed oak tree in the field beyond, but I was getting anxious about the hill between us and home. It was a lovely peaceful evening, such long shadows from the elm trees on the grass.

I wrote this much, soon after I came home, but being busy, laid it aside and can now only piece out from a rough note, which I am sorry for, for a diary, however private, brings back distinctly the memory of what in this case seemed like a most pleasant dream.

LENNEL, COLDSTREAM

Tuesday, July 17th. Came to Lennel, Coldstream, on Tues. July 17th. 94. Left King's Cross ten in morning, got in about seven, after much slow shunting at Tweedmouth.

The house large, rambling, roundabout, and not over clean according to the servants, but sanitation good, and standing high.

A perfectly awful garden full of broken bottles, rats and piebald rabbits, but much honeysuckle, briar and Lancaster roses among the weeds, and a splendid view over the valley to the Cheviot Hills. My father groaned intolerably about the untidiness for several days. If I can form an independent opinion I am disposed to like the place, and it is delicious fresh air.

Sunday, July 22nd. Very hot. Sat on a wall all afternoon and sketched the river. I think it is a very beautiful stream and grows upon one. There is no impressive volume of water like the Tay, but it winds about in a sweet fashion, setting the meadows now on the north, now on the south and reflecting cliffs and trees in the deeper reaches. All along the field edges there are strips of pebbles, many coloured, and a shelf of sandbank under the turf where sandmartins burrow. There are stockades of planks here and there, and the tangled grass in the trees shows what the flood can do in its time.

At present it is very low, a mere ripple of water over the Ford below Lennel village. The Scotch riders are said to have crossed that point to drive the English cattle, it is almost too peaceful now to accord with salmon nets.

I was so fortunate as to see them take a grilse.[4] It was very exciting but not a fair fight for the fish. We sat on the north bank in the dusk and watched them drag up two boats from the next station, a shieling with a yard staked for the wet nets. They dragged the flat-bottomed, sharp-prowed boats up the stream, an old fellow in waders going in to push at the ford. Three other men, one with a club-foot.

One man composed himself at the top of a rough wooden ladder, the other three lit their pipes and sat on the bank some thirty yards higher near the boat. The man on the ladder watches the shallows intently. How he can keep his mind on it I wonder, the present take being only two or three fish during a night.

They fish by moonlight. It does not, of course, pay, but the gamekeeper said he had seen twenty salmon at a haul. In this instance there was a doubtful cry of 'boat' within five minutes, and at a second louder cry the men rushed at the boat, and the watcher came down headlong. The old fellow rowed out quickly, the net gliding out over the stern of the boat. When half way across he turned down.

The salmon follows the stream at the south side, and as soon as the old man had met and passed it there was a shout of 'home', and he pulled frantically ashore. The net was dragged in on the shingle considerably below the point where the salmon was surrounded, but they seemed under no apprehension of losing it, though it splashed. It is not sport, but after all less cruel than the gaff. It was a silver grilse about 4 lb. It was caught on Monday, not the sabbath, but they are sufficiently near the border to scare crows with a gun on Sunday.

Monday, July 23rd. Photographed in the afternoon, excessively hot. Pretty sheep in the meadows, very tame, but I believe the property of Mr Lilicoe the butcher. What a curious reflection it is, that every lamb which is born, is born to have its throat cut. In the meantime they lie in the sun under the sandbank and sneeze defiantly at the camera.

Friday, July 27th. Discovery of bugs in back premises, an event which overshadoweth all things else, but I believe I went for a drive up the Duns road.

★

Wednesday, August 1st. Started with papa to go towards Swinton, very lowering and obliged to turn back. The roads are singularly quiet and well kept. At one point we overtook a troop of farm-labourers, perhaps twenty men and half a dozen women, coming away from hoeing turnips.

Some of the men are immensely tall stout fellows. The women are dark and on the whole good-looking. A type with dark eyes, sunburnt complexions and white teeth. Their dress in the fields is in this wise peculiar, that it is impossible to say without peeping under their sun-bonnets and pink handkerchiefs whether it is an old woman or a young girl. My father was rather taken aback, on passing the time of day to one whom we overtook, to see her turn round the face of a child.

There is a funny specimen in the village, apparently the property of lodgers, a pretty little imp of eight or nine with yellow curls, in the neatest of little blue and pink combination knickerbockers riding a bicycle. A very tippity-twitchit. It is indeed the thin edge of the wedge if children grow up to them. I herewith record my conviction that we are at the edge of the reign of knickerbockers, a very different matter to the bloomer mania which excited Mr Punch.

The weak point of that fad, and of the divided skirts, was the endeavour to assert that they 'didn't show', and ought to be worn universally and on all occasions. To wear knickerbockers with more or less overskirt, frankly as a gymnastic costume, for cycling or other more or less masculine amusement is a different matter, and whether desirable or not has a definite reason, and I shall be much surprised if, within a very few years, a lady cannot appear in them without exciting hostile comment.

The only specimen I noticed before leaving town, on a bicycle in the High Street, did not look so queer as might have been expected. On the other hand I heard reported a stout middle-aged lady in green trousers with straps under her boots. Also the pioneers of the movement parade in procession smoking cigars. There is no custom that is not liable to abuse, but if females go in for gymnastics, wherein I include the stiles of this country, they should wear the costume. In my opinion they make all the difference in the world in the comfort of scrambling, but are hot.

★

Tuesday, August 7th. To Alnwick with papa, much interested with the journey through the Cheviots, North Britain, Kirknewton the point for hills, Yeavering Bell. Also rather good collection of stuffed birds in signalbox.

The Bowmont is a fine stream. The stream at Wooler and others in that part are horrid, torrent-beds of bare stones. Very fine, wild country at Edlingham, a ruined town near station and fine crags. Very steep line in loops. Remarkably good stations, whence they cultivate tomatoes in plots in the waiting room.

Alnwick itself some very old houses, wide cobbled streets and Market-place. Castle very large, and resembling Carlton Jail, so very bare as seen from park. The entrance striking with its black, dark gateway, and the odd statues on the battlements in quaint threatening attitudes.

There was a most absurd elderly lady got in at Wooler, a little off her balance, but luckily accompanied by a stout country maid 'Jane'. I was sorry for Jane, she was so extremely embarrassed and kept bringing things out of her bag and fiddling to break the flow of the old lady's indiscreet conversation.

She seemed a clever, amiable old lady, and when she spoke to the Stationmaster or papa (at which point Jane's face was a study), she spoke very pleasantly, but her prattle to herself, or Jane, caused papa to look out of the window occasionally. It was unfortunately too gossipy to be of interest, except the description of a blizzard in New York when she had her petticoats blown off.

She had reddish hair, was arrayed in a bundle of crêpe and bombasine, but had well appointed luggage and kept her feet jealously on her *dispatch box*. She appeared incapable of holding her tongue or her limbs, which I rather misliked when there was a tunnel.

Thursday, August 9th. Thurs. 9th. was devoted to violent showers and the Coldstream Sports, which proved most amusing, but I did not go after dinner luckily, for there was a thunderstorm and torrents of rain, which bogged the heavy oats woefully.

In the morning there was a Regatta, in the pool above Coldstream Bridge. First for youths swimming, very shivery, and then the small boys, which caused shrieks and shrill shouts from the younger spectators. The two leading boys got mixed up and began to claw each other, coming in last.

Obstruction seemed to be the great object also in the boat-races, six or seven heats, two or three boats each time. The skill consisted in running the opponent on to the shingle opposite the marshbank's column, and if possible getting the prow of his boat against your stern, so that the more he rows the faster you are propelled.

The boats sometimes got locked nose-to-nose when rounding the barrel, and the competitors occasionally dropped their oars to push and shove. When it comes to propelling with your oar against the opponent's broad back there is a certain probability of temper, but the fun to the spectators is uproarious.

I thought the match was unfair in one respect, as a certain blue-painted new boat won about five times in six, but possibly that may have been part of the game if the fishermen reward the boats of their respective stations. Mr Turnbull and family walked about in state. The racing was confined to the fishermen and tradespeople. One race in which an elderly, bald tailor rowed away from two shoemaker's apprentices caused much excitement. The old men's race was rowed *down* the course only, and won by Mr Scott whose age I did not hear, but he was a great-grandfather, a fine old fellow.

The company was very broad Scotch and very amusing, not in the very least degree rough at this stage, there being a large sprinkling of comfortable old farmers with their stout wives in bonnets in the height of good temper, 'just delightful to view', and auntie Grizzy and Miss Charlotte strangely rigged out, and commending the weather till it absolutely rained.

The babies sat at the top of the cliff and there were dog-fights, the leading warrior being an awful terrier from the Newcastle Arms with a head as large as a wild boar. The farm-family whom I sat beside had a fox-terrier Snip, which Miss Nicky choked periodically with the hoop-handle of her umbrella. She and a nice fat girl sat flat on the edge of the cliff, to the terror of the elder part of the family who were too far back, standing perched on the wall, to see the nature of the slope, 'Eh woman, be careful, it makes my head skirl to luik at ye!'

It was as well the old farmer should stand back, for he fairly danced on his perch shrieking 'It's a fool! its a fool!' when the boats collided. There was a stampede to the wall on the arrival of the Kelsie Band, nine trumpets and two drums, who played The Bonnie Woods of Craigelee very sweetly, and five other tunes.

I was also amused with two holiday mill-hands, one of whom would aye live in the country, and thought Caw'sram was a bonny place, 'I think it aye bonnie every time I see't' – but the other lass said 'It was no to compear wie Newcastle where we hey a park wi seats! and theatres', whereon the other lassie, very quietly, 'she never went into one'. Blessed are they that are contented.

I know few more striking views than from the High-Level Bridge at Newcastle on a starlight night – or a glimpse of moonlight through the smoke, for the stars are down below along the quays.

Saturday, August 11th. We drove to Ford,⁵ up and down through Crookham, much puzzled by the inability of Northumbrians to pronounce the letter 'R'. It is remarkable what a real division the Border is here, the people talk broader Scotch at Coldstream than at Dunkeld, and yet at their railway station, Cornhill, a mile south of the Bridge, they are English, queer English to understand, but emphatically not Scotch, nor in prejudices and religion. I am told the exception is Wark, which speaks Scotch for some reason.

Ford village exasperated me in a way that was somewhat silly, but I hope never to see another village where they do not keep cocks and hens. I am not clear whether children are allowed except in perambulators and under control, but there was a peacock stalking about.

The walks are laid with red dust, the little grassplot shaved and trimmed, the trees trimmed, the door steps whitened. I do not know whether the inhabitants are permitted to empty out soapsuds from the back windows, but I wonder anyone can be induced to live there. If I did, I should let loose a parcel of sighs.

If they had been Almshouses it would have been very quaint, but applied to a live north country village it provoked feelings of the Radical in my mind. I did not think the taste was absolutely perfect either, for instance, the stone moulding of a Smithy door in the shape of a horse-shoe. Now a cat-hole in a barn is properly round, but when applied to a door intended for the use of horse or man, it shows a lack of that appreciation of the fitness of things which is the soul of artistic taste.

Thursday, August 16th. Up a long, straight road towards Mindrum, turning near Downham Station. I got behind a flock of lambs, and was delayed going up till an impatient baker came up and insisted on a passage. Large rolled stones in a hedgerow near East Learmouth.

I thought, looking up at some of the larger, overshadowing *Druths*, here larger and tumultuous and the lane crossing under their lea, I had a sudden imagination of the towering, resistless ice, piled as high as the clouds above me, grinding over the top of the Cheviots, swaying round it as the current sways round a stone under water.

Whether it is that one has not previously considered geology, or that there is a sense of awful power in the track of the ice, I don't know, but I think the view looking from the spurs of the Cheviots across the wide strath to the Lammermoors is magnificent. Some people call the hills lumpy, but to see a mass like Dunslaw rounded as though a lump of clay, is more impressive than a Highland crag which has come down by frost and the laws of gravitation.

Saturday, August 18th. Went again to the wood near Hatchednize suspecting funguses from the climate, and was rewarded, what should be an ideal heavenly dream of the toadstool eaters.

The wood is insignificant on to the road, a few yards of beeches and old brush, but spreads at the back of the fields into an undreamed wilderness full of black firs. There was a sort of grass track, or I should have been afraid of losing my bearing amongst the green fogginess and tangle. There were wild privet bushes and much tangle.

The fungus starred the ground apparently in thousands, a dozen sorts in sight at once, and such specimens, which I have noted before in this neighbourhood. I found upwards of twenty sorts in a few minutes, *Cortinarius* and the handsome *Lactarius deliciosus* being conspicuous, and joy of joys, the spiky *Gomphidius glutinosus*, a round, slimy, purple head among the moss, which I took up carefully with my old cheese-knife, and turning over saw the slimy veil. There is extreme complacency in finding a totally new species for the first time.

Tuesday, September 4th. In the afternoon a long, delightful but withal anxious voyage over the table-land above Wark and Carham. Went up by West Learmouth, noting a number of sea-fowl and a heron standing up to his thighs in a pool. Turned up to the left after passing the queer, solitary little penfold with its greys, I immediately came upon a long, solitary stretch of road.

The road could not be said to be bad, apart from grass, and we toiled on manfully, up a most fearful hill to Pressen, where I discovered I had gone wrong if I had any intention of getting into the Mindrum road. I felt disinclined to go back down the hill, and moreover a stream at its foot was rather deeper than at first expected.

We forded about four streams, and there were most magnificent views, but I don't like the sort of road which becomes indeterminately broad on the boulder of a hill, it is a direct invitation to the steed to turn round, but happily appealed in vain to the immaculate Nelly who descended the mountains of the harvest moon with singular gravity and caution, and spun merrily home along the flat, high road.

A shock-headed reaper, a lad with a red head and a reaping-hook twisted round with straw, was sitting under a hedge. I asked if it was the road to Carham, and he replied in a shy mild voice that it was a fine day, and, after repeated enquiries, that he didn't know. I was not a little amused to hear such soft sweet talking from such an unpromising appearance.

I understand that there is a habit here of bargaining with the tramping reapers at so much an acre of corn, a good plan for the farmer when weather is uncertain. I heard of a dispute between the farmer's offer of sixteen shillings and the reaper's demand of twenty-one shillings, I don't know what was the final rate or how many men were on the job. The large farms are probably independent of tramp labour.

When we got near Wark Common we met a troop of labourers going to a field. They seem almost always to walk separately and very silently, the men in front. They stared a good deal, the lasses with mild enquiring eyes, like cows. They are uncommonly handsome, as far as can be seen, in their curious headgear, invariably a pink, check-handkerchief round the face and shoulders like a nun's wimple, and black, straw, mushroom hats lined with red, which throws a pink shadow on the face, though I suspect the complexion needs no external help. They all wear blue aprons and very short petticoats.

I got over a narrow, steep bridge near Sunilaws station, and was relieved by the sight of the well-known postman with Coldstream on the bands. The road came down opposite Carham Hall. All along to Wark the high road was littered with barley-corn in sluttish plenty, corn is not worth gleaning except with a horse-rake. What fields and fields of barley on the solitary uplands!

The sun came out very warm and pleasing as I was driving home. The prettiest sight was the coneys[6] at Wark, the timid people who live in the hedge on the side of the kaim and scoop out the white river gravel. They were sitting all along the bridge in the evening sunlight, fifty or sixty of them, a garrison in keeping with the Castle.

Monday, September 10th. To Berwick, very hot, almost too brightly glaring. We went after dinner, which is not a good thing, as there is less stirring among the fishers, and on this day, the tide being down, the seaweed smelled in the sun.

Mamma and I went down to the beach, getting astray on the grassy ramparts up above where there were washerwomen spreading out clothes, and people sitting on the grass in the hot glow. Down on the beach the smell of the seaweed soon drove us away.

It was cloudless, and the harbour like burnished gold looking back from the breakwater, and some abominable persons in a boat shooting gulls. The birds were provokingly tame or stupid, wheeling round and round. I saw a flock of little snipe startled by the gun, but the shooting was neither gastronomic nor scientific, but at large, as fast as he could load, and a black retriever tearing across the mud. I have seldom felt more thoroughly irritated.

I was glad to get back to Berwick station and a cup of tea. We seem fated to dawdle away a good deal of time in that somewhat dilapidated erection, but a station on the main line is never uninteresting. A train was waiting, and I looked vaguely up and down for Caroline Hutton who was probably travelling by the East Coast, and moreover this train was going south when it went.

I never saw anything more beautiful than the golden haze over the sea, and the bridges and little red roofs. Inland, the cornfields and woods steeped in gold which grew softer and dimmer as we approached Cornhill, and great flocks of starlings, like a cloud, whirred up from the stubble and slid along the tops of the woods.

★

Tuesday, September 11th. I must confess to having been in an excessively bad temper being rather tired and very much vexed that I could not have the Hutton girls. There is only one spare bedroom, and that so dirty that no one will sleep therein (*experto crede*),[7] but the sting of my annoyance was the knowledge that this was regarded as a convenient excuse. I am afraid that it would have resulted in rubs, but I would so very much have liked to have Caroline, and I am afraid they rather expected to be asked.

I was also today much provoked because my mother will not order the carriage in the morning or make up her mind, and if I say I should like to go out after lunch I am keeping her in, and if she does not go and I have missed the chance of a long drive, it is provoking.

Wednesday, September 12th. When passing Twizel in the train I saw an absurd sight, a black cat and a hedgehog in a field. The cat was retreating, lifting its paws up, but turned and again approached the enemy with its tail on end. I should very much have liked to see the next round. It was a very large hedgehog and quite unconcerned.

Thursday, September 20th. Some of the small children in the village with great solemnity reported this strange circumstance – 'That Bob Turnbull had found a baby in the Rockingwell (a dipping cliff two miles down the river), a very little one, and he'd taken it home and kept it!' I should like to know whether this euphonious legend was a spontaneous invention of Mr Turnbull's, or a last flickering gleam of the worship of the Scandinavian goddess Friga Holda of the Well, Frau Holt, the gracious house-mother, good wife of the spinning-wheel, and the gossamer threads that she hangs on the rose bushes on autumn mornings and bleaches on the grass. Hers by right is the round Catherine window at Dryburgh Abbey, taken over by the monks to the service of their ascetic saints, whose reign has come and gone in this land of sheep.

Are not the little white lambs that lie round the sun mother Holda's flocks?, as the wild grey clouds that race before the west wind are the Horses of Woden and Thor, in realms that still reverence the stork and the ladybird, and where childhood clings to the cult of Red Riding-hood and Puss-in-boots?

★

Tuesday, September 25th. Papa and I to Smailholm Tower, having telegraphed for a carriage to be ready at Kelso station, and this time there was no hitch, only our nerves were rather startled by the sight of some cattle up the railway bank between Sprouston and Kelso.

I had not time to count them, but there were perhaps eight or ten, half-grown two-year olds, the leader a white bull with horns, plunging wildly to get back through the hedge where its fellows were lowing to the trespassers. We spoke to a porter at Kelso who seemed moderately concerned and looked along the line in an incapable manner. It was a shuttle-train. I have heard no report of accident either to the train or the cattle.

The drive all the way to the turning was the same as that to Dryburgh, outside the Floors' wall. We turned up a steep, sandy side road with a slip of fir wood, and right through the farmyard and corn-ricks of Sandyknowe, where the farm labourers stared gravely as is their custom, and the driver took us up a very rough track where the horses shied, close opposite the town.

There is a large dam overgrown with weed with farm ducks on it, and at the upper end an amphitheatre of rocks, and on the neck, perched on an isolated boulder, the Tower. It is much the best view of it because both brook and tower are seen end on, which adds to the height.

It is in singularly perfect preservation, but barbarously bare, (not so pretty as Edlingham for instance), but, as a specimen of a real Border fortress in original state and situation, it is most striking. The curtain-wall and out-buildings are down, but the tower itself and the surrounding moor must be singularly unchanged in their barren desolation.

Two crows were eyeing us over the ridge of the roof, but disappeared. I noticed their litter of straw and wisp of sheep's wool from a window-sill at a giddy height. We had some very greasy pies in a paper bag, which I was requested to carry and conceal from these birds.

Up the staircase round and round, very dark, and then an opening in the third floor which was gone, and only a few modern planks here and there, then round and round again on to the level of the garrets, and a giddy long way down to the floor of the hall. The opening on to the roof, where one could have stood safely with a wall breast-high, was at the opposite side, and between was a stone shelf about a yard and a half wide, being the roof of the passage and closet below.

It was perfectly safe, but the yawning chasm on the left down to the stone floor of the hall was too much for my head. I went half across to a window, but was glad to slide back along the wall feeling sick. I should very much have liked to go out, but being by myself, and a black stair behind me, have seldom had such a turn.

There was a similar ledge and outlet to the south side of the roof at the other end of the hall, but inaccessible, the intervening floor being gone, as was likewise a door on the second floor to a closet or stair, for the same reason. The few loose, modern rafters look as though some one thought of putting in the floors again. I should have extremely liked to go out but I durst not.

The view is of course not very different from the windows, and, to say the truth, rather disappointed me. It is vast but not clearly marked. The Cheviots are too far off, and the same may be said of the woods of Merton, indeed the woods and fields are rather indistinguishable, and I could not make out the Tweed. It is only fair to say it was not perfectly clear.

I came down and found my father very hot, photographing every view but the right one, the sun being wrong. I posted away to the end overlooking Eildons, through a curious valley of rocks. The plateau ends very determinately: down below were corn carts creeping about like flies. I came back along the south slope, the turf very dry, short-cropped, but came across a flower that pleased me, *Dianthus deltoides*.

It was almost too dry for funguses, but much white *Hygrophorus* and some gigantic red ones, also a *Cortinarius*, brittle and graceful on bleached horsedung in the bog. My father hotter than ever, and rather huffed about the mutton-pies and some straps which he could not carry. A boy was throwing stones at the ducks and an old woman staring at us from the farm, whence the hum of the thrashing engine was audible. I waited about and found *Annularia charcarhas*.

Went with my father up the first flight, but he was so concerned about his descent that he would scarcely look round, and positively refused to go higher. I posted off to the north across a peat moss marked with old cuttings. An easy supply of fuel, but do not know where they got their water, the pond seemed fairly outside, besides being to a greater extent a modern artificial dam.

The ground boggy but dry, too dry for funguses. I found three little scarlet *Peziza aurantia*. I just got up the slope across the bog as the carriage appeared.

The high ground shades off more indefinitely to the north. There was a farm-track. It was sharp, frosty air driving back, and into Kelso we met flocks of sheep. We had tea, very refreshing at the Cross Keys, but had to wait a long time while he spread the table, and then drove home with our own conveyance.

Thursday, September 27th. Had thought of Jedburgh, but papa was tired. Went with the pony in the morning up the steep road to Coldstream Mains, passing a flock of sheep and the shepherd with a steel crook. Wondered if he holds by the fleece, the short-sheep have no horns.

Just over the hill I met the farm-horses, five or six pairs coming from the plough, such great sleek bays, I should have liked to photograph them.

At the corner, a great flock of starlings flew up and kept in front of me, passing from tree to tree in the hedgerow whistling and spluttering uninterruptedly. The starling is a joyous bird, he sings base and treble with the same breath, and claps as well. I delighted to see them manoeuvering in a great pack, turning sharply to right or left like a well-drilled regiment. They all seem to alight at a moment in the branches, and all their heads in the same direction. I never see any white ones.

There is a rook always all summer at a point in the road opposite Wark, with a dash of white, i.e. each elbow when the wings are spread. Once or twice I have seen others with it, but it is generally alone, always at the same place. We see a great flock every morning streaming over the house towards Ladykirk. Sometimes so low that we hear the rustling of their wings and a queer husky croak. I think it is the old birds who are asthmatical, I wonder how old they are, whether any of the rooks at Pallinsburn saw Flodden?

Monday, October 1st. Went to Coldstream to shops.

I came home the lower side road from Homebank. The air so

warm and mild and spring-like, mildness one feels sometimes in the end of the year. The Cheviots so blue and peaceful, not a breath of wind, but high up the *carry* was topped and drawn-out in gossamer threads, in unpoetical word 'Aaron's beard'. The rabbits sat out at the edge of the woods in the sunlight.

I shall not have many more drives this autumn here. The autumn is a time that makes one think there is no time like the present, and the present is very pleasant. Let me record my hearty thanks to Mistress Nelly, who is as near perfection as a lass or pony can be. There may not be much style, but commend me to a horse which will stand still, go any distance, face the steepest road and never stumble once the whole season, and take an amusing and intelligent interest in geography.

Tuesday, October 2nd. Another delicious autumn day, crisp hoarfrost, rising up in mist under the reach of the warm slanting sunbeams. I wanted to go to Mindrum to photograph, but chose a shorter distance to the Willow Burn in deference both to my own endurance and the pony's, having been out late the previous afternoon.

I had no cause for disappointment except the unavailing regret of a last sight of the pretty stream, sliding so silently under the great burdock leaves. The streams here have no joyous boisterous rush like Highland burns, but there is a happy peacefulness about them, especially the solitary Bowmont. Such gentle solitude, no howling wilderness, but corn, cattle and sheep, rich and prosperous and well attended beyond the seeming capacity of scattered herds and farm-labourers.

I am sure, driving for miles among these lonely cornfields and deep silent woods, and on the grassy slopes of the still more quiet hills, I have thought the whole countryside belonged to the fairies, and that they come out of the woods by moonlight into the fields and on to the dewy grass beside the streams. There are not many hedgehogs, which are fairy beasts, but there are the green sour ringlets whereon the ewe not bites, and how without the aid of the fairy-folk of fosterland could there be so little mildew in the corn?

Wednesday, October 3rd. We went up to Branxton, still misty and the light wrong, but I enjoyed it. We went through on the stubble at the back of the church, the next field to the Piper's Hill. To my great pleasure I picked up a very thin, rusted strip of iron about the size of the palm of my hand. My father said it had come off a midden with the manure. It might indifferently be an old kettle or a fragment of armour, but I was quite satisfied. I went a long way across the stubble staring intently. I had a sore eye unluckily. Any bone would be stained red in that ferrugineous soil. I roused a great, brown hare. I did not get over into the Piper's Hill as there was grass after barley, the bare stubble being oats.

I have it all in theory in my mind, if imaginary no matter, it is ingenious. That the English did not come straight over the middle of Pallisburn, because there is even yet a swamp. They formed at the back of this swampy ground, that the Centre and Right crossed at the Cornhill side, but the Left by Crookham, where the Lancashire bow-men turned the fate of the latter by getting close to the Scotch Right among the involved, steep druths above Crookham, (3 min.), and shooting up at them.

The druths there are so short-sided and steep, that unless the men rushed down into the gullies the bowmen would get close below them. I think Lord Stanley turned the flank of the Scotch Centre by coming along about on the level of the upper part of the road from Crookham, that is to say, on the church ridge, not the higher level of Branxton Hill Farm. Had he been on the higher ridge he would have turned Lord Home, the Left wing, too.

This goes to prove that the King *was* killed as far forward as the Piper's Hill. Lord Home I take to have been higher up between Branxton and Monylaws, the Centre originally on Branxton Hill ridge, but by the King's impetuosity getting down forward, and liable to be taken in the flank.

It was particularly peaceful and sunny, someone playing the harmonium in the ugly little church. We spoke again to the short-petticoated old woman. She had some vague knowledge of the discovery of bone in a pit in the south west side of the church some years ago, but denied that anything was ever found during ploughing.

Monday, October 8th. Misty but warm, and a glimpse of blue sky. Bertram hoped to get bats out of a willow, but they had been scared away. The village children gave him one, rather large, I think Pipistrelle, which he put in a small wooden box fastened by two nails.

The very next morning that horrid old jack jay, being left alone to bathe in a wash basin, opened the box and destroyed the poor creature. I fancy he found it ill-flavoured, but he pulled out its arms and legs in a disgusting fashion.

Last week I had the misfortune to lose the toad, but trust that he is enjoying himself as nothing was found below. He got off from the first floor window-sill. I was sorry to lose him as I had had him more than a year and very tame, turning sharply round for food when I put my hand near him.

Then, that there is writing on both the sashes in the round bedroom, which I noticed by chance standing on the broad ladder, 'Daniel Calder, Painter from Edinburgh, July 8th. 1821', written in round copy-book hand, in pencil. I suppose the house had not been painted since, nor I may add 'washed'.

There was a stirring-up of the annoyance the last week, owing to the Hamiltons desiring Mr Gray to clean those rooms in which 'some persons supposed that they had seen bugs'. An innuendo which was effectually silenced by papa's diary. Aug. 8th. two, etc. Aug. 11th. another, etc. One of the creatures was found in a book being read by Sarah, whether sermons I must enquire, but I never wish again to see such a funny mixture of uncleanliness and godliness. However, it was such a large, scrambling house, that being once pretty well assured by experience that there were none in the front part we really were not seriously inconvenienced.

Wednesday, October 10th. On this last morning, Wednesday the 10th., having finished packing up my fossils in a little box, I went down to the river and proceeded to get more. Very aggravating at the end, besides the autumn funguses.

There was mist and a gleam of blue sky through the hazy clouds, no wind, but a faint autumn breath of dead leaves. Autumn is the pleasantest season of the year, none the less pleasant for being the end, as the last breath of sweets is sweetest last.

I found a very curious fossil, but the Tweed smelled so nasty from the village sewage, that, after filling my little tin case with water-plants, I was glad to sit on the twisted roots of the large sycamore looking down the river under the black shadowy leaves, very tired and peaceful. The autumn colours were bright in the woods lower down. I never saw it look prettier.

I was very sorry indeed to come away, with a feeling of not having half worked through the district, but I have done a good summer's work. The funguses will come up again and the fossils will keep. I hope I may go back again some day when I am an old woman, unless I happen to become a fossil myself, which would save trouble. The fatigue and petty annoyance of a removal rather painfully obtrude the advantages enjoyed by disembodied spirits.

It is not a country which will change for the worse by overbuilding, for the population is not increasing, and the state of the old castles is due not to the ravages of time but to quarrying, they will alter very little now, except an occasional stone sprung out by frost.

We were somewhat nettled during the last week by the activity of that idle person Mr Hopkirk, the gardener, who made a frantic effort to get the place straight for his own employer after our departure. I have seen him lie flat on his face in a gravel walk, to weed with a little knife.[8] Another thing he did was to leave the strawberry nets on the ground for weeks, till overgrown by a forest of weeds. I thought he would never have got them off, but he did by a superhuman effort.

It is somewhat trying to pass a season of enjoyment in the company of persons who are constantly on the outlook for matters of complaint. I and Elizabeth the housemaid were the only persons who were thoroughly pleased, whereof I take to be the moral that Elizabeth and I had better go there some day for a holiday, to lodgings.

In my opinion it is a country where only man is vile, and it is the most thinly populated that I have ever been in, the ratio being about one cottage every two miles. I imagine it may be dull country for foot-walking, being spread out over a great extent, and hedges; but for driving it is perfect. I made out fifteen drives besides some cross-roads on which I never went at all.

My photography was not very satisfactory, but I made about forty careful drawings of funguses, and collected some interesting fossils, one of which I find labelled at the Museum, *Arancarioxylon*[9] from Lennel Braes, a lucky find since I know nothing about it.

For the rest I read sundry old novels, in good old calf binding contemporary with the house, Galt's *Annals of the Parish; The Heart of Midlothian*, by the author of Waverley; Moore's *Lalla Rookh* in a little thumb edition; the preposterous Southey and the matter-of-fact Crabbe, some of which I had read before. There are one or two fine descriptions in the *Curse of Kehama*, but it is utterly devoid of any sense of the absurd, or of the melody which when flavoured and toned by old prints and old binding gives a real charm to the tales of the veiled prophet.

For the rest I also learned four Acts of *Henry VIII* and ought to have learned all, but I can say this for my diligence, that every line was learnt in bed. The 4th. Act is associated with the company of a robin who came in at daylight attracted by sleepy flies, and sat on the curtain-pole or the wardrobe, bold and black-eyed. He only once sang. The swallows used to fly round the next room. Mice were also an amusement and extremely tame, picking up crumbs from the table.

There is a line in *The Tempest* about the green, sour ringlets,[10] which I meant to investigate but left too late, with the white *Paxillus*. That the real reading is green sour, not sward, that Lord Bacon would know that there is actual acidity in the spore of the large *Paxillus* especially, which blue deadens the actual grass blades and merely sours the root too, but this requires observation.

I see no mystery in the enlarging ring myself. The funguses grow from the mycelium, not the spore direct, and the mycelium grows from that spore which falls outwards on unexhausted ground.

Then, that I know *Richard III* right through, *Henry VIth.* four fifths, *Richard II* except three pages, *King John* four Acts, a good half the *Midsummer Night's Dream* and *The Tempest*, half way through *The Merchant of Venice* and *Henry VIII*. Then that I learnt six more or less in a year. Never felt the least strained or should not have done it. It is a singular fact that I know them better when seasoned; the last two I always know worst.

1895

'The cooking is not so handsome as the bill'

LONDON

A PRIVATE VIEW AT THE ACADEMY

My dear Esther, my aunt and I went to the private view this morning. I don't know to whom we owed the unusual favour of tickets, they were sent by the Council.

I suppose instigated by either Thornycroft or Mr Prince, for Sir J. Millais' would have been signed, and Mr Brett disclaimed the favour.

As to the pictures, we saw them splendidly, but for the company, unfortunately neither my aunt nor I knew who people were, except Mr and Mrs Gladstone, whom we met continually round corners.

If my uncle had been with us no doubt he could have 'named' a large proportion, however, I was well entertained, and I could not have had his information without the sauce or rather with sugar.

Personally I confess to appreciating once in a while the privilege of basking amongst the aristocracy, and it was so very select. My aunt pointed out one lady and gentleman as the Duke and Duchess of Westminster, which I'm positively certain they weren't. However, there were many pretty dresses and a few sweet faces, and I daresay some (at least) of the haggard gentlemen were Dukes, and the smart ones, lights of literature, and I judged them all up to my own satisfaction.

There was a delicious, refined odour diffused through the building, emanating not from the aristocracy, but from banks of lilies and azaleas which were arranged in the lecture-room and down the sides of the grand staircase, where two officials in strange scarlet cloaks, covered with tags, took the tickets.

I did not recognize a single Academician except Mr Brett, who looked very comical with a tile hat superadded to his velveteens, and very rampant as to the hair which ornaments his countenance. We saw no one else to speak to except 'my brother Abel' a Lancashire cotton worthy.

WEYMOUTH

Tuesday, April 9th. Came to Weymouth, April 9th. 95, Tuesday, by London and South Western from Waterloo, very tedious, the best way by Paddington, which though longer in mileage takes a shorter time and better carriages. Much surprised by the extent and dreariness of the New Forest, which was increased by the fact of the gorse having been browned or almost killed in the late severe winter. The state of the shrubs here, euonymus, bay and ilex, is deplorable.

We are staying at the Imperial Burdon Hotel, expensive but very comfortable, old-fashioned *and* clean, quiet, a civil waiter 'if *you* please, sir', and good cooking. The one drawback being fan-lights over the doors which makes it awkward to change photographic slides.

The town is a good size but very old-fashioned and empty, very few new houses, probably almost unchanged since Fanny Burney was crowded into an attic, and met Mrs Siddons[1] walking on the sands and found her decidedly dull.

King George's visit appears to have been the last event of any importance, the other municipal excitement being the worship of Sir Henry Edwards the late member, of whom there is a very fearful statue on the parade. King George's Jubilee Monument is still worse, but comical, erected by the grateful inhabitants, and with a long rambling inscription which refers pathetically to the prisoners in France. The King holds a most gigantic sceptre and there is a crown as large as a clothes-basket. Much other furniture, a unicorn, and the most singular presentment of the British lion which ever I have seen.

There is a wide expanse of muddy sand, a bank of shingle, a parade where they turn the gas out at 9.30, and a long line of well-built old houses. Those about the harbour have little wooden bow-windows and projections and steep tiled roofs. There is an octagonal, ugly modern building, but the narrow winding harbour is decidedly picturesque.

A curious feature of the harbour is the swans, sailing amongst the ships and occasionally out to sea, almost out of sight. In the evening a pair may often be seen flying along towards Lodmoor or over to the Radipole breakwater. There are numerous cormorants and graceful, black-headed gulls wading in the marsh.

Friday, April 12th. We met troops of blue-jackets, most of them lads belonging to the training ship *Wanderer* lying at that time in Portland Roads. There was no particular invasion of the town.

We drove in the afternoon to see Chalbury Ring, which we had some difficulty in finding as the driver had apparently never heard of it, and all the downs seem equally scored.

I thought we had a beautiful drive, the light was so beautiful on the Downs at the back of Chalbury Hill. The narrow, white, unbordered roads on a great expanse of turf give an impressive feeling of size and solitude, increased by the great earthworks on the solitary slopes. The most inexplicable are the terraces; they occur at the head of nearly every valley amongst the Downs, two or sometimes three broad steps on the slope at either side; some of them which resemble steps at the head of valleys may possibly be beaches.

Sunday, April 14th. Very horribly windy. In the afternoon sauntered about with papa, and sat a long time on a seat in the Dorchester Road looking at the Sunday-school children and the little gardens. Thought rather sadly what a strange thing it was for him to do. In the morning I picked up a strange little red fish which I painted.

Tuesday, April 16th. Morning, walked about, got out of the wind, and sat on a bench reading the papers, with some amazement at the reported treaty between China and Japan.

Drove to Abbotsbury afternoon, should have done better to go by rail had we known it was so near the station, at the other end. It is a very long drive, and the country, after the pattern of most country at the seaside, as nearly dull as country can be to an intelligent person, though not without a dreary poetry of solitude in certain effects of light and mist.

★

Wednesday, April 17th. Papa photographed in the harbour, then Persian cat, and a particularly fine child with a proud father in the Boatbuilder's yard. We went to the backwater and found the tide was out. Again after lunch the same disappointment, caused by some letting down of gates for repairs.

Afterwards took a row up from the ferry with a worthy of most reverend appearance, but stone-deaf, who explained that, when the tide went down too far for the landing steps, it was the deuce of a job. He also made relevant remarks upon potatoes, Beecham's pills and a body which he had picked up in the backwater partially devoured by rats, *black* rats he said, but I conclude an epithet only. Saw an odd, yellow-black toad-like dead fish, but could not get it as the rain came on furiously. They were fishing for flounders, stirring up the mud with a bit of chain at the end of a pole. We sheltered in a saw-shed; examined the complicated machines.

I succeeded in finding two or three new sorts of shells which I knew of and wanted. I very much regret not having had an opportunity of going out dredging. My scientist's endeavours have been a failure, the only one thing I was set on doing was to photograph Chesil Bank. However, I saw enough to perceive that it is a very good place for fossils.

A quiet town and plenty of lodgings, the air and water most excellent. The Burdon Hotel we found most excellent, but extortionate, £20. 9. 0 for one week, three persons, a sitting room but no table d'hôte. This decided us not to stay the fortnight, so we moved to Salisbury. Odd names in Weymouth, *Jesty, Dominy, Meech, Kiddle, Barnicolt.*

SALISBURY

Thursday, April 18th. Salisbury, Thurs. 18th. by very shaky rail over country which became pretty as we approached the Avon. Went to the White Hart, a good Inn, rather emphatically an inn with a powerful smell of beer and a noise of people going late to bed, but very clean and good attendance.

We were much delighted with Salisbury, especially the Close, with its fine elms, green meadows and old red-brick houses in gardens where the *Ribes* and *Pyrus japonica* are coming into flower, and the walls are covered with Cape jessamine. Several have steps and curious old ironwork in railings and gateways. I was much pleased with a sun-dial on the side of a house, 'life's but a walking shadow'.

The Cathedral is very beautiful, a thing of perfection externally. The inside rather painfully bare and plain. We had a curious illustration of the height of the roof, a pigeon flying wildly up and down during Service. A very beautiful organ, the fourth sweetest I have heard. The choir-boys wear white frills, we saw them playing football in the Close afterwards, and one round-faced cherub careering about the turf on a bicycle, the frills have a most curious effect.

The eggs also have frills at the White Hart. The house is old, but nothing like the five-hundred years which the Inn is said to have existed. The presiding geniuses are certainly cats, especially a very black one with yellow eyes. They supply iced-water, and there is currant-bread at lunch. The cooking is not so handsome as the bill.

Friday, April 19th. After lunch, to Stonehenge, I think that I was more impressed by the Plain than by Stonehenge, where behold the ubiquitous game of golf, two other carriages and a camping-photographer; his pony was wandering about in a sack. More in keeping, a great flock of sheep and lambs, with bells, attended by a shepherd, drinking in a shallow pond near the Stones, but they wandered off over the grass roads before I could get my camera ready.

The Plain is anything but flat, and most of it is broken up in cultivation, but there are no hedges, and someways, open undulating land gives one a strange feeling of size. There seemed to be no cattle whatever, great flocks of sheep, but most of them still penned. The corn just beginning to show green, thousands of skylarks singing and running among the tussocks. Signs of hares which we did not see.

The first view of Stonehenge is disappointing, not because it is small, but because the place whereon it stands is so immense. The stones are large enough to satisfy anybody, but I had not the least idea that they were all crowded together in a grove, I do not think a larger space than our back garden. The number of mounds like gigantic mole-hills, and the straight Roman roads are almost as striking.

We passed fine Earthworks at Old Sarum and Amesbury. Came back by Lake House and the valley of the Avon. Very sweet. We drove a long way over the springy turf, most curious. It must be a fine place for funguses, gigantic fairy rings appeared on the slopes.

I had the misfortune to twist my ankle getting out of the carriage, not badly, but a singularly indiscreet choice of location, the middle of Salisbury Plain! I fell over a certain camera of papa's which I opportunely broke, a most inconveniently heavy article which he refuses to use, and which has been breaking my back since I took to that profession. Should I get a camera of my own it will not be a bad bargain. N.B. I did no particular damage, but it was the last straw of clumsiness. We had fortunately taken a long walk in the morning round the water meadows of the Avon.

We went by Crane Bridge, looking over at the great trout in the beautiful, clear, chalk stream. Further on we saw others, and the water was alive with shoals of grayling and minnows. It was the first warm, mild feeling of spring, and we heard the cuckoo. It was hot dragging home along the road. I noticed when we were driving on the Downs we were coming with the wind, under the shadow of a cloud, and several times when we almost overtook the edge of the shadows I could feel and see the hot dither from the ground, where the sun had recently been ousted, an instance of the amount of heat refracted from the chalk.

I am afraid I shall never have a very reverent memory of Stonehenge by reason of certain shells which I found behind some nettles right under one of the standing stones. I thought they were uncommonly fine ones for such bare pasture, but failed to find a single live one, which was not surprising, for they were periwinkles. That part of the story is very fine so long as one finds it out for oneself.

Saturday, April 20th. On Sat. my foot being painful I went round the town in a bathchair, and didn't like it. It was market-day and I had an unintelligible chair-man who stopped in the middle of streets to point out objects of interest, and I was too inexperienced as to powers of endurance of that species of draught-horse to venture to remonstrate.

The Poultry Cross, restored, is very curious. There is the site of the Blue Boar in the market square where Buckingham was beheaded by Richard III. We afterwards came round by the river and into collision with another *pram* containing a very dirty boy.

DENBIGH

Tuesday, May 28th. May 28th. Went to Gwaynynog near Denbigh to stay with the Burtons for one week, and very fortunately came home again unbroken.

I do not know what has possessed uncle Fred, he has taken to driving the carriage-horses, and such horses, of the very worst type of hansom. One of them is unsafe even for the coachman, having bolted twice in Manchester.

Uncle Fred is quietening into a little old man, deaf, placid, rather dateless, excessively obstinate, very mean as to ha'pence, unapproachably autocratic and sublimely unconscious of the fact that he cannot drive.

The coachman appeared to be a very nervous man and suavely moribund, but it was enough to frighten anybody. I trust he will overturn in a dry ditch, and not injure Alice. I give up my aunt who, sauf votre respect, is tiresome, and as penny wise as he is, in keeping a beast which cannot be worth £20, and will end in smashing the carriage.

The whole establishment is not on the same footing of respectability and stinginess which, notwithstanding the real affection and respect which I have always felt for uncle Fred, was rather too much for my gravity.

It is very odd, a date on the back premises 1571, the front black and white, and the more modern garden-front, stone. Two large rooms, dining-room and music-room 1776, the most modern. Upstairs all up and down and uneven, low beams and long passages, some very fine chimney-pieces, and one room panelled.

It was the ancestral home of the Myddletons, who by a lavish prodigality were reduced to living in the kitchen. Uncle Fred dwelt upon their dissipation with unction, also the literary association of the house with Dr Johnson.

The present library consists of one Bible, Shakespeare, the

Waverley Novels, Dickens, six standard poets, a set of the *Cornhill Magazine* and about a dozen odd volumes not including the dictionary.

However, he hath whitewashed and papered the house all over and furnished it in perfect taste. I never saw rooms more faultless in scheme of colour or Sheraton, more elegant without being flimsy. Moreover, he pays his way, and, if he keeps only four maids, they are the most obliging, merry servants ever met with, more especially Polly.

The table was better fed than usual, thanks to an unlimited supply of vegetables, and eggs at twenty to the shilling, but chickens exorbitant at three shillings each. Coal twelve shillings per ton. We had a fire twice in the gunroom on wet nights. The cartage was very heavy, and also they objected to the merchant who drove a team of donkeys and goaded the poor little beasts up a long hill.

I could not exactly determine what distinguished the Welsh type, but it is marked, particularly among the women and girls; something about the forehead, eyes, and the fall of the nose, and a rather vacant mouth, a perfect mouseface sometimes. They all wrinkle up their eyes as though in a strong light, the eyebrows usually arched, the forehead round and the nose long. Dark or blue eyes, red or black hair, an occasional fair, fat type, rather idiotic.

There appear to be many extremely old persons in spite of starved looks. The only well-grown man I saw was the Gamekeeper, a jovial lively party who went about with a big stick looking for poachers. They net the river, steal the scanty game and commit petty thefts in spite of the solemn warning of John Evans's notice boards, 'Who ever will be found taking watercress out of this pond shall be prosecuted'.

There are no shutters to the house for serious crime, but a farmer who overturned in his gig was picked up by the market people, but a considerable sum of loose money which rolled from his pockets was not forthcoming.

The race is said to be deteriorated by much intermarriage. The Denbigh Asylum seemed populous. I thought it very singular that the lunatics should walk in the Park and come up to the garden-railings. I saw a party of perhaps twenty, with keepers, which I at first took for a cricket match.

My aunt seemed to consider the old women amusing. One had appeared and stopped to tea in the servants' hall. There is a standing reward of five shillings for strayed ones, not worth the risk in my opinion. A man had knocked at the back door and much bewildered Polly by talking about Mr Gladstone. He fortunately took himself off and presently the keeper arrived in search of him.

Another individual, described as very dangerous and prepared to kill anybody, got into Miss Foster's garden, and being after dark could not be found, so a watch was set in the house, and the following morning he was found sitting among the potatoes, very damp.

These pleasing incidents were scattered over several years, but in my opinion they constitute a drawback to the neighbourhood. I should not care to live amongst the same natives either, it is an uncomfortable, suspicious state when so few can understand English. The climate also I did not like, extremely muggy and relaxing, though no doubt it was aggravated by the thunder.

It is rich, undulating country, woods and pastures, all up and down, the hills really high, but lumpy: not definitely fine landscape but beautiful in detail, especially the den below the house, where there is a little glaring-white cottage buried in wood, sacred to the memory of Dr Johnson. A winding path up the dell leads to an urn erected to that worthy's memory before his death, which seems to have provoked his commonsense.[2]

A doctor in Denbigh seems to have done the same thing on his own account, perhaps because no one was likely to do it for him. He presented a little slip of garden to the town, and set up an obelisk and his statue exactly opposite his front door. His name was Pearce, he died a few weeks since and lay in state in a scarlet hunting coat. He would turn in his grave if he knew that my uncle had dug up a litter of foxes.

We had a picnic-tea at Dr Johnson's, provided by Polly, a very taking young woman, tall, thin and freckled. She made a most excellent treacle-pudding which, combined with the thunder, had disastrous effects upon Alice and me, and finally Polly herself, who took to her bed with two pills and a seidlitz-powder. I should doubt if the air suits young people.

I thought cousin Alice rather quiet. She solaced herself with a little old dog called Toby, a chestnut riding-mare, and interminable conferences with the coachman Gibbon, a good-looking nervous young man whose conversation appeared to be harmless and restricted to horses. Stable-talk in broad Lancashire always sounds quaint. They certainly are simple about horses.

One morning they put the little chestnut Pearl in the gig to go to Nant-y-Glyn. She certainly behaved very well, much to the congratulation of Alice and Gibbon as they didn't think she had been twenty times in harness, and only once that season. She had on a wrong bit and a large collar belonging to *Bootles*, and at the first hill showed symptoms of lying down.

We went up an awful road with sharp corners and narrow bridges, but the coachman led her up and down, and she went beautifully on the flat. I believe it was very fine country, but I was sitting on the edge of the back-board prepared to roll off.

The garden is very large, two-thirds surrounded by a red-brick wall with many apricots, and an inner circle of old grey apple trees on wooden espaliers. It is very productive but not tidy, the prettiest kind of garden, where bright old fashioned flowers grow amongst the currant bushes.[3]

Outside in the straggling park, beyond the great oak trees, were two large quarries where I found many fossils, corals, encrinites and a few shells. One of the latter of obstinate hardness led to an acquaintance with John Evans, who chipped it down most neatly and said it was very natural. He worked in a large shed between carpenter's chips and an anvil, a little wizened, warped Welshman who looked at things sideways with one eye and talked a laboured foreign English. He also had been terrified by uncle Fred's driving, having gone to the mountain on the back seat of the trap.

WINDERMERE

Friday, July 26th. July 26th. we came to Holehird, Windermere, where we tarried in the summer of 89 when I could hardly walk at all, for which be thankful. I am very much struck with the difference. I had never been on the hill behind the house, only once in the copse.

We found the pleasant old gardener dead and gone, and a bustling self-important personage in his place, who amused me but exasperated Bertram by giving him permission to pick raspberries. Mr Anthony Wilkinson ('by gum its währm'), very much alive, ('I – los – my second in – a – con – finement!') also one of the same carriage-horses, the worse for wear. We had rather wet weather, arriving on the heels of a thunderstorm.

Wednesday, July 31st. Went to Wray Castle July 31st., delighted to see old Foxcroft and Jane. The old man eighty-three, not a bit deaf, and funnier than ever, sitting in the sun in carpet-slippers. The house topsy-turvy after the tenancy of Mr Lumm who had left it, 'its filthy'.

One day a party arrived to look over Holehird which is on sale. Mr Edward Partington and family from Glossop. I was amused showing them round, but think father double-locked himself in retirement and indignation.

I had some good luck finding funguses in the rain.

Aunt Clara and Miss Gentile arrived, and the weather was atrocious. Aunt Clara heavy and out of spirits, Miss Gentile odious.

Wednesday, August 7th. My first great day of fossils Aug. 7th. when I drove up Troutbeck, overtaking a young farmer with a string of horses. Left the pony in the road and walked up Nanny Lane leading to the foot path up Wansfell. I had to go high, nearly level with the quarries across the valley before I came to a part where the walls were crumbling stone.

I found many shells, and when I had turned to come down, spied something sticking up grey on the top of a wall. I took it for a sheep's horn till I had it in my hand. It is a very steep, wide lane between high walls, a wonderful view. I could see the glint of a window or glass across Lancaster Sands.

Thursday, August 8th. Drove with aunt Clara and Miss Gentile to Coniston and back by Tilberthwaite. Miss Gentile has as much sentiment as a broom-stick, and appeared principally interested by the *sit*-uation of the Hotels, aunt Clara half asleep. The only place where she showed any animation was the turn of the valley towards Holme Ground.

There is a great wreckage of fir trees in the gap at the top of the hill above the Marshalls, down which we came faster than I approved. I seemed to remember every bush on the road, and through the opera glass, on the hill-side above Coniston Bank. Not that five years is long, but I had so much forgotten this in six. I think I must have been in very weak health when I was here before, though not conscious of it to complaining at the time.

I was very much struck with the ideal beauty of Coniston. It was a perfect day, but apart from weather it is in my opinion far the most beautiful of the larger Lakes. Esthwaite and Blelham being reckoned with the small. It is so compact and the ground and vegetation so varied. Close down to the Lake the wild flowers were lovely.

I parted with aunt Clara and the interminable Miss Gentile and posted along the dusty road in the hot sun, looked at the exact spot in the roadside where Billy Hamilton, the blind man used to stand, also I heard in the village that the good-tempered, amiable creature was dead, two years since.

Blind men are reputed to be saints, but they are generally sour. Billy must have absorbed the baking sunshine through his pores as he stood in the ditch. He came boldly up to the pony-carriage holding his hands like a scoop, and never failed to thank 'Mr Potter' by name, with broad grins. He also went about with a wheel-barrow collecting sticks, entering thickets with the immunity of the men of Thessaly; he fulfilled the pious service of supplying chips for the stove in Coniston Church.

I had a long talk with the postmistress, a lame girl on crutches. I went afterwards to see Miss Hanes in an old row of cottages above the Sky Hill – a little, thin, elderly woman with black hair and eyes, in spectacles, with a clean cottage and soapy hands.

I heard a long history of her daugher Jane, a girl to whom we took a great fancy, which seems to have been mutual unless butter entered into our conversation. I heard the history of Jane not marrying a coachman who took to drinking, and lost his place after the banns were put up; but the queer part of it was the way the course of events was taken, not as a disappointment but as a positive success, in the very nick of time, and he had turned out so very badly since.

Then I turned to cats, caäts, a he 'cart', a black Persian named Sadi whom we had bestowed on Jane. I should fail to give an impression of old Mrs Hanes looking over her spectacles and gesticulating in the middle of the flagged kitchen, nor would the joke be perceived without previous knowledge of Sadi, whom I saw last as a splendid half-grown kitten of diabolical temperament. 'He wad stand on the table and clar ye,' she thought the world of that caät. Also he was 'moross' which I can well believe from what I saw of him.

When they took him to Liverpool he led them a dance, Jane wad be up ladders and over walls. Mrs Goodison thought the world of that caät. Mr Goodison didn't. It used to go to sleep in his arm chair and he was afraid to stir it. It was a trojan. It died of a consumption when it was only three.

I walked after lunch as far as Tent Lodge, and much regretted I could not go on to Coniston Bank to see Barnes and especially Mrs Barnes, a fine old Cumberland farmer's wife, homely and comely. We drove home by Yewdale and Skelwith.

Saturday, August 10th. In afternoon went with the pony up Troutbeck and put it up at the Mortal Man which looks a very little inn. Papa and I walked up Nanny Lane and got over a stile into the heather, sweet and heavy with honey. There was a thunder-haze, no view, but very peaceful, except that the stone walls were covered with flying-ants.

I did not find many fossils, but we had great pleasure watching a pair of buzzards sailing round and round over the top of Wansfell. There was an old shepherd half way up the side of Troutbeck, much bent and gesticulating with a stick. He watched the collie scouring round over stone walls, coming close past us without taking the slightest notice. Four or five sheep louped over a wall at least three feet high on our right and escaped the dog's observation, whereupon the ancient shepherd, a mere speck in the slanting sunlight down the great hillside, this aged Wordsworthian worthy, awoke the echoes with a flood of the most singularly bad language. He gesticulated and the dog ran round on the top of dykes, and some young cattle ran down with their tails in the air.

It is most curious how sound travels up either side of the steep Troutbeck valley, but in keeping to be greeted with the classical but not time-honoured phrase addressed by *La Pucelle*[4] to invaders. We passed him sitting on a wall as we came down, a pleasant, smiling old fellow. We asked him which was Ill Bell and he leant over the wall, 'we'll perceive I'm rather hard of hearing', then heard that the prize-pup at Kelso Show was named 'Sandy Walker'.

Tuesday, August 13th. 11.12 when aunt Clara left, and also the greater part of Tues. 13th. was very wet. The German Emperor was expected to pass on Tues. but did not, owing to weather. Many took the trouble to go down, but I, not being keen, put off to the eleventh hour, and a man came past on horseback taking word to Troutbeck.

I had a long, beautiful drive in the afternoon going up by Pull Wyke to the barn gates. Then I remembered a pleasant lane down to Skelwith Bridge, and the woman at the inn assured me that the *sharies* came that way. All I can say is that we met a gig half way down, and could not have passed it had not it on two wheels been next the bank.

It was very beautiful under Black Fell but I was rather nervous. I walked up to see the Force[5] which was in deafening flood, one of these foolish lambs in the meadow below the bridge knee deep.

We consumed three whole hours waiting to see the Emperor, not very well worth it. I had seen him in London. I think he is stouter.

I was not particularly excited. I think it is disgraceful to drive fine horses like that. First came a messenger riding a good roan belonging to Bowness, which we could hear snorting before they came in sight, man and horse both dead-beat. He reported that the Emperor would be up in ten minutes, but it was twenty.

The procession consisted of a mounted policeman with a drawn sword in a state approaching apoplexy, the red coats of the Quorn Hunt, four or five of Lord Lonsdale's carriages, several hires, and spare horses straggling after them. There were two horses with an outside rider to each carriage, splendid chestnuts, thoroughbred, floundering along and clinking their shoes.

They were not going fast when we saw them, having come all the way from Patterdale without even stopping at Kirkstone to water the horses, to the indignation of mine host, and an assembly of three or four hundred who had reckoned on this act of mercy. I think His Majesty deserved an accident, and rather wonder he didn't have one considering the smallness of the little *Tiger* sitting on the box to work the brake.

The liveries were blue and yellow and the carriages much yellow, singularly ugly low tub, with leather top to shut up sideways. The

Emperor, Lord Lonsdale and two ladies in the first, Lady Dudley etc. in the second.

There was a considerable crowd and very small flags, German ones bad to get at short notice, but plenty of tricolours. Lord Lonsdale is red-headed and has a harum-scarum reputation, but, according to Mr Edmonstone, less 'stupid' than his predecessor whom he had seen 'beastly droonk' in the road on a Sunday morning.

Saturday, August 17th. Kirkstone in the coach with papa. Fetched back by carriage middle afternoon. Very pleasant, silent air on the hills, curious place. Began to have enough of it during afternoon. Three pairs of buzzards nesting unmolested on Red Screes in one quarry. Innkeeper said he could hear the young birds crying in the morning.

Coming down we stopped at the wonderful view over Troutbeck Tongue, and blue shadows creeping up the head of the den.[6] The Troutbeck valley is exquisite when it is fine, which is but seldom.

Sunday, August 18th. Went to the Troutbeck Chapel – Rev. Parker. I wonder why Dissenting Ministers are so very unpresentable. The congregation were quite clean and had their hair cut. He preached on a long text on the Angel appearing to Manoah and his wife, better than I expected, though very homely.

The Congregationalists are more liberal than the Methodists and Baptists, and this shock-headed, earnest preacher got forth a rational, amiable interpretation, finding sermons in stones and heavenly messengers in every blessing, – yea – even in those afflictions which at first sight appear to be 'emissaries of Satan'. I thought the singing very sweet, two favourite hymns – *Oh early happy, lasting wish – We faintly hear, we dully see, in differing phrase we pray*, and a young woman behind me singing *Angels of the night* in a clear, firm voice. Lancashire folks sing through their teeth so to speak. I suppose very young, but quaintly earnest.

Friday, August 23rd. There was a hound-trail and sheep dogs in Troutbeck which I did not know of in time. I had, however, a lovely drive in the afternoon to Blelham, curling and blue under the crisp, fresh breeze. The boggy ground was literally dry, and I waded through the sweet bog myrtle to look for the long-leaved sundew, which I remembered covering the black peat like a crimson carpet. I found it near Scanty, past the season.

I went along the Causeway to the projecting knoll of firs where I found *Boletus badius*. I did not venture far into Randy Pike Wood because I could see a drove of cattle through the trees, and memories of a bull, which caused me to dodge them.

Saturday, August 24th. Went to see Ginnet's Circus at Ambleside and had a good laugh. I would go any distance to see a Caravan (barring lion-taming), it is the only species of entertainment I care for.

Mr Ginnet himself hath gone-off in appearance since I saw him last on the same spot ten years since, when he rode a young red-roan bull. He has subsided into a most disastrous long frock-coat and long, tight trousers with about a foot of damp at the bottom of them, and cracked a whip feebly. Were I inclined to weave a romance I might suspect that he had had reverses not unconnected with the bottle.

The Circus has fallen-off in the way of horses which represent capital, and stronger in the variety line. Probably a boisterous element introduced by growing lads. The neat little jockey had developed into a big, loutish, rough rider, very gentle however with the little child Millie Ginnet. She was exceedingly pretty and nice-mannered in her clothes, and indeed seemed too well clothed under her bathing-drawers, a marvellous little bundle, by no means painfully proficient.

The scornful Madame Ansonia was arrayed in blue and silver, and, alighting from her piebald, put on goloshes publicly in the ring. The fair-haired enchantress did not appear unless indeed she had shrivelled into Madame Fontainebleau, who displayed her remarkable dogs in an anxious cockney accent, and twinkled about in high-heeled French boots and chilly apparel. Tights do not shock me in a tent associated with damp grass, they suggest nothing less prosaic than rheumatics and a painfully drudging life.

Most people are vagabonds, but the rain washes away part of their sin, and the constant change of audience is better than leering at the same idle youths night after night. But for ignoring her company (and half the scarves which she ought to jump), commend me to Madame Ansonia. She was a good looking young woman with dark hair and eyes.

The other madame (there were but two), displayed an old, very old iron-grey mare with a long, thin neck, and a long, thin tail which it swished in cadence with the music. I think it was the oldest horse I ever saw in a circus, and the best dancer, going through its piece with avidity just in front of the band, but so very, very old that I was apprehensive about its rising when it curtseyed.

The other horses were the piebald, a steady property-horse with a broad back, two creams, not by any means a pair, and two ponies, the smaller Joey very clever in the way of temper. The most amusing thing was a race between these two, which Joey won by cutting across the turf-ring to the immense delight of the school-children who composed three-quarters of the audience.

Then any gentleman whatever was invited to ride, which they did with bashful courage and no success, the ponies going down on their knees and tumbling them right and left.

There was a great sale of sweets and the occasional variety of streams of rain through the tent, and the opening of umbrellas. The circus-dogs who mingled freely with the audience were demoralized by a fox terrier on the stalls, otherwise a rickety erection covered with carpet. One bench of school-children was overturned by Joey.

The most skilful performers were two men on parallel bars, and Herr Wartenburg the Barrel-King, who climbed on to a high seat and, having wiped it with a pocket handkerchief, laid himself on his velveteen back with his heels in the air, and danced wrong side up to the tune of *The Keelrow* against a cylinder, and then an immense barrel, I suppose inflated with gas. He danced his feet most gracefully, in little pointed shoes.

The performing-dogs turned back-somersaults with agility, and one small poodle dressed in clown's jacket and trousers skipped energetically on its hind legs, two persons turning the rope. A stray dog appeared in the ring but was chivvied out.

The entrance to this scene of joy was through some yards of stone fall thrown down on a dunghill, which afforded a gentle slope to the meadow below.

I regret to state that for the last week in August we had almost unceasing rain accompanied by storms of wind. I had plenty to do indoors, but our time is running out.

★

Monday, September 2nd. Sept. 2 being very fine we went to Coniston. Rowed to Coniston Bank and saw Mrs Barnes in great trouble, and as she expressed it, 'topsy-turvy', Barnes having received notice and failed to find another situation.

It is not possible to give an opinion without knowing both sides, but unless he was very much to blame the case is hard. He has lived there twenty-eight years under three different masters, and now Mr Docksey who has had it but two years has turned him out in a quarrel.

Whatever the merits of the case I am sorry for the old woman, who was feebly turning out a collection of dusty rubbish from her cupboards. She seemed to consider Mr Ruskin 'collective', which she wasn't herself, 'but very quiet'. She used to be rather proud of her acquaintance with him, he sometimes took a cup of tea with her. She says he knows her if he meets her.

Monday, September 9th. Hot, hazy day, the hottest of the summer. Drove to Dungeonghyll Hotel, two post-horses, one old stager with the hogged-mane, the other mare a chestnut, rather unpleasant up hills; a thick haze.

Noted the glaciation with much curiosity, especially the loose mound on that canny desolation, Elterwater Common. I never saw a spot more strickled with herd and ducks, many of the former garnished with knickerbockers, and the very sheep of shortest wool and every colour, like those recorded in Rob Roy!

There are some beautiful exposures of rock along the new road between Skelwith and Elterwater, a road whose newness may enrage sentimentalists but strikes me as a good thing well done. I cannot find a single decided scratch on the boulders or rocks that are exposed to the weather (i.e. the mechanical action of wind and rain), for the grit and volcanic rock do not perceptibly weather in the fashion of the Coniston limestone, which very completely rots about four feet, for which reason I take it boulders of that stone are hardly likely to exist on the surface. The grit and volcanic boulders are eroded so to speak, smaller *muffins* dug out of pits in the hill to break to mend roads, and often observably scratched. I should have exceedingly liked to photograph that clearing.

We were rather surprised at the amount of company at the Hotel,

Monday, a trip day. A most marvellous family from Chicago, lavender kid-gloves, jewellery and bonnets.

Tuesday, September 10th. To Wray with Elizabeth to see the Foxcrofts, a howling wind, but fine, blowing evening, rather cold. I drove the old lady sixteen miles with her tassels blowing, 'hey! the *funny* lugs'. Jane says they look like a wedding. A new idea; I don't feel like a wedding.

Elizabeth and I could not find anyone for some time, and took stock of the groceries and new articles, 'two housemaid's boxes and twelve water-cans'. We went all over the downstairs rooms and finally found Jane and Mary sewing carpets on the back top-landing. We had previously seen Anne and Sid Foxcroft at the cottage.

I am afraid I shall never see him again, a sweet, gentle old man, with the funniest lisping way of talking like a child, and a bird, with his head on one side. To me no tongue can be as musical as Lancashire.

MANCHESTER

Tuesday, September 24th. Sept. 24th., very sultry. Went to the Institution and saw a poor show, but there are some very fine Millais' among the permanent collection. Afterwards to shop, bought a map. I never before quite mastered the geography of Manchester.

Went to look at the Bright statue. I think the front-face fine, the side-face does not seem to me the right shape of head. The effect of the figure does not strike me as correct. Every statue that has ever been made of Mr Bright endeavours to give dignity by *height*. No man's figure ever had more when he held himself up, but it was from *sturdy* mass. My father, a competent judge, considers this statue far away the best.

After lunch to call on cousin Mary Harrison, and to tea, aunt Sidney sitting in her rocking chair as if she had not moved from it in the last two years. A little thinner in the face, a little discomposed at our sudden entrance, her voice a little weak, but very much herself. When old aunt Sidney, the last of her generation, has gone to rest, cousin Louisa will be the nearest portrait of her mother, her voice and figure very like. The former more jerky and interrogative and her features more strongly marked, but many tricks of tone and manner strongly resembling.

My father afterwards in sentimental mood went to call on the Miss Gaskells,[7] but the sentiment was too gushing for the sentimental. He kept referring to it all evening. For one thing they had become exceedingly stout. Neither of their parents were so. There is a tradition that Mrs Gaskell, a very elegant woman, had even served as a model for sculpture in the days when sculpture was voluminously draped! I never saw her.

LONDON

Thursday, September 26th. Next day we went home. Sept. 26th. I should like to have stayed longer. I enjoy Manchester. There is one odd sensation, one is constantly jostling against people who look like relations. I saw one degraded party the very image of a deceased uncle. The women are like our 'lizabeth, the girls like cousin Alice, and though he would scorn the imputation, the young men are like my brother in features.

Friday, September 27th. To call on Mrs Moore[8] whom I found in bed with a cold and very cheerful, talking as hard as possible, very hoarse. I was afraid of catching it.

She presently sat up in a state of excitement the two boys being on the balcony leaning round to the window. The nursery governess was also in bed with a cold. The little girls on the other hand were endeavouring to go up the chimney. The little sweeps were most engaging but rougher than I had previously seen them. The cat had kittens.

I was somewhat taken aback to hear of Mrs Moore in bed. What a thing it is to have a family, but vicariously I was exceedingly amused, and having found face to deposit an old silk dress was much relieved to find it received with effusion.

Friday, October 4th. To call on little Miss Rosie Carter,[9] which for once seemed a kind action, for she was overflowing with talk and a little tearful. Worldly affairs pretty well, but she has lost her two friends, one retired into the country, the other to a boarding-house 'for more society', leaving that sociable little person quite alone, and moreover with the most miserably forlorn stock of furniture.

She was about to move into new lodgings, and I was almost convulsed with the precautions which she had taken to find out whether they were respectable. Not but what it was exceedingly proper and wise, but the lady is so terrifically plain. She is most bright and industrious, but something like the Australian aborigine.

There were two French professors, than which nothing can be imagined more nasty, on the other hand the son of the landlady was a choir-boy, which is next good to a cherub (when so be they are not 'emissaries of satan') and the third boarder was an 'independent old lady'. The clergyman to whom she had applied seemed to have been exceedingly kind in making enquiries.

Monday, October 11th. Mamma was taken very ill, sick from eight on Monday morning till three next morning. If it had gone on longer I should have been frightened as there began to be haemorrhage, but it stopped as suddenly as it began. She was upstairs nearly a fortnight, mending, without any shock, but I had a weary time, bother with the Servants as well.

There is supposed to be some angelic sentiment in tending the sick, but personally I should not associate angels with castor oil and emptying slops.

It is an odd experience sitting up all night, sweeps in the lane at four o'clock, the street-lamps put out at 4.45 in pitch dark, and towards six, workmen going to town on bicycles with lights, in the dusk, and others trooping along, all walking in the road.

I had no difficulty in keeping wide awake and never knew a night go faster, but became so frightfully hungry I had to go down to the larder at four in my stockings.

Having been indoors almost continually I caught a violent cold in my head, and my father being troubled with gravel again, and every prospect of a hard winter, I have become lower than is the habit with me, a cheerful person.

Sunday, November 3rd. Went to the Paget's. Sir William Flower came in but did not recognize me, it was dark. I wonder if people know the pleasure they may give a person by a little notice. Not that I think that Sir W. Flower is very kind, but absent minded. He knows me occasionally, but generally not at the Museum, and I always thought perhaps if I happened to meet him at the Paget's he would speak to me.

Must confess to crying after I got home, my father being as usual deplorable, and beginning to read Gibbon's *Decline and Fall* from the beginning again, after having waded to the 4th. vol. of seven, and forgotten the three first. It is a shade better than metaphysics, but not enlivening.

Monday, November 18th. Mrs W. Bruce's children to tea, nice little girls but very shy. Peter Rabbit was the entertainment, but flatly refused to perform although he had been black-fasting all day from all but mischief.

He caused shrieks of amusement by sitting up in the arm-chair and getting on to the tea-table. The children were satisfied, but it is tiresome that he will never show off. He really is good at tricks when hungry, in private, jumping (stick, hands, hoop, back and forward), ringing little bell and drumming on a tambourine.

Wednesday, December 11th. I fretted so wearily that I went privately to see Dr Aikin Dec. 11th., and had it out with him. He was very kind. I told him plainly I thought it was very startling to be told to go abroad for five months of the year. If my father cannot stand the English winter it is a matter to consider, but seriously we could not stand living five months in an hotel. Now another house on the top of our present arrangements, it would mean a complete change of habits.

He told me nothing which I did not know before and agree with, but I was relieved that he took a cheerful view of mamma's ailments. He was strong for our going to Falmouth, as I suggest. I only fear papa will refuse to move before he is ill. I am anxious to do my best, but I really cannot face going abroad with him.

Saturday, December 14th. I was feeling very much down for a few days. I derived much quiet pleasure from reading Matthew Arnold's letters. I believe I like them because I obtain much consolation at present from reading the Old Testament and Wordsworth; set after

Shakespeare, however, of whose existence Matthew Arnold seems to have been almost absolutely unconscious.[10]

I also increasingly derive consolation from a less elevated source, the comfort of having money. One must make out some way. It is something to have a little money to spend on books and to look forward to being independent, though forlorn.

In the meantime comes the American panic, and my father nearly beside himself.

Saturday, December 21st. to Tuesday, December 31st. We had not a pleasant Christmas, wet, dark, Bertram sulky, and interminable rule of the sums and stock-broking calculations which would never come right.

By the middle of the week papa was ill, very ill he looked last night, but today, New Year's Eve, the weather has providently become as warm as spring. He has got rid of a good deal at no particular loss, and is unloading the rest gradually. Ellis', the brokers who kept cool in the crisis, don't favour American Railroads for a nervous person.

By way of relaxation, the amusement of the last month has been the question whether Sir Lewis Morris is married or not, that hypocritical Welshman having suddenly electrified his most intimate friends by sending out cards Sir Lewis Morris and my Lady. How he has possibly kept it quiet so long, living at an address in Maida Vale with his christian name spelled wrong in the Blue Book, I cannot imagine. He has always passed as a bachelor. Luckily, too frightfully ugly to break hearts, but a certain elderly lady, now justly enraged, is said to have taken gratuitous trouble to introduce him to likely parties.

He has not told any of his Club friends, and the only two of them who ventured to tax him got not much information, except that he had been married 'some time'. One report saith a boy at Westminster, another saith a boy at Eton, two girls just coming out, but yet another rumour that the eldest is twenty-eight.

Miss Bruce, overcome by curiosity, called, but couldn't make much of it, she appears to have used her eyes to the effect that there was good china and Lady Morris wore the 'stiff silk' dress, and there was a litter of cards ready to post and some of them were shilling ones!

I am ashamed to say I have been much amused. I think his poetry beneath contempt, but he has been the poet laureate of ladies' schools and respectability.[11] Was not there once a skit in Punch 'I am he that opened Hades, to harmless persons – and to ladies!'

1896

'There is a largeness and silence going up into the hills'

LONDON

Tuesday, January 7th. To Museum, studying labels on insects, being in want of advice, and not in a good temper, I worked into indignation about that august Institution. It is the quietest place I know – and the most awkward. They have reached such a pitch of propriety that one cannot ask the simplest question.

The other Museum is most disagreeable with the students, but if I want to find out anything at the library there is not the slightest difficulty, just pay sixpence and have done with it. At the Natural History Museum the clerks seem to be all gentlemen and one must not speak to them. If people are forward I can manage them, but if they take the line of being shocked it is perfectly awful to a shy person.

The sweetest spectacle I have lately seen, the Store's cat, its paws folded under its white chest, its ears and white whiskers laid back, ignoring the roar of the Haymarket, in a new red morocco collar, couchant in a pile of biscuit canisters.

Monday, January 13th. Lunch at the Paget's. Old Mr Paget, Miss Paget, Mrs Price, Mary, Kathleen and W. Rathbone's grand daughter, an immensely tall young girl with an odd likeness to the dawdling languid manner of her aunt Elsie (not but I admire Miss Rathbone who has reason to look tired) but in a younger person it looks lazy.

The lunch was surprisingly clean, with one exception of a live dormouse on one of the hot plates. Old Mr Paget was very funny, stone-deaf, obstinately, amiably bland, with a high voice and a fine old-fashioned politeness, somewhat disconnected, 'No I will not eat an-y cheese be-cause I am go-ing out with Mis-es Paget, I tell you I will *not*.'

He keeps jumping up, he despises lunch and modern feeding, especially does he despise rich pudding, it is reported that he once refused some, with the explanation that he had 'not been recently confined', and a further magisterial comment to the effect that 'The only use for a rich pudding is to put your foot in it.'

Old Miss Swanwick remembers, when living with her mother and sister at Liverpool, that late at night some gravel was thrown against the windows, and, looking out, a voice cried that the Reform Bill had passed.[1]

Wednesday, January 22nd. Walking in the afternoon met a news-boy with a placard of the death of Prince Henry of Battenburg, not an interesting personality to the world, but very sad for his family.[2] Mourning almost universal and of the sort I call genuinely sympathetic. Not so much show, suits of complete black, and every female wearing something, either hat or petticoat. There was a horrid rumour on Friday morning that the Queen was dead, I cannot imagine how started.

Sunday, February 2nd. Sunday morning, papa taken suddenly very ill, as usual. Did not really look so ill as at Christmas, not being much troubled with the gravel, but shocking pain. Obstruction lasting till Wednesday, and took an extraordinary amount of morphia.

Dr Aikin most exceedingly kind. Also uncle Harry, only I begin to regard him in the light of a corbie or hoodie-crow, he comes in at these times. After papa got better I had a cold, and much done-up.

Tuesday, February 11th. Unveiling of Mr Bright's statue at Westminster Hall. I did not go because of cold, and also not clear whether to ladies. Sorry afterwards because Sir H. Howorth there, whom I have a curiosity to see. I wonder why I never seem to know people. It makes one wonder whether one is presentable. It strikes me it is the way to make one not.

The statue is so frightful that the Duke of Devonshire winked at John Gilbert.[3] The latter is indignant, and yet the Duke says that

Mr Gilbert made *three* different clay figures. I think he is very uneven, an eccentric individual. There was a story of someone finding him at lunch upon strawberries and treacle.

Sunday, February 23rd. To Chapel, sitting behind that old person Lord Dysart, to my displeasure, for in addition to the erratic behaviour incident to his blindness, the poor man has a sort of twitch. A most singular-looking individual, very large and upstanding, high features, arched eyebrows and nose, very red hair, cropped, very stout and bristly, staring and rolling grey eyes, wide open. A personality calculated to distract attention from a more engrossing discourse than little Mr Freeston's.

There was the annual meeting afterwards, not without friction, the Minister receiving a not undeserved dressing from Mr Beal with regard to certain political indiscretions. They are the mischief with Dissenters. I cannot say that I feel the slightest interest or pleasure in that Chapel, apart from going with my father.

I shall always call myself a Unitarian because of my father and grandmother, but for the Unitarians as a Dissenting body, as I have known them in London, I have no respect. Their creed is apt to be a timid, illogical compromise, and their forms of Service, a badly performed imitation of the Church. Their total want of independence and backbone is shown by the way in which they call their chapels churches, and drag in the word Christian.

We are not Christians in the commonly accepted sense of the term, neither are the Jews, but they are neither ashamed nor shamed. Then a profane saying of Ben Brierly's, quoted by Elizabeth 'They put their 'ed in their 'at and count twenty.'

Tuesday, February 25th. Met Lady Millais in Gloucester Road.[4] She was being bullied by a lady in a velvet mantle, so I merely insinuated the remark that I was sure that she must be receiving more congratulations than she could attend to, whereupon she seized my arm to cross the street, expressing a wish to die together, there being a procession of female bicycles. I thought it a characteristic mixture of graciousness and astute utility, she walking with a black crutch-stick, but most amusingly elated.

Sir John Millais told Mr F— he supposed he must take the damned thing.[5]

SWANAGE

Monday, April 13th. to Saturday, April 25th. We came to Swanage April 13th., a fortnight, to the Royal Victoria Hotel, Miss Vincent. Clean, civil, rather poor for the money, and singularly tough food.

I am writing this at the end of an idle fortnight, chequered by toothache, but on the whole a very pleasant impression, apart from east wind and the annoyance of wasting expensive wet days.

The town is not exciting, but *small* and there are places of interest and beauty. Studland near Poole Harbour, one of the sweetest pictures of white sand, blue sea, and background of fir and sandy heaths, which I have seen. Also Rempstone among the Downs with a splendid view, cowslips and the first cuckoo.

One day to Wareham in a gale of wind, a sleepy, shrunk little market-town inside mounds, an absurd Fair in the town-ditch, ponies, scraggy horses, Hereford cattle, and a young bull rushing about, finally dragged out of a hedge by the tail, I behind a lamp post.

Corfe massive, bare, except for jackdaws, and a suspicion of iron railings to cope with trippers. I should think this place is swarming in the summer.

I should like well to come again some day, to better lodgings, and at my leisure.

I find it better not to expect or worry much about geology, but got one amusing afternoon among the quarries. The quarrymen quiet, and a curious community. It is not a place one can pick up much, unsafe cliffs and underground quarries. With opportunity I fancy the Corfe clay-pits would have been more satisfactory.

With opportunity the world is very interesting. I fear this corner will fall into the grip of Bournemouth, but it is much more exposed to east wind, and the railway has been open ten years without much increase. Is amazingly under the spell of Mowlem & Burt, Contractors.

The flowers and singing-birds have been pleasant. My father was very unwell one day, but I have seen worse outings.

I forgot to set down on Sun. April 12th. a few minutes after eight I saw a fine meteor. I should say a large one a long way off in the north. I was surprised to find no mention in the paper.

It was at a height of about 30 degrees and scarcely dropped at all before going out, which it did without the slightest appearance of explosion. It appeared rather larger and more striking than Jupiter, *white* with a *red* compact trail. There was still some slight glow of light in the north west.

My bedroom was dark, I was just going to get the book of Daniel. It is odd, but in the instant of looking at it I was irresistibly reminded of those photographs of a bullet at the museum. I can hardly suppose the waves visible, I suppose the labouring motion and hot train of light in the furrow gave the impression of ploughing through the air. I believe it is the generally accepted explanation, but I did not know it would be apparent.

I supposed it to be very distant (geographically) from its motion appearing comparatively slow, less steady and less rapid than an express train, but more like that sort than the undetermined slant of a falling star. I was much impressed by it, a strange visitor from the outside of the world.

I do not often consider the stars, they give me a *tissick*. It is more than enough that there should be forty thousand named and classified funguses.

LONDON

Tuesday, May 19th. Uncle Harry in to see papa in the evening.[6] In a sudden fit of kindness of conscience he proposed the next day taking me to Kew. It had slipped so often.

I was rather agreeably surprised before getting up next morning, to receive a message, Sir Henry's love and would I be ready to start at half-past nine, which romantic elopement took place in a gale of wind via Earl's Court Station. I was rather flattered to find that only myself was going. I think he rather wanted to see Mr Thiselton-Dyer,[7] but he was most exceedingly kind.

We travelled third, and discoursed upon motor carriage, Pretoria posters, bicycles; uncle Harry deaf, sententious and very good-tempered. Just before the last station he got into a whisper about the umbrella-handle of the opposite young woman, which was decorated with two carved love-birds, coloured to nature. I had for some time been apprehensive that he would observe it. There is nothing like impudence, we certainly did well.

I only hope I shall remember separately the five different gentlemen with whom I had the honour of shaking hands. Not that uncle Harry was presumptuous (there is a shorter word), on the contrary, he assumed a bland and insinuating address, a solicitous and engaging simper which caused me to observe him with surprise, not having previously seen him exhibit that phase of deportment.

We first saw Mr Morris[8] who disclaimed all knowledge of fungi – 'I am exclusively tropical', he was sorting crumply papers containing very spiky, thorny gums from Arabia, fastened down by multitudinous slips. A funny little house up and down. Covered with creeper, one in beautiful flower against the chimney.

We went out and across Kew Green to the Herbarium, a fine old red house with wainscotting and a fine staircase. I think it is one where Fanny Burney dwelt. There we saw Mr Hemsley,[9] and stacks of dried papers, whereof such contents as I happened to see were either spiky or of the everlasting race, and there was a decorous flavour of herbs.

We saw Mr Massee[9] whom I had come to see, a very pleasant, kind gentleman who seemed to like my drawings.

Outside we met Mr Baker,[10] the librarian, who bowed profoundly in silence upon presentation to uncle Harry. A slim, timid looking old gentleman with a large, thin book under his arm, and an appearance of having been dried in blotting paper under a press, which, together with white straw hats and white trousers, was the prevalent type, summery, rather arid and very clean.

We returned to the Director's office, and found him, a thin, elderly gentleman in summery attire, with a dry, cynical manner, puffing a cigarette, but wide awake and boastful. He seemed pleased with my drawings and a little surprised. He spoke kindly about the ticket, and did not address me again, which I mention not with resentment, for I was getting dreadfully tired, but I had once or twice an amusing feeling of being regarded as young.

Uncle Harry was afraid of missing his train and we trudged across grass, under showers of red blossom and across the rock-garden, and a distant glimpse of the two young women presumably in knickerbockers tying up flowers.

Mr Thiselton-Dyer puffed his cigarette, vituperated the weather, the rate of wages, discoursed vaingloriously upon his Establishment and arrangements, and his hyacinths, better than the Dutch. His anecdotes were too statistical to recall without a note-book, much of great interest and informative, for instance how the British occupation and property in Egypt has destroyed the English onion industry.

I followed behind them, kept going by a providential peppermint in my pocket. We sat on a seat on the platform, and the two gentlemen got into deep conversation about London University where there is apparently some hitch.

Uncle Harry became somewhat maudlin, 'Now Gladstone, poor old devil – he knew no more about science than my boot-jack, and now there is Salisbury – I *cannot* understand,' and 'Devonshire' appeared to be the leading delinquent.

Mr Thiselton-Dyer showed himself a Radical, if no trades unionist. I shot in one remark which made him jump, as if they had forgotten my presence; not political. I got home without collapse, a most interesting morning.

WINDERMERE

Father, mother and I to the Ferry Hotel to look about for houses. We went to Kendal one day to see Mr Hanes, a fine big fellow, the first Land Agent I ever saw who struck one as a gentleman. A queer, steep old town, much thronged, being market day (most choice white piglings in coops), and a Hiring-Fair for farm-servants.[11]

Our stay was not eventful, only I noticed on the journeys I was allowed to undertake the luggage. I judged as a melancholy satisfaction I managed well.

LONDON

Saturday, June 13th. I went to Kew again to see Mr Massee. I was not a little amused again – I hope not disrespectfully. He seems a kind, pleasant gentleman. I believe it is rather the fashion to make fun of him, but I can only remark that it is much more interesting to talk to a person with ideas, even if they are not founded on very sufficient evidence.

He was growing funguses in little glass covers, and, being carried away by his subject, confided that one of them had spores three inches long. I opine that he has passed several stages of development into a fungus himself – I am occasionally conscious of a similar transformation.

It was very hot (ours went up to 130°, but no one believed it), and I had more than enough to do during the last week or two.

I took certain things to the Museum to make out, and was further edified by the slowness of the officials. They do not seem anything but very kind, but they do not seem to be half sharp. Mr Kirby, however, stutters a little. Mr Waterhouse (beetles), – two ladybirds rotating in a glass pill-box – is so like a frog we had once, it puts me out. I should like to know what is Sir W. Flower's subject besides ladies' bonnets.

From this contumelious disquisition I except Mr Pocock, and a gentleman with his head tied up, who were sufficiently pleased with my drawing to give me a good deal of information about spiders. They are almost too much specialists, they really seem less well informed than an ordinary person on any subject outside their own, and occasionally to regard it with petulance.

SAWREY

Wednesday, July 15th. Came to Lakefield on Esthwaite.[12]

Thursday, July 23rd. Drove along the Graythwaite road through oak coppices, a blind-road, the least pleasing in the neighbourhood. The wood scattered with poor specimens of the poisonous *Agaricus phalloides*, and not without a suspicion of adders. It is too dry for much funguses.

One has a pleasant sensation sometimes. I remember so well finding *Gomphidius glutinosus* in Hatchednize wood, and now today, under a beech tree on a large flat chip, I spied the dark hairy stalks and tiny balls of one of the Mycetozoa.

After tea, up the hill, a little way up there is a remote hennery whence proceeded singular thumpings and bumpings. I making a circum valley observation, with suspicion of mills or gipsies, and the assistance of sheep, the best of outposts, discovered that it was caused by two nasty broody old hens shut up in a barrel. Afterwards watched a hedgehog.

Saturday, July 25th. Most tremendous rain. Funguses came up extensively, but small. Poked about amongst the lumber in the attics, and watched the rain rushing down a sort of runnel into the cistern. There are some ancient pistols and an ancient case and velvet hunting-cap. Bertram turned out a portfolio of chalk drawings, figures and heads, in the style of Fuseli, such as young ladies drew at school sixty years since.

Played much with Peter Rabbit.

Sunday, July 26th. Blowy, soft air. Afternoon went a long dragging walk on the top of Stone Lane with Bertram, not without a sense of trespass, but the air and wild herbage very pleasant.

Cutting across to get back to our moor, in the middle of half a morass, wading through heather and bracken, came across a small but very lively viper, which we killed with a stick. Should not have in gaiters, but think the dogs run some risk of being bitten.

We cut off the head which soon ceased to nip, but the tail was obstreperous for an hour and still winced after another hour in the spirit – I hope mechanically! They are exceedingly pretty.

Tuesday, July 28th. A perfect, hot summer day, cloudless, but evening when it rolled up like thunder round How Fell.

I am thirty this day. I felt a certain irritation upon receiving congratulatory letters from the Hutton girls, for one thing I can never remember theirs. They told me of poor Kathleen Hutton, dead at nineteen. I remember so well the first I saw her and Carrie, such handsome Irish children, gathering the sacred cabbage roses in Putney Park garden.

I feel much younger at thirty than I did at twenty; firmer and stronger both in mind and body.

Edith's little Molly to tea. Master Jim in disgrace, having gone against orders with the gardener to the running of a fallow deer escaped from Curwen's island. That boy is a tyke. Walked home part way with the gossipy roly-poly Anne, assisting to push the mail-cart. Very pleasant evening-light, and village people up and down the road in the flowery little gardens.

Saturday, August 8th. To see Edith. Went up into the loft to see Mrs Frisky, who had been loose the previous night, let out by Miss Molly, and caught with much difficulty with a candle among the hay. I should think it is very unusual for squirrels to breed in confinement. The lady in question could not help herself, having been caught in a cage-trap four days before the event.

There are two young, supposed to have been four originally. She was sitting on them like an old hen, looking very pretty. They appeared about the size of mice; they are five weeks old. They were naked at first and blind for four weeks.

Thursday, August 13th. Sir John Millais died Aug. 13th., interred into rest. He would have gone long ago if he had been an ordinary poor man. We pity the poor when they are sick, but this was surely the other extreme.

I saw him last in November, walking in Knightsbridge, 'How is my little friend?, can't speak, can't speak!' He looked as handsome and well as ever, he was one of the handsomest men I ever saw, apart from the defect of his eye, and the odd mark across his forehead which the tan stopped, but perhaps the sunburn may only have been noticeable in Scotland.

There is a Scotch saying 'his face is made of a fiddle'. I think it must have been particularly applicable to all the Millais', for people to whom they were rude, to the extent almost of unkindness, were just as much fond of them. I am not speaking of ourselves, for in London society they were in a different light, we in none at all, and meeting them casually, they were always exactly like old times.

They might be considered selfish, but they made no pretensions and I should always take such as I found them – for the moment very pleasant – a little hard, but with a background of feeling and trouble, which I hope the world had forgotten and not known.

I shall always have a most affectionate remembrance of Sir John Millais, though unmercifully afraid of him as a child, on account of what the papers call 'his schoolboy manner'. I had a brilliant colour as a little girl, which he used to provoke on purpose and remark upon at times. If a great portrait painter's criticism is of any interest this is it, delivered with due consideration, turning me round under a window, that I was a little like his daughter Carrie, at that time a fine handsome girl, but my face was spoiled by the length of my nose and upper lip.

He gave me the kindest encouragement with my drawings (to be sure he did to everybody!), vide, a visit he paid to an awful country Exhibition at Perth, in the shop of Stewart the frame maker (who invited him), but he really paid me a compliment for he said that 'Plenty of people can *draw*, but you and my son John have observation.' Now 'my son Johnnie' at that date couldn't draw at all, but I know exactly what he meant.

He sent me a little note when I was in bed with the rheumatics, take the world as we find it. He was an honest fine man.

Wednesday, August 26th. The larch peziza came into flower. I took it very calmly being so firmly persuaded it would come.

Afternoon – Drove to Ambleside and, at one of the corners between Out Gate and Randy Pike, was banged into by another female driving a gig. I was rather aghast at the moment, but afterwards convulsed with laughter. I am persuaded it is upon the conscience of the other party because she was so rude, asked me why I did not get out of the way. Had I responded in like spirit I should have said something about the old gentleman and the deep ditch.

We were dragging up hill at a walk, she coming down very fast hit the box of my hind wheel with the *tyre* of hers. When two boxes scrape an inch is as good as an ell, but I do not think I could have gone three inches nearer the ditch.

There is apt to be a difference of opinion on these occasions. I have driven in much funnier traffic in London and never touched anything in my life.

Friday, September 4th. To Holehird, very pleasant and silent on the hill. I am very fond of Troutbeck. There is a largeness and silence going up into the hills. I think because it is on the edge of a vast waste.

★

Sunday, September 6th. Went to the Friends' Meeting at Colthouse. I liked it very much. It is a pretty little place, peaceful and sunny, very old-fashioned inside, with a gigantic old key to the door.

I thought it so pleasant in the stillness to listen to a robin singing in the copperbeech outside the porch. I doubt if his sentiments were religious.

There were between twenty and thirty. I was the second to arrive, following in a roly-poly stout lady in a black silk dress who shook hands and demanded my name, which I pronounced, whereupon she said 'never heard of it', and I diffidently added I was a visitor to the neighbourhood, to which she affably replied that she was visiting the Satterthwaites, I think their aunt?

Our conversation was interrupted by the arrival of two friends from Kendal, a lady and gentleman, on *bicycles*. The gentleman spoke very well, but I could not quite get over his being in knickerbockers. Mr Satterthwaite read the 103rd. Psalm slowly and reverently.

There is something in the sentiment of a Quaker Meeting so exactly quaint and fine that a very little oversets the balance, and to an ordinary Philistine it is never comprehensible at all, but to those who can feel the charm, like Charles Lamb, it is exquisitely pleasant. There was one child present, a little boy, who sat behind me on the women's side. He was very quiet, except for audibly sucking sweeties and sighing deeply at intervals. I fear, but do not wonder, that backsliders are numerous in the young generation.

In the afternoon we again had that old person Tom Thornely. It is my opinion he is half-baked, not two minutes would he talk about one thing except ghost stories, whereby he made my mother very uncomfortable.

Tuesday, November 17th. I have neglected to write this up for a very long time. We came home on October 6th., Bertram going north on 5th.

I was very sorry to come away in spite of the broken weather. It is as nearly perfect a little place as I ever lived in, and such nice old-fashioned people in the village. Poor little James Rogerson kept up in a dejected state at the end, but was seen with his knuckles in his eyes as he shut the gate.

I went the last evening to say goodbye to Mary Postlethwaite who made a very pretty picture in the fire-light dandling her fat baby. Little Josie was there rocking backwards and forwards, repeating 'The Cat and the Fiddle' and 'Sing a Song of Sixpence' in a rapid gabble.

Perhaps my most sentimental leave-taking was with Don, the great farm collie. He came up and muddied me as I was packing up Peter Rabbit at the edge of dark. I accompanied him to the stable-gate, where he turned, holding it open with his side, and gravely shook hands. Afterwards, putting his paws solemnly on my shoulder, he licked my face and then went away into the farm.

I have a pleasant memory of Hawkshead another day, when I went to Tyson's shop and bought two striped petticoats. There was a pleasant, friendly, middle-aged lady in the shop who said, 'I think I ought to know your face,' and oddly enough I thought the same, but it was Mrs Beck of Esthwaite Hall.

I went up afterwards part way up the steep road towards Grizedale, left the pony and walked across some rough intakes to the edge of a copse getting funguses, and back near a little tumbling stream and some flaming wild hollies. The hawthorns down below were a sight in the sun.

I was followed a long way by two cockerels because I had a basket. I got rid of them by bestowing a round peppermint which puzzled them sadly. It was a bright, sunny day, blue sky and mist.

I think one of my pleasantest memories of Esthwaite is sitting on Oatmeal Crag on a Sunday afternoon, where there is a sort of table of rock with a dip, with the lane and fields and oak copse like in a trough below my feet, and all the little tiny fungus people singing and bobbing and dancing in the grass and under the leaves all down below, like the whistling that some people cannot hear of stray mice and bats, and I sitting up above and knowing something about them.

I cannot tell what possesses me with the fancy that they laugh and clap their hands, especially the little ones that grow in troops and rings amongst dead leaves in the woods. I suppose it is the fairy rings, the myriads of fairy fungi that start into life in autumn woods.

I remember I used to half believe and wholly play with fairies when I was a child. What heaven can be more real than to retain the spirit-world of childhood, tempered and balanced by knowledge and common-sense, to fear no longer the terror that flieth by night, yet to feel truly and understand a little, a very little, of the story of life.

MEMORIES OF CAMFIELD PLACE

My dear Esther, you ask me again still more pressingly to write to you from Camfield. I begin obediently, but I much fear this will break short like the other letters I have tried to write. There is something so sad in deliberately writing for the time when these things shall have utterly passed away from me.

To me all is bound up together in fact and fancy, my dear grandmother, the place I love best in the world and the sweet balmy air where I have been so happy as a child. I shall never want a record to remind me of this perfect whole, where all things are a part, the notes of the stable clock and the all pervading smell of new-mown hay, the distant sounds of the farmyard, the feeling of plenty, well-assured, indolent wealth, honourably earned and wisely spent, charity without ostentation, opulence without pride – or if I reflect, I have lived long enough to know that time destroys long memory as well as friends remembered. If I reflect that I shall one day think with perfect equanimity of days that are no more, does that knowledge encourage me to write with tender enthusiasm of my Blakesmoor[1] in Hertfordshire.

Besides there is something awkward and absurd in describing to you a place which you know so well. Can you not see in your mind's eye, as plainly as I who am here, the windy north front on its terrace, with the oaks moaning and swaying on winter nights close to the bedroom windows, and at their feet the long green slope of meadows down to the ponds, and have you not been wakened on summer mornings by the persistent crying of a cuckoo in these same oaks, twenty to thirty. I believe the record was fifty-two cries before seven o'clock, till tired of counting.

You have drawn up the window-sash and looked out. A slight mist still clings to the beech-wood over against the ponds. Further east, beyond the sweep of grass-land and scattered oaks, the blue distance opens out, rising to the horizon over Panshanger Woods. If you get on any rising ground in this neighbourhood you would fancy Hertfordshire was one great oak wood. There are trees in every hedgerow, and, seen from the moderate elevation of our hills, they seem to stand one against another. In summer the distant landscapes are intensely blue.

The autumn frost spreads a ruddy glow over the land. I shall never forget the view I once saw from Essendon Hill, miles upon miles of golden oak wood, with here and there a yellow streak of stubble, and a clump of russet walnut trees behind the red gable, and thin blue smoke of a farm.

Not less beautiful is the winter, when the oaks are clothed in a delicate tracery of snow and hoar-frost, they sometimes look quite orange-coloured in the sunshine against the sky, and yet the hoar-frost scarcely drips. My grandmother says when it snows in Hertfordshire it lies all winter. Have you ever noticed what a peculiar blue the snow is during a white frost? I know no colour like it except that milky lemon-blue which you find in the seed of wild balsam. At such times of frost and snow the two great cedars on the lawn look their best. The snow lies in wreaths on their broad outstretched arms, or melting, trickles down the dusty green bark with red stains. Both are magnificent trees in their prime. The cedar on the right nearest the house grows low, its branches resting on the ground, mixed up with summer growth of wild parsley and coarse grass.

Between the cedars the upward slope of the lawn is crowned with a bank of rhododendrons and trees, behind which appear the tops of the pink chestnuts in the carriage drive. Here also, almost concealed by lignum vitae, is an artificial ruin or grotto, one of the efforts of Capability Brown[2] who planted the cedars and laid out the grounds about the year 1800. A hideous thing it must have been before it was weather-stained and smothered with ivy, but we will forgive him his grotto for the sake of two charming old summer-houses, real houses, not rickety little boxes, and it is down by the ponds.

I believe it is the fashion to make game of Capability Brown, but, if this place is a fair example of his skill, I do not agree. The grouping of the trees is particularly fine, and more striking from the contrast to my grandfather's muddled and over-crowded efforts.

With the exception of cedars, (which had been planted), Brown confined his choice to herbaceous trees. The only planting of my grandfather's which has been really satisfactory are the pink chestnuts. His Northerns, pines and hollies, struck up wonderfully fast at first, and were the pride of his heart; he had a Wellingtonia which had climbed half its first hundred feet – but now they have got down to the blue clay and every year one or two fall off.

A few years ago there were scores of tall lignum vitae bushes, trees almost, some planted by my grandfather, some old established, but at least half of them were uprooted and overturned by an unlucky snowstorm. A cedar fell into the pond at the same time but is not missed.

Another weak point during snow is an enormous hollow elm opposite the kitchen windows. It is braced up with iron bands and a useful receptacle for a wheel-barrow, brooms, etc. It has had two tragedies within my memory, the first time smashing on to the roof and kitchen wall, but it always sprouts again like the phoenix. What fun it used to be climbing up into the holes looking for owls and starlings. It is a paradise for the birds.

I remember when I was a child lying in a crib in the nursery bedroom under the tyranny of a cross old nurse – I used to be awakened at four in the morning by the song of the birds in this elm. I can feel the diamond-pattern of that old yellow crib printed against my cheek, as I lay with my head where my heels should be, staring backwards over my eye brows at the plaster heads on the chimney piece, and a large water-colour alpine scene which I regarded with respectful awe.

What a great deal we lose in growing wise! Pictures, which seemed almost alive and with a real scene as a child, now are mere daubs of paint and woefully out of drawing, and the plaster of Paris busts which seemed almost real people in the twilight, – I am afraid that Musidora squints,[3] Sir Walter Raleigh is a stick, and the lady who leans on a rock in a corner above the hot-water pipes is absurdly too tall; she used to be my ideal of elegance. To be sure their complexions have never been the same since Zipperah took to washing them in hot water at the spring-cleaning. But the loss is much more with myself.

I have always liked the old part of the house best, although the new part is more associated with my grandmother, who has not been down the stairs into the old part for several years now. The new rooms are not bad in taste, though made before present art enlightenment, but they are rather uncomfortably large, handsome is the word, and perhaps my having felt shy there as a child may have had something to do with it.

There are two tall mirrors facing one another on the stairs, miles of looking-glasses and little figures in white muslin. I never durst look in them for fear of another head besides my own peeping round the corner. I now regard it as a curious study in perspective. You, Esther, will not suspect me of superstitious fear if I confess I prefer the back staircase even yet after dark.

The long corridor has particularly painful associations with my grandfather, in the largest, barest bedroom at the far end he died. He used to hold on to the carved post at the head of the stairs when they tried to get him to bed, away from my grandmother when he was out of his mind.

No such painful memories spoil the old part of the house, the dear realms of *Nanny Nettycoat*, that little old lady with white woollen stockings, black velvet slippers and a mob-cap, who must have been just like my grandmother. The only pity is that the realm is so circumscribed.

When my grandfather bought Camfield Place from the Dimsdales, (who were by no means the original owners, however), it was a good-sized small-roomed old house of no particular pretensions, the outside, red brick, white-washed.

There was one oak-panelled room, destroyed alas, where the Lord of the Manor had held some sort of Court or Session in Elizabeth's reign. My grandfather pulled down a certain part, perhaps half, at the eastern end and built a large addition curiously joined to the old part with steps and stairs. Were it not for this difference of elevation and a slight twist, you would be able in the upper part of the house to look along the old passage and the new corridor from one end of the house to the other. About 44 paces.

This new part, built of yellow terracotta, contains six sitting-rooms and a porch below, six bedrooms and two dressing rooms above, with a good deal of wasted space under the gables. The old house though of the same external height is in three stories.

Report says that the Court-room was a considerable size, but the only large old room left now is the kitchen, whose height always

surprises me and is full of flies by the way. There is a large scullery
with a stone oven and a great vat for making broth, also a curious
smoke-jack in the chimney, and a plague of another sort of jacks
which are black.

The servants' hall projects beyond the back door and is modern.
On the opposite side of the flagged passage, garnished with hams,
to the kitchen, is the coal-hole and various offices, including a
larder, so cold that my grandfather complained that the hot-baked
meats are hard with the frost – also a breakneck stair leading as I
understand to the men's rooms, which I conclude to lie behind the
blank party-wall on the north side of the passage upstairs. But the
geography of that part of the house is a delicate mystery to me, so
is the stained yellow window at the end. Half of it, with rails that
you cannot get to, is above the level of the upper passage, and the
lower half ought by ordinary reasoning to be visible in the kitchen
passage below but it isn't. It will not open and looks out on to
inaccessible leads, a fine subject for a fanciful child. I used to sit
there for hours looking into the stable yard and wondering if there
was an enchanted Prince below; but he made no sign. I was very
much afraid of losing my dormice into the mysterious depths.

Then once the family were consternated by puffs of smoke which
came out behind the wainscot of this passage wall, and were
supposed to be connected with the kitchen chimney. How that was
compatible with the chimney's being swept through a little door in
a wall cupboard in No. 10 I don't know – my subsequent acquaintance with depraved human nature leads me to think the smoke may
have been tobacco.

I cannot clear up another problem in an equally commonplace
way. The wisdom of centuries will not explain why the closet where
the teacups are kept in the nursery does not make a corresponding
bulge in the wall surface of No. 10. The passage length, too, seems
greater than the inside of the rooms. I believe still if there was a
little chimney-sweep to go up my bedroom chimney he would run
no risk of sticking fast.

I left off in the stone passage. There is one more room on the
north side, the pantry; large, low, with a flavour of string and flower
pots (Zouche once waited all dinner with half a yard of bass matting
hanging out of his trouser's pocket) and a suspicion of not being
over-clean. At the opposite side is a little old room which is spotless,

such funny old linen cupboards up to the ceiling, doors opening in the panels without rhyme or reason. It has a light-coloured paper, the presses, chimney-piece and the high wainscot are painted white, and the sunlight dimples on the whitewashed ceiling. The flower bed outside is level with the broad window-seat, it is planted with wall-flowers every spring and a *Pyrus japonica* peeps in at the window.

That ends the old rooms downstairs. There is a heavy swing-door with diamond brass in the windows, I always push it wrong way. Then comes an interregnum up and down steps, with store rooms and lavatories which are certainly new, and a back staircase of which the banisters at least are old. It leads, – past a housemaid's closet with a bewilderment of taps, and a glass door which is kept closed with rather inconsistent care, considering the well of the stairs is of course open, – up to the servants' bedrooms.

I may finish off this part by saying they are numerous and airy, mostly super-added when the house was enlarged. There is also a rickety door opening on to the roof where I was once locked out. It is very large and commands a fine view. Otherwise it is like other roofs, with smuts, starlings, a fine bell, and awful views down skylights, just like looking over the edge of a boat into Derwentwater! The largest skylight is at the top of the back staircase which is almost dark in winter in consequence of the snow on the glass. During thunderstorms the noise of hail on it is tremendous.

I may mention that all about the passages are shelves with fire-buckets, which are occasionally repainted but never by any chance contain water. Also hose which probably leak. The plugs out of doors are all right because the gardeners use them for watering. As to the fire-bell, it is a case of 'Wolf, Wolf' for it is used to call folks out of the garden.

Coming through the glass door and round the well of the stairs, past the jam-room which is new and over the new store-room, the passage runs along over the kitchen passage. It is full of corners, in one an ottoman containing sheets and housemaid's napery, in another the hot-air slab and the sentimental lady before referred to. Half way along are two short flights of steps, four and three, the space between curiously illuminated by a shaft up to the roof into which a window opens from the servants' rooms.

The steps are wooden, all warped and creaking. When I was a

child I once slipped on the sloping boards and sprained my right wrist badly. But I bear no grudge for that, for it proved an excuse for breaking off music lessons. One can scarcely figure ladies in hoops and sacks coming along this old-fashioned passage. I can touch the whitewash with my finger. They must have stooped their heads to go under the crooked doors into what must have been the lady's parlour.

The rooms are used as a day and night-nursery when there are grandchildren at Camfield. They cannot have made very large parlours but they are high and airy, with an old-fashioned folding-door between, wonderful for trapping little fingers and getting broken backed. In both rooms are wide lattice windows with little panes, and one door in the middle that pegs open. A single iron bar was across. I used to hang upon it, children never will sit up if they can lounge, looking down at the yellow roses on the kitchen screen-wall below, or up at the old elm with its birds' nests. There was a tame robin who sat on this wall when not in the house.

At dusk the bats hawked up and down between the wall and the kitchen window, doubtless a rich harvest of flies were attracted by the heat and smell from the windows. Mouse-bats as Grimes called them, and occasionally the excitement of a great grey 'raat baat' sweeping over the roof with a piercing twitter.

The pleasantest association of that pleasant room for me is of our teas there in the twilight. I hope I am not by nature greedy, but there was something rapturous to us London children in the unlimited supply of new milk. I remember always the first teas of the visit when we were thirsty and tired. How I watched at the window for the little farm-boy, staggering along the carriage-drive with the cans! It came up warm in a great snuff-coloured jug which seemed to have no bottom, and made the milk look blue.

I seem to hear the chink of the crockery as the nurse-girl brought it out of the closet in the wall and laid the coarse, clean table cloth. I think the earthenware had a peculiar cool pleasant taste. *Nanny Nettycoat* presided in the middle of the table, guttering, homely, lop-sided with fascinating snuffers in a tin dish.

Then we had eggs, so new that the most perverse kitchen-maid could not hard-boil them, and next morning, joy of joys, the sops were made of Spriggins bread, 'sunt qui dicunt', that bread of Spriggins is sour. If that be so I can only say I do not like it sweet.

It may have been heavy but it never kept me awake, and as to tough crust (dusted with flour) why in those days we had teeth.

I think our London servants had some sort of tiff with the Spriggins or rather with their niece, a flirtatious young lady with ribbons. They live at a pretty cottage with sweeties in the window half way down Wild Hill. Miss Spriggins has grown into a stout matronly body, having married the spectacled Mr Polter, who poses as a martyr on account of having thrown up gardening at *Dollymops* rather than vote Tory and mend her gates without any nails.

My dear granny sometimes gets Mrs Polter's letters when her correspondents cross the 'L'. I remember her opening one at breakfast which began 'My dear Mary and the chicks'.

There was not much furniture in the two rooms. Some dwarf elbow-chairs, and a stumpy low table on which we made sand-pies without damage, and sailed therein as in a boat when wrong side up, which reminds me there was a drugget very tight stretched. There was also a rocking chair, we had none at home.

There was a book-shelf hanging on ropes which swayed about when you replaced anything. A work-box banished for its old-fashioned ugliness. American cloth on the round table which became sticky when we rested our chins on it. How short we were in those days.

The green curtains slid on a long brass pole. I have reason to know it was hollow, for once we took it down to extract a tame fieldmouse.

(Written about 1891)

THE LONELY HILLS

I have been listening to a Danish girl distilling melody from an old spinet. Her fingers caress the yellow ivory keys. Notes come tinkling forth like the sound of a harp; like a hesitating breeze, away, far away amongst hemlocks. The limpid undertones are the song of a brook that ripples over pebbles. J. Sebastian Bach composed his minuet for such an instrument; an old-fashioned piano propped against the wainscot on seven fluted legs. The maker's name, 'Clementi', is painted above the keyboard in a wreath of tiny flowers.

Music strikes chords of memory. Big golden-haired Ulla spoke of Copenhagen; of Hans Christian Andersen; of the little bronze mermaid sitting on her stone upon the strand where Danish children bathe and play beside the summer sea. She spoke of long frosts in Denmark; of skating on lakes and canals. No letter – another month and still no letters from Denmark; poor Denmark; poor Europe; silent behind a blank curtain of fear.

For me the pretty jingling tunes bring memories of Merry Nights and of our English Folk-Dance Revival twenty years ago. The stone-floored farm kitchen where first we danced 'The Boatman' and heard the swinging lilt of 'Black Nag'. The loft with two fiddles where country dancers paced 'The Triumph', three in arm under arched hands. The long drive home in frosty starlight with a load of rosy sleepy village girls wrapped up in rugs. Coniston, and the mad barbaric music of the Kirkby-Mazzard Sword Dance, when a beheaded corpse springs up and holds a wheel of wooden swords aloft. Chapel Stile in Langdale where we came out into deep snow from a dance over the store. 'Haste to the Wedding', 'Pop Goes the Weasel' and 'We Won't Go Home Until Morning'! The Morris bells and baldricks! The plum cake and laughter. Fat and thin, and high and low, the nimble and the laggard, the toddler and the gray-haired gran – all dancing with a will.

There were summer festivals, also, most lovely to remember. Quivering heat and smell of trodden grass, the lawns of Underley Hall, a stately setting. Deep below the woods and hanging gardens the River Lune meandered in wide sweeps through Kirkby Lonsdale meadows. The 'County' perched precariously upon a grandstand made of planks. A fine wind and string band with big drum and bassoon, very hot and thirsty, fiddled furiously under a tree, a lime scented bloom. At Underley the dancers were marshalled behind lilac bushes and azaleas. They danced on in converging strands of colour to weave a tapestry that glistened like shot silk.

I remember another unforgettable pageant, held on the Sportsfield at Grasmere. The fells towered around like a wall, and white clouds were piled over Helvellyn and Stone Arthur, with distant rumblings of thunder. And the dancers! The merry dancers! They had come in their hundreds from all over the north, a rainbow-hued kaleido-scope. In spite of roughish turf I have never seen better Morris, or prouder beauty than the Durham reels danced by girls in corn-coloured smocks. The reels pleased me especially. Folk dancing, if it is to take real hold, ought to be an indigenous revival. 'Three Reels', 'Petronella', and 'The Triumph' were traditional in this border country. My farm servants danced them at our Christmas suppers long before Morris dancing was introduced from the south. Well-trained Morris dancing is a miracle of graceful agility; a display for international meetings. But give me the swinging, roaring reels – the sparkling pretty long sets – the maze of intricate dances surprisingly remembered – follow the fiddle, forget your feet! Or dance with style and bend and sway; a bow and a curtsy for man and maid; and an inextricable tangle of laughter for beginners! Give me reels and spontaneous unsophisticated country dancing all the time for dancing in a north country village.

Another time all by myself alone I watched a weird dance, to the music of Piper Wind. It was far away in that lonely wilderness behind the table-land on Troutbeck Tongue. In the midst of this waste of yellow-bent grass and stones there is a patch of green grass and stunted thorn. Round the tree – round and round in measured canter went four of the wild fell ponies. Round and round, then checked and turned; round and round reversed; arched necks, tossing manes, tails streaming. I watched a while, crouching behind a boulder. Who had taught them? Who had learned them to 'dance the heys' in that wilderness? Oftentimes I have seen managed horses cantering round the sawdust ring under a circus tent; but these half wild youngsters had never been handled by man.

I stood up. They stopped, stared, and snorted; then galloped out of sight. While I was watching them I remembered how I had been puzzled once before. In a soft muddy place on the old drove road I had seen a multitude of little unshod footprints, much too small for horses' footmarks, much too round for deer or sheep. I did not know at that time that there would be ponies on the Troutbeck fell; though I knew they were at Haweswater and Mattisdale. I wondered were they footmarks of a troop of fairy riders, riding down old King Gait into Hird Wood and Hallilands, away into Fairyland and the blue distance of the hills. Over the ferry where mountains are blue, the finding of those little fairy footmarks on the old drove road first made me aware of the Fairy Caravan.

In the calm spacious days that seem so long ago, I loved to wander on the Troutbeck fell. Sometimes I had with me an old sheep dog, 'Nip' or 'Fly'; more often I went alone. But never lonely. There was company of gentle sheep, and wild flowers and singing waters. I listened to the voices of the Little Folk.

Troutbeck Tongue is uncanny; a place of silences and whispering echoes. It is a mighty table-land between two streams. They rise together, north of the Tongue, in one maze of bogs and pools. They flow on either hand; the Hagg Beck in the eastern valley; the Troutbeck River on the west. They meet and re-unite below the southern crags, making the table-land almost an island, an island haunted by the sounds that creep on running waters which encompass it. The Tongue is shaped like a great horseshoe, edged by silver streams, and guarded by an outer rampart of high fells. From the highest point of the Tongue I could look over the whole expanse: Woundale and the Standing Stones; Sadghyll and the hut circles; the cairns built by the stone men; the Roman road; Hallilands and Swaindale, named by the Norsemen; and the walls of the Norman deer park stretching for miles – 'Troutbeck Park'.

Far away in Dalehead the black Galloway cattle were dark specks moving slowly as they grazed. Sometimes I came upon the herd on the lower slopes of the Tongue; which was a reason for not taking

Nip. The little shaggy cows were quiet with me, but fierce in defence of their calves against dogs. Sometimes I timed my ramble to cross the track of the shepherds when they drove down a thousand sheep from the high fell for dipping. Rarely, I saw a hiker who had lost himself. Once there were two ravenous boys who had been out in a mist all night on Caudale moor. Usually I saw nobody, the long day round.

Mist is beautiful I think, though troublesome for sheep gathering. It takes strange shapes when it rises at sunset. During storms it rushes down the valleys like a black curtain billowing before the wind, while the Troutbeck River thunders over the Cauldron. Memories of 'old unhappy far-off things and battles long ago'; sorrows of yesterday and today and tomorrow – the vastness of the fells covers all with a mantle of peace.

(From *The Horn Book*, May 1942)

NOTES

The Code-Writing

1. (p. 46) These studies of spore development are contained in the collection of Beatrix Potter's Fungi paintings at the Armitt Library, Ambleside, Westmorland. The Collection contains some 270 paintings covering the period 1887–1901, most of which were done between 1893 and 1898. (L.L.)

1881

1. (p. 49) The family lived at Gorse Hall, Stalybridge, near Manchester.
2. (p. 50) The coachman. (L.L.)
3. (p. 51) Their old maid. (L.L.)

1882

1. (p. 53) Miss Hammond was Beatrix Potter's governess. (L.L.)
2. (p. 54) John Bright (1811–89), Radical orator and politician.
3. (p. 54) Charles James Fox (1749–1806), Whig statesman and a noted gambler.
4. (p. 54) It was from this paragraph that the key to the code-writing was found. (L.L.)
5. (p. 54) Exeter and Rufus were two of Mr Potter's horses. (L.L.)
6. (p. 54) John Everett Millais (1829–96), celebrated Victorian painter.
7. (p. 55) Princess Marie of Russia (1853–1920), sister of Czar Alexander III, wife of Alfred, Duke of Edinburgh, second son of Queen Victoria. Princess Mary Adelaide, Duchess of Teck

(1833–97), cousin of the Queen and mother of the future Queen Mary. Millais' subject was Princess Marie (1875–1938), subsequently Queen of Rumania. Beatrix Potter was to view the portrait on 10 June. 'Hands and arms very well painted, face too pink.'

8. (p. 55) Millais moved from Cromwell Place to his new home in Palace Gate, Kensington, in 1878. (L.L.)

9. (p. 55) Princess Alexandra of Wales (1844–1925) was Danish, the eldest daughter of King Christian IX.

10. (p. 55) The novel was *Ruth* (1853).

11. (p. 56) Dwight Lyman Moody (1837–99), American-born evangelist, toured Great Britain 1881–4.

12. (p. 57) On the west side of Lake Windermere, about two and a half miles from Hawkshead.

1883

1. (p. 62) James McNeill Whistler (1834–1903), Anglo-American painter.

2. (p. 62) A member of the Pre-Raphaelite Brotherhood, of which Millais was among the founders.

3. (p. 64) At no period since the beginning of the agitation for Home Rule was England feeling more incensed against Irish-Americans than during the years 1883–4 when these dynamite outrages took place. The policy of dynamite had been boldly proclaimed by the *Irish World*. Attempts were made to destroy the Offices of the Local Government Board and to blow up London Bridge. (L.L.)

4. (p. 64) William Ewart Gladstone (1809–98), Liberal politician, was four times Prime Minister: 1868–74, 1880–85, 1886, and 1892–4.

5. (p. 64) Lady Florence Dixie (1859–1905) was well known for her advanced views on female emancipation.

6. (p. 65) Prince Louis Bonaparte (1856–79), son of the former French Emperor Napoleon III, was killed in action in the Zulu War.

7. (p. 65) Ellen Terry (1848–1928), celebrated actress.

8. (p. 66) Miss Carter was Beatrix Potter's new governess. (L.L.)

9. (p. 66) Is she referring to Reynolds' picture *Faith*? (See final paragraph of her entry for 13 January 1883.) (L.L.)
10. (p. 66) Benjamin Disraeli, 1st Earl of Beaconsfield (1804–81), Conservative Prime Minister 1868, 1874–80.
11. (p. 66) Members of the Irish Nationalist movement, Sinn Fein.
12. (p. 66) Movement organized by Michael Davitt, designed to ease the burden of rents on Irish tenantry.
13. (p. 66) Charles Stuart Parnell (1846–91), Irish political leader.
14. (p. 67) She evidently meant Victoria Station as there was no direct route between Brighton and Waterloo. (Sir E. Henderson was Chief Commissioner of Police.) (L.L.)
15. (p. 67) Henry Labourchere, a well-known journalist of the time, was commonly known as 'Labby'. (L.L.)
16. (p. 67) Princess Louise, Marchioness of Lorne (1848–1939), fourth daughter of Queen Victoria.
17. (p. 67) The Wellington Arch, erected in 1828 near Hyde Park, was moved to its present position on Constitution Hill in 1883, when the equestrian statue which had surmounted it since 1846 was removed and re-erected at Aldershot.
18. (p. 67) Dalguise House, on the bank of the River Tay near Dunkeld, Perthshire, had been rented by Mr Potter year by year since 1871. (L.L.)
19. (p. 68) Tim Kelly, a twenty-year-old coachbuilder, was one of the murderers of Lord Frederick Cavendish, Chief Secretary of Ireland, in Phoenix Park, Dublin, on 6 May 1882. Owing to disagreement on the part of the jury he was tried three times before conviction.
20. (p. 69) Mrs Catherine Booth (1829–90), wife of William Booth, founder of the Salvation Army.
21. (p. 70) A house in Hertfordshire, about a mile south of Camfield Place, home of the Potter grandparents.
22. (p. 71) Verulamium, the most extensive Roman remains in southern Britain, lies a short distance to the west of St Albans Abbey (since 1877 a cathedral).
23. (p. 73) Lady Elizabeth Eastlake (1809–93) was the widow of Sir Charles Lock Eastlake, architect, painter and President of the Royal Academy of Art. She was a well-known art critic in her own right.

24. (p. 74) Rosa Bonheur (1822–99), French painter of animal subjects.
25. (p. 74) Jean Meissonier (1815–91), French Romantic painter of large-scale historical subjects and battle scenes.
26. (p. 74) George Du Maurier (1834–96), artist and novelist.
27. (p. 74) John Ruskin (1819–1900), art critic and social philosopher. *Modern Painters*, his first major work, appeared in five volumes between 1843 and 1860.
28. (p. 74) Dante Gabriel Rossetti (1828–82), poet and painter, a founder member of the Pre-Raphaelite Brotherhood.
29. (p. 74) Published in 1883.
30. (p. 74) Edmund Burke (1729–97), Irish political writer and orator; John Dryden (1631–1700), English poet and dramatist.
31. (p. 76) Believed to be a family of garden snails. (L.L.)
32. (p. 76) Richard Doyle (1824–83), book illustrator and humorist.
33. (p. 76) John Leech (1817–64), popular cartoonist.
34. (p. 76) Hablot Knight Browne ('Phiz') (1815–82), illustrator of many of the novels of Charles Dickens.
35. (p. 77) Gustave Doré (1833–83), popular artist and book illustrator.
36. (p. 77) John Brett (1832–1902), English painter.
37. (p. 78) In the 1880s a number of houses in the style that became known as 'Pont Street Dutch' were being built in London's western suburbs. Their cheerful brickwork, elaborate gables and small-paned windows were in marked contrast to the appearance of Number Two Bolton Gardens.

1884

1. (p. 81) Son of the Potters' coachman. (L.L.)
2. (p. 81) Man-servant of Mr Millais. (L.L.)
3. (p. 84) Leopold, Duke of Albany (1853–84), fourth and youngest son of Queen Victoria; Arthur, Duke of Connaught (1850–1942), third son of Queen Victoria.
4. (p. 84) Grandmamma Leech's house, Gorse Hall, near Manchester. (L.L.)
5. (p. 86) Beatrix Potter's great-aunt, Mrs Sydney Potter. Cousin Louisa was her eldest daughter.

6. (p. 86) The Reverend William Gaskell (1805–84), Unitarian minister and husband of the novelist Elizabeth Gaskell.

7. (p. 89) The celebrated painting of a stag by Sir Edwin Landseer (1802–73).

8. (p. 93) Sir William Vernon Harcourt (1827–1904), Home Secretary.

9. (p. 93) Joseph Chamberlain (1836–1914), Liberal politician, at that time President of the Board of Trade.

10. (p. 94) Sir Edward Burne-Jones (1833–98), English painter.

11. (p. 94) William Morris (1834–96), poet and craftsman.

12. (p. 94) William Holman Hunt (1827–1910), Pre-Raphaelite painter. *The Light of the World* is hung in Keble College Chapel.

13. (p. 95) As a child, Beatrix Potter had a warm affection for Mr Gaskell; she knitted him a comforter for a Christmas present in 1874, at the age of eight. Referring to this present in a letter of thanks, he wrote, 'Big as I am I know I could not have done it one-tenth as well. Every time I put it round my neck – which during this weather will be every day – I shall be sure to think of you.' (L.L.)

14. (p. 97) No. 2 Palace Green was inhabited by Joseph Bravo, a West Indian merchant, whose stepson Charles Bravo was allegedly murdered in 1876 in Balham. His wife Florence came under suspicion at the second inquest, but was never sent for trial. Her father did not own land in New Zealand, but in Australia.

15. (p. 97) Lord Randolph Churchill (1849–95), politician and father of Sir Winston Churchill.

16. (p. 98) Oscar Wilde (1854–1900), dramatist, writer and wit.

17. (p. 99) Millais' son-in-law. (L.L.)

18. (p. 99) The British army, under Sir Garnet Wolseley, defeated the Egyptian leader, Arabi Pasha, at Tel-el-Kebir on 13 September 1882.

19. (p. 100) Bush Hall, on the River Lea, Hertfordshire, was the property of Lord Salisbury. It seems likely that 'week' is a mistake for 'month'. (L.L.)

20. (p. 100) Robert Cecil, 3rd Marquess of Salisbury (1830–1903), Conservative Prime Minister 1885–6, 1886–92, 1895–1902.

21. (p. 102) The Grosvenor Gallery opened on 1 May 1877, and

became a centre of the Aesthetic movement. 'A greenery-yallery, Grosvenor Gallery, / Foot-in-the-grave young man!' – W. S. Gilbert, *Patience* (1881).

22. (p. 102) George Frederick Watts (1817–1904), painter of portraits and symbolic pictures. Beatrix Potter thought poorly of his work.
23. (p. 104) One-horse hackney carriage. (L.L.)
24. (p. 104) Assumed to be some early type of searchlight. (L.L.)
25. (p. 104) Robert Blake (1599–1657), Admiral.
26. (p. 104) George Villiers, 1st Duke of Buckingham (1592–1628), was assassinated in Portsmouth by John Felton.
27. (p. 108) Believed to be Karl Heffner, born 1849. (L.L.)

1885

1. (p. 110) Sir Herbert Stewart (1843–85) was in command of the army sent to relieve the British forces in Khartoum, capital of the Sudan, which was being besieged by the rebel forces of the Arab religious fanatic known as the Mahdi.
2. (p. 110) Charles Bradlaugh (1833–91), controversial politician and freethinker.
3. (p. 111) Khartoum fell to the Arab forces on 26 January; General Charles George Gordon (1833–85) was killed. Sir Charles Wilson (1836–95), who took over the command of the relieving forces following the death of General Stewart, entered Khartoum on 28 January.
4. (p. 111) Sir Redvers Buller (1839–1908), Chief of Staff of the Relief Expedition to Khartoum.
5. (p. 115) The International Inventions Exhibition at South Kensington. (L.L.)
6. (p. 116) Sir Laurence Alma-Tadema (1836–1912), English painter of classical subjects.
7. (p. 116) Police, so called from the lanterns they carried. (L.L.)
8. (p. 116) The original Benjamin Bunny, commonly called Bounce, was a handsome tame Belgian rabbit. He was succeeded by Peter. They both appear in *The Tale of Benjamin Bunny*, 1904. (L.L.)
9. (p. 121) The well-known picture by Millais, later called *Bubbles*. (L.L.)

1. (p. 126) In the winter of 1885–6, when trade was bad, the Social Democrat Federation leaders organized meetings and marches of the unemployed. On 8 February 1886, a Meeting held by them in Trafalgar Square led to considerable disorder, the mob doing much damage to houses and property on their way from Trafalgar Square to Hyde Park, afterwards to Oxford Street. For this, four notable men – H. M. Hyndman, John Burns, H. H. Champion and Jack Williams – were prosecuted at Bow Street; but in April an Old Bailey Jury acquitted them after a four-day trial. Similar unemployment disturbances occurred in Manchester and elsewhere. (L.L.)

2. (p. 129) Janos Water was a Spa water, like Harrogate Water, and was put up in foreign bottles – long slender necks; possibly from Austria or Hungary. Apart from wine shops, it was also obtainable from such establishments as Boots Cash Chemist. (L.L.)

3. (p. 129) Archibald Philip Primrose, 5th Earl of Rosebery (1847–1929), Prime Minister 1894–5.

4. (p. 131) See note 1 (for Tuesday 9 February).

5. (p. 133) The Polygon still exists in the Ardwick Green area. During the nineteenth century it was one of the most select residential thoroughfares. (L.L.)

6. (p. 134) The Reverend Charles Beard, minister of the Gee Cross Unitarian chapel. (L.L.)

7. (p. 136) There appears to be no record either of an Eccles Road or a Swinton Lane in Manchester dating back as far as this period. (L.L.)

8. (p. 137) William Edward Forster (1818–86), Chief Secretary for Ireland 1880–82.

9. (p. 137) Franz Liszt (1811–86), Hungarian pianist and composer.

10. (p. 137) This should have been 'Thirlmere', where the lake was converted into a reservoir. Manchester never considered Tilberthwaite as a source of water. There is no lake there. (L.L.)

11. (p. 138) 'B flats': bugs. (L.L.)

12. (p. 140) A point of dispute had arisen with regard to a legacy to Mrs Potter. (L.L.)

1890–91

1. (p. 142) Esther is believed to be an imaginary person. (L.L.)
2. (p. 145) Fanny Burney (1752–1840), novelist and diarist.
3. (p. 145) Believed to be her brother, Walter Bertram Potter (1872–1918).
4. (p. 145) Believed to be her uncle Sir Henry Roscoe (1833–1915).
5. (p. 148) Mrs Hugh Blackburn, née Weddurburn (1823–1909). Her work was admired by Millais and Ruskin.
6. (p. 149) *Birds Drawn from Nature* by Mrs Hugh Blackburn, James Maclehose, Glasgow 1868, bound in cloth. (The first edition, 1862, art paper, boards, contained about half the number of Plates.) (L.L.)
7. (p. 149) Stamford Hutton, a cousin of Mr Potter. (L.L.)
8. (p. 151) Younger sister of Stamford Hutton.

1892

1. (p. 152) Written from memory after her return. (L.L.)
2. (p. 152) The Great Western Railway abolished the Broad Gauge on 21 May 1892. (L.L.)
3. (p. 153) The Reverend William Gilpin (1724–1804), travel writer and authority on landscape and the picturesque.
4. (p. 154) A Quaker family. (L.L.)
5. (p. 169) The pier, which would probably be admired today, was built in 1884, damaged in an air raid in 1941 and demolished in 1953.
6. (p. 173) Beatrix Potter was puzzled that a Villa should have such a 'fine name', but Mr Ross who built the house called it by that name because heather grew all over the field, and *Park* in Scots means *grass plot*. Later it was changed to *The Lodge* because the other name was thought to be misleading. (L.L.)
7. (p. 174) A building. (L.L.)
8. (p. 174) A woman's or child's linen cap. (L.L.)

9. (p. 174) This was the year Mr Potter first rented Dalguise House, when Kitty became their washerwoman. (L.L.)
10. (p. 174) A gamekeeper living at Inver. (L.L.)
11. (p. 175) The loch is shown, but not named, on the Ordnance Survey Map, about a mile from Dunkeld, on the Pitlochry Road. (L.L.)
12. (p. 177) Now Rothmells Farm. (L.L.)
13. (p. 177) Wife of the gamekeeper at Dalguise. (L.L.)
14. (p. 178) A donkey. (L.L.)
15. (p. 179) Dr Culbard was medical man in this district from May 1857 to February 1901. (L.L.) Beatrix Potter portrayed him as a mole in one of her drawings.
16. (p. 180) The Marquis Deguillies came over from France bearing a letter from King Louis around 1745 and seems to have taken quite a part in the Atholl affairs as well as the Rebellion. In 1892 Anne Atholl was an old lady and although it could not have been the same Deguillies, there is always the possibility of a descendant. From the reference, he sounds as if he was still *sponging*. (L.L.)
17. (p. 183) Barclay Field of Drumour died September 1893. (L.L.)
18. (p. 185) 'Carry' is an old Cumberland term meaning the movement of direction of the clouds, 'It'll be fair today, because t' carry's frae t'west.' (L.L.)
19. (p. 185) Beatrix Potter's way of rendering the local pronunciation of the word 'sock'. (L.L.)
20. (p. 188) This presumably refers to the translation in the Book of Common Prayer of the Church of England.
21. (p. 188) Drumclog, a boggy moor, was the scene of an engagement fought between the Royal Forces under John Graham of Claverhouse and the Covenanters, on Sunday 1 June 1679. The battle features in Scott's novel *Old Mortality* (1816).
22. (p. 188) Rullion Green in the Pentland Hills was the scene of the defeat of the Covenanters by the Royal forces in November 1666. (L.L.)
23. (p. 188) The open-work spire that crowns St Giles's Cathedral, Edinburgh. The church served as a cathedral only between 1633–9 and 1662–90.

24. (p. 190) Aberdeen Angus cows. (L.L.)

25. (p. 190) Beef or mutton pies with gravy in them. (L.L.)

26. (p. 191) Julia Neilson (1868–1957), well-known actress, married to the actor Fred Terry.

27. (p. 191) Arthur James, 1st Earl of Balfour (1848–1930), philosopher and politician. Conservative Prime Minister 1902–5.

28. (p. 191) Albert, Duke of Clarence (1864–92), elder son of the Prince of Wales, died of inflammation of the lungs on 13 January. His betrothed, Princess Mary ('May') of Teck (1867–1953), later married his brother, the future King George V.

29. (p. 191) The weekly illustrated *Black and White* which preceded the *Graphic* and *Sphere*. (L.L.)

30. (p. 192) Samuel Johnson (1709–84), lexicographer, poet, critic and biographer.

31. (p. 193) The camera. (See entry for 1 October, paragraph 2.) (L.L.) (p. 196)

32. (p. 194) The name of the place at which Bella lived. (L.L.)

33. (p. 195) George Leveson-Gower, 3rd Duke of Sutherland (1828–92). He reclaimed much of the waste land in the Highlands.

34. (p. 198) Their former maid. (L.L.)

35. (p. 202) The Roman nettle, *Urtica pilulifera*. (L.L.)

36. (p. 203) A young bullock or heifer, usually between one and two years old. (L.L.)

37. (p. 204) This was a primitive system of cultivation. The soil was ridged and rounded with furrows for drainage between the ridges which might be anything up to four or more feet across. The crop was sown on top. When Duncan Cameron 'had run up his kit-rigs' he had ploughed them over or levelled them. This would explain why Kitty said 'Then there'll be some bad meal.' (L.L.)

38. (p. 204) Alfred, Lord Tennyson (1809–92), Poet Laureate.

39. (p. 204) Sir Lewis Morris (1833–1923), Welsh-born patriotic poet.

40. (p. 204) George Saintsbury (1845–1933), journalist and literary critic.

41. (p. 204) Alfred Austin (1835–1913) succeeded Tennyson as Poet Laureate, a notoriously unsuitable appointment.
42. (p. 204) Coventry Patmore (1823–96), Catholic poet and literary critic.
43. (p. 204) Frederick Locker-Lampson (1821–95), poet and writer of light verse.
44. (p. 204) Algernon Charles Swinburne (1837–1909), though among the most admired poets of his time, was a self-proclaimed free-thinker. For many readers he would have been an undesirable candidate for the Laureateship.
45. (p. 205) Sir Theodore Martin (1816–1909), author of the five-volume *Life of the Prince Consort* (1875–80).
46. (p. 205) Jean Ingelow (1820–97), Lincolnshire poet.
47. (p. 205) Christina Rossetti (1830–94), poet, sister of D. G. Rossetti.
48. (p. 207) A popular narrative poem by Sir Walter Scott, published in 1810.
49. (p. 208) James Payn (1830–98), novelist and journalist. Beatrix Potter is unlikely to have been alone in misspelling his name with an 'e'.
50. (p. 208) Meaning 'besides cats'. (L.L.)
51. (p. 209) The old ruins at Salachill are believed to be the many ruins of small buildings that are dotted on the whole face of the hill which bears the name Salachill. These small houses probably belong to the so-called clearances which followed the arrival of the sheep-farmer, and are visible evidence of the great change that has taken place in the uplands of Scotland. (L.L.)
52. (p. 209) General George Wade (1673–1748) from 1726 onwards was in charge of the building of roads designed to open up the Highlands and thus discourage (ineffectively in 1745) further risings against the Hanoverian government. According to Leslie Linder, Beatrix Potter was incorrect in supposing this particular track to be a Wade road.
53. (p. 210) Charles Macintosh of Inver (1839–1922), the local postman. In 1883 he was elected Associate of the Perthshire Society of National Science, to which he contributed many Papers. He made a study of mosses and fungi, and his work can still be seen at the Perth Museum. He used to walk many

miles each day delivering mail, and it was during these walks that he studied the natural history of the surrounding country. (L.L.)

1893

1. (p. 215) Sir Henry Irving (1838–1905), celebrated Shakespearean actor.
2. (p. 215) Princess Helena (1846–1923), third daughter of Queen Victoria, married to Prince Christian of Schleswig-Holstein-Sonderburg-Augustenburg.

1894

1. (p. 220) The Gloucestershire home of Beatrix Potter's cousin Caroline Hutton.
2. (p. 220) In 1956 Caroline Hutton (Mrs Caroline Clark) remembered this first visit and wrote: 'I am always glad that in spite of her mother's objections I managed to get her to my old home. She said B. was so apt to be sick and to faint; and I, regardless of the truth, said I was quite accustomed to all that; and of course she could do most things, quite long walks included, and very soon she made friends with my father who called her "The busy Bee". She was very anxious to photograph him, but he refused; so she got a volume of Milton and asked him a question about it; while he was looking it out she got two very good photographs of him, both of which, one framed, are here in the dining-room. I often think of her – I am now nearly eighty-six, and am glad she has escaped extreme old age.' (L.L.)
3. (p. 224) Vicar of Painswick. (L.L.)
4. (p. 227) A young salmon that has been only once to sea. (L.L.)
5. (p. 232) A rough and uncultured place which was turned into a model village by Lady Louisa Waterford in the middle of the nineteenth century. (L.L.)
6. (p. 235) Rabbits. (L.L.)
7. (p. 236) 'Take this on the word of one who has tried.' (L.L.)
8. (p. 243) In a letter to her publishers in February 1942, the year

before she died, Beatrix Potter, in writing about the origin of Peter Rabbit, said: 'Peter was so composite and scattered in locality that I have found it troublesome to explain its various sources . . . Mr McGregor was no special person unless in the rheumatic method of planting cabbages; I remember seeing a gardener in Berwickshire extended full-length on his stomach weeding a carriage drive with a knife – his name I forget – not McGregor. I think the story was made up in Scotland.' By that time she had forgotten the name, 'Hopkirk'. (L.L.)

9. (p. 243) This particular fossil occurs in the so-called Calciferous Sandstone stratum in Berwickshire. (L.L.)

10. (p. 244)　　　'. . . you demi-puppets, that
　　　　　By moonshine do the green sour ringlets make
　　　　　Whereof the ewe not bites . . .'
(*The Tempest*, Act V, Scene I) See entry for 2 October, third paragraph (p. 240).

1895

1. (p. 246) Sarah Siddons (1775–1831), renowned actress and tragedienne.

2. (p. 253) Johnson visited Gwaynynog with the Thrales in 1774, and later wrote to Mrs Thrale on 18 September that the 'erection of an urn looks like an intention to bury me alive. I would as willingly see my friend, however benevolent and hospitable, quietly inurned. Let him think for the present of some more acceptable memorial.' One suspects that Beatrix Potter would have reacted in a similar manner.

3. (p. 254) In 1909 Beatrix Potter used this garden for the setting of *The Tale of the Flopsy Bunnies*. (L.L.)

4. (p. 257) Joan of Arc. (L.L.)

5. (p. 258) Skelwith Force, a waterfall on the river Brathay a short distance below Elterwater lake.

6. (p. 259) A valley is called a *den* in parts of Scotland, but not here, except by someone like Beatrix Potter who knew Scotland. (L.L.) The term, however, is not quite unknown in the Lake District: the head of Great Langdale is called Mickleden.

7. (p. 264) Marianne (Meta) and Julia Gaskell, the second and the youngest of the novelist's four daughters.
8. (p. 264) Formerly Miss Carter, Beatrix Potter's governess. Mrs Moore was the mother of Noel, Freda and Norah, for whom *Peter Rabbit*, *The Tailor of Gloucester* and *Squirrel Nutkin* were written. (L.L.)
9. (p. 264) Sister of Mrs Moore. (L.L.)
10. (p. 267) She must have been unaware that Matthew Arnold was the author of a sonnet on Shakespeare which begins, 'Others abide our question. Thou art free.'
11. (p. 268) Sir Lewis Morris was a fluent writer of whom it is said that he had the faculty of writing what looks like poetry till one begins to examine it a little. (L.L.)

1896

1. (p. 270) The first Reform Bill was passed in 1832.
2. (p. 270) Prince Henry of Battenburg (1858–96) was married to the Queen's youngest daughter, Princess Beatrice.
3. (p. 270) John Gilbert (1817–97), painter and sculptor. The statue was the work of W. Bruce Joy.
4. (p. 271) Lady Millais (1828–97), the former Euphemia Gray, had been married first to John Ruskin. The marriage was dissolved in 1855, whereupon she married Millais.
5. (p. 271) Sir John Millais had just been elected President of the Royal Academy of Art. (L.L.)
6. (p. 273) Uncle Harry was Sir Henry Roscoe.
7. (p. 273) Director of the Royal Botanic Gardens. (L.L.)
8. (p. 274) Assistant director of the Royal Botanic Gardens. (L.L.)
9. (p. 274) Principal assistants. (L.L.)
10. (p. 274) Keeper, Herbarium and Library. (L.L.)
11. (p. 275) Hiring-fairs were held in various parts of the country up to the early days of this century. At these hiring-fairs, which usually lasted about three days, farm-labourers were hired by the year; shepherds walked about with tufts of wool in their hats, and carters with whip-cord, to indicate their calling. In the past, even indoor servants were hired by the year on farms. (L.L.)

12. (p. 276) A large country house in the village of Sawrey (now 'Ees Wyke'), with meadow-land stretching down to Esthwaite Water, situated just behind Hill Top Farm. (L.L.)

Memories of Camfield Place

1. (p. 283) Blakesmoor in a celebrated essay by Charles Lamb was in real life Blakesware, a country mansion, where as a child he spent many happy hours with his grandmother who was the housekeeper. It gave him recollections that he never forgot. (L.L.)
2. (p. 284) Lancelot Brown (1715–83), influential landscape gardener. His nickname derives from his habit of assessing the landscape in terms of its capability for development.
3. (p. 285) Could this have had an association with Gainsborough's picture *A Nymph at her Bath*, later known as *Musidora*, with its derivation from a Renaissance statue by Adriaen de Vries, or with a Nymph called Musidora in Thompson's poem *The Seasons* (Summer), which was a very popular work at that time? (L.L.)

INDEX